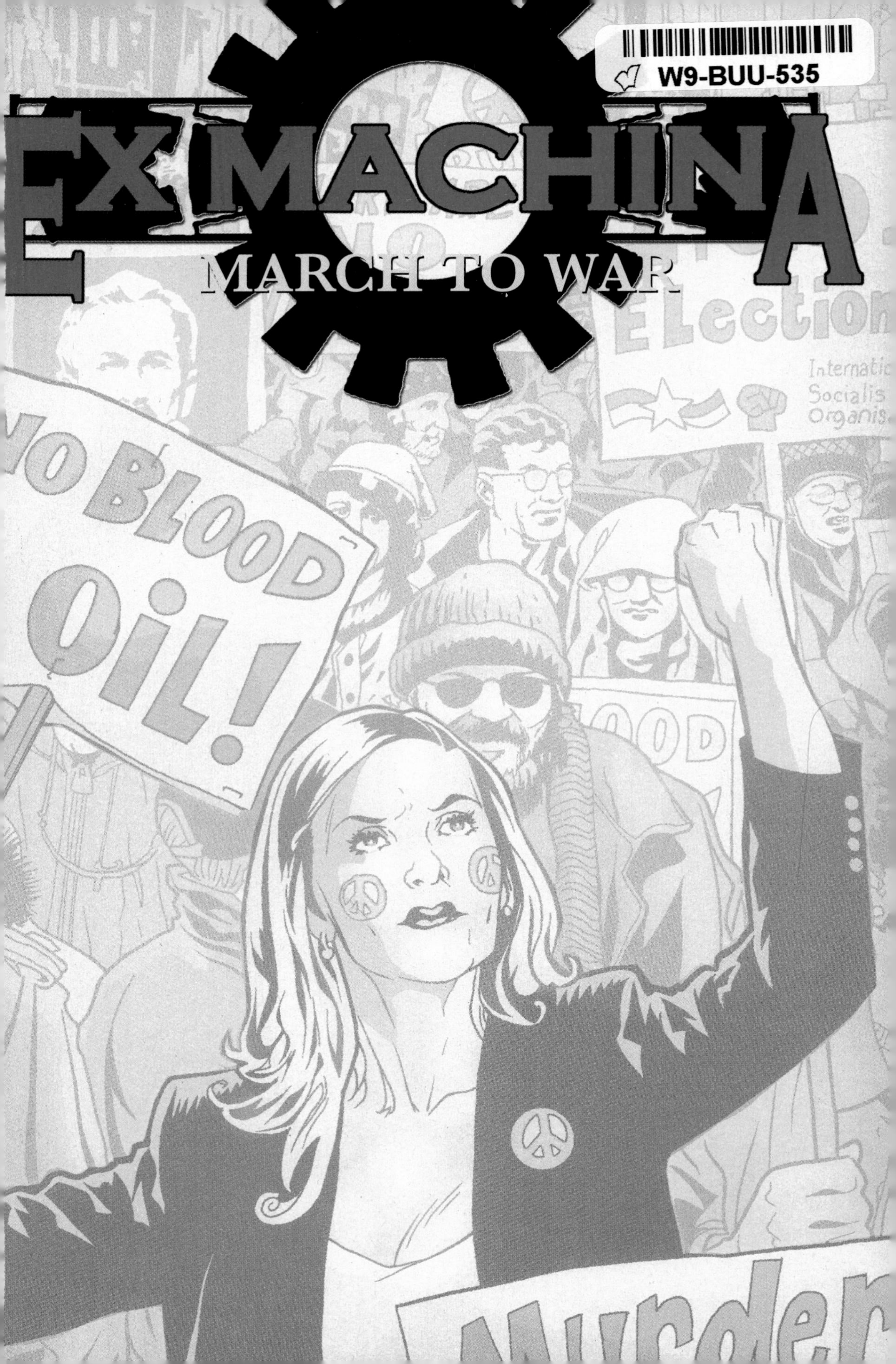
EX MACHINA
MARCH TO WAR
BLOOD
OIL!
Election

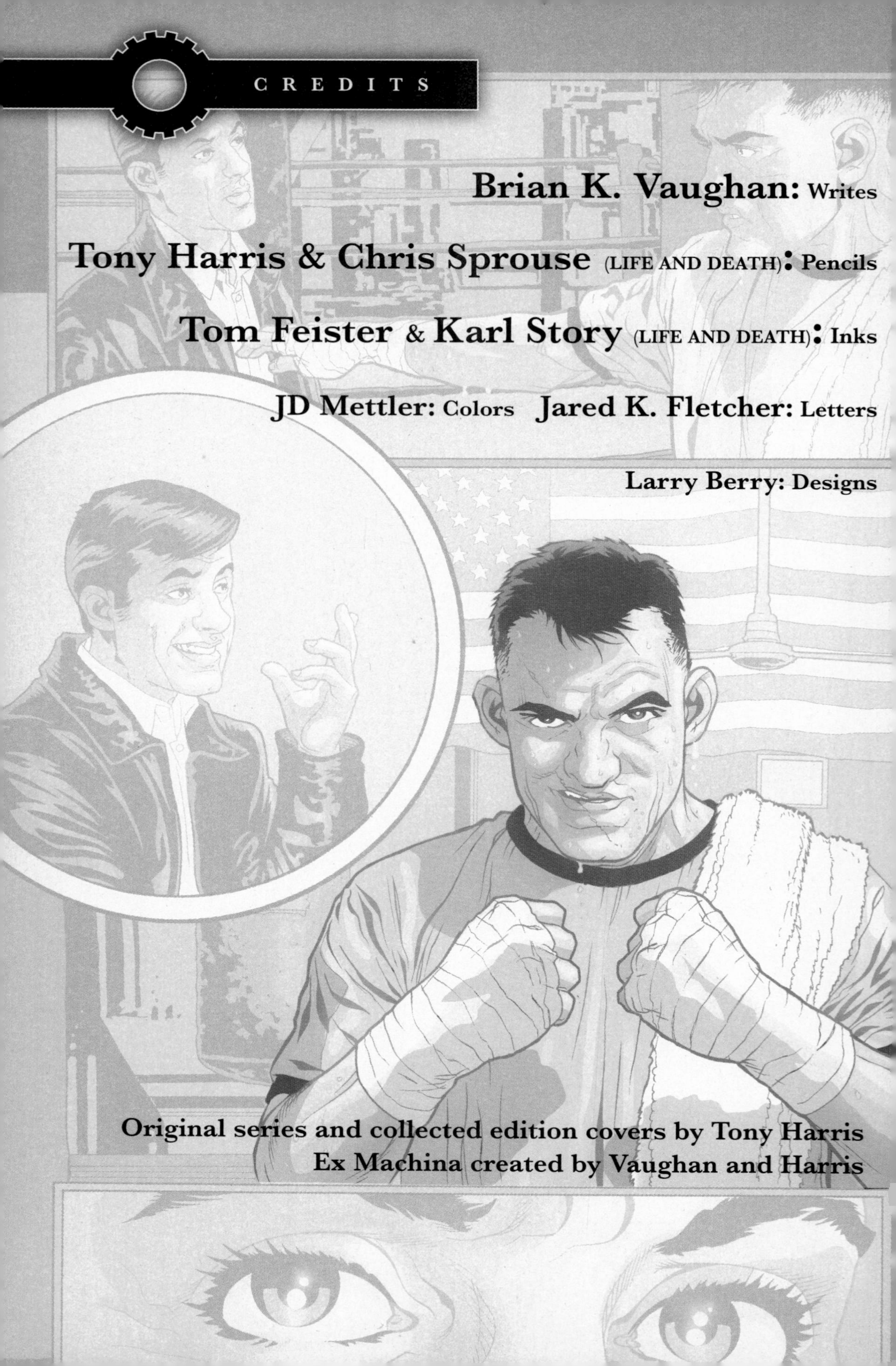

CREDITS

Brian K. Vaughan: Writes

Tony Harris & Chris Sprouse (LIFE AND DEATH): Pencils

Tom Feister & Karl Story (LIFE AND DEATH): Inks

JD Mettler: Colors   Jared K. Fletcher: Letters

Larry Berry: Designs

Original series and collected edition covers by Tony Harris
Ex Machina created by Vaughan and Harris

LEGAL

Jim Lee, Editorial Director **John Nee,** VP—Business Development **Scott Dunbier,** Executive Editor
Ben Abernathy, Editor **Kristy Quinn,** Assistant Editor **Ed Roeder,** Art Director **Paul Levitz,** President & Publisher
Georg Brewer, VP—Design & DC Direct Creative **Richard Bruning,** Senior VP—Creative Director
Patrick Caldon, Executive VP—Finance & Operations **Chris Caramalis,** VP—Finance **John Cunningham,** VP—Marketing
Terri Cunningham, VP—Managing Editor **Stephanie Fierman,** Senior VP—Sales & Marketing **Alison Gill,** VP—Manufacturing
Hank Kanalz, VP—General Manager, WildStorm **Lillian Laserson,** Senior VP & General Counsel
Paula Lowitt, Senior VP—Business & Legal Affairs **MaryEllen McLaughlin,** VP—Advertising & Custom Publishing
Gregory Noveck, Senior VP—Creative Affairs **Cheryl Rubin,** Senior VP—Brand Management
Jeff Trojan, VP—Business Development, DC Direct **Bob Wayne,** VP—Sales

ISBN:1-4012-0997-1   ISBN-13: 978-1-4012-0997-1

EX MACHINA: MARCH TO WAR. Published by WildStorm Productions, an imprint of DC Comics. 888 Prospect St. #240, La Jolla, CA 92037. Cover, compilation copyright © 2006 Brian K. Vaughan and Tony Harris. All Rights Reserved. EX MACHINA is ™ Brian K. Vaughan and Tony Harris. Originally published in single magazine form as EX MACHINA #17-20 and EX MACHINA SPECIAL #1-2 © 2006 Brian K. Vaughan and Tony Harris.

PTER
1

March to War

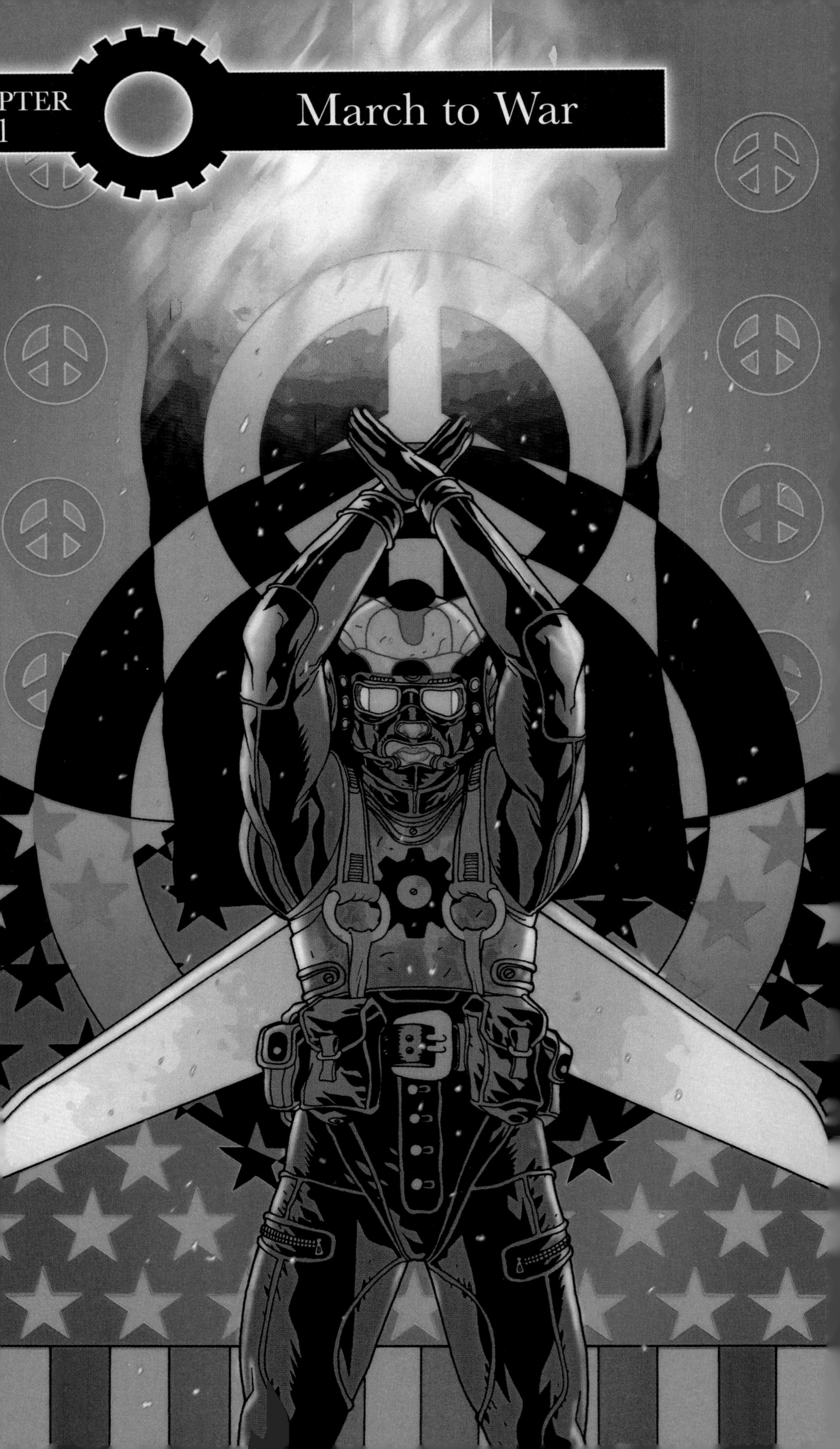

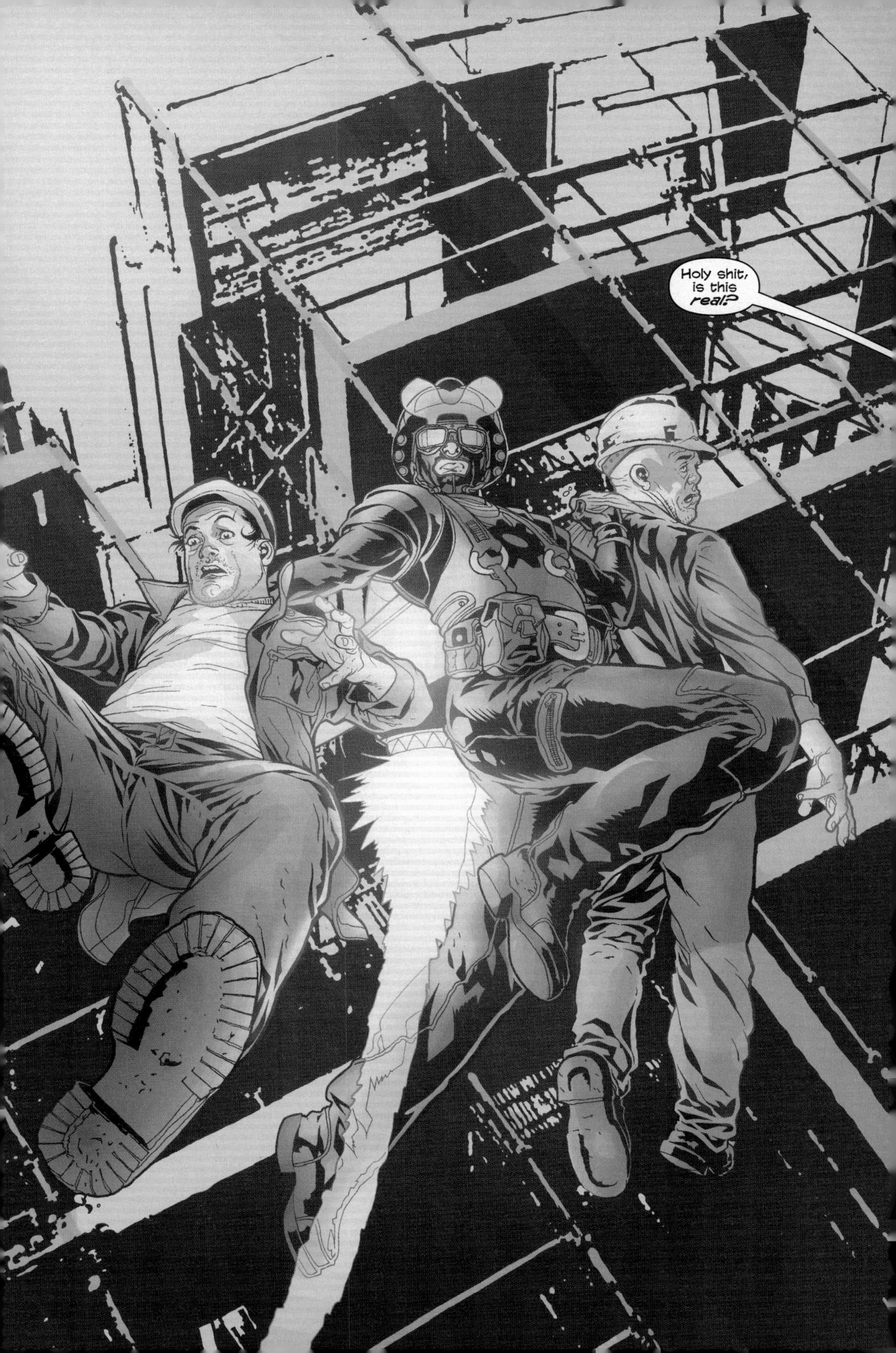
Holy shit, is this *real?*

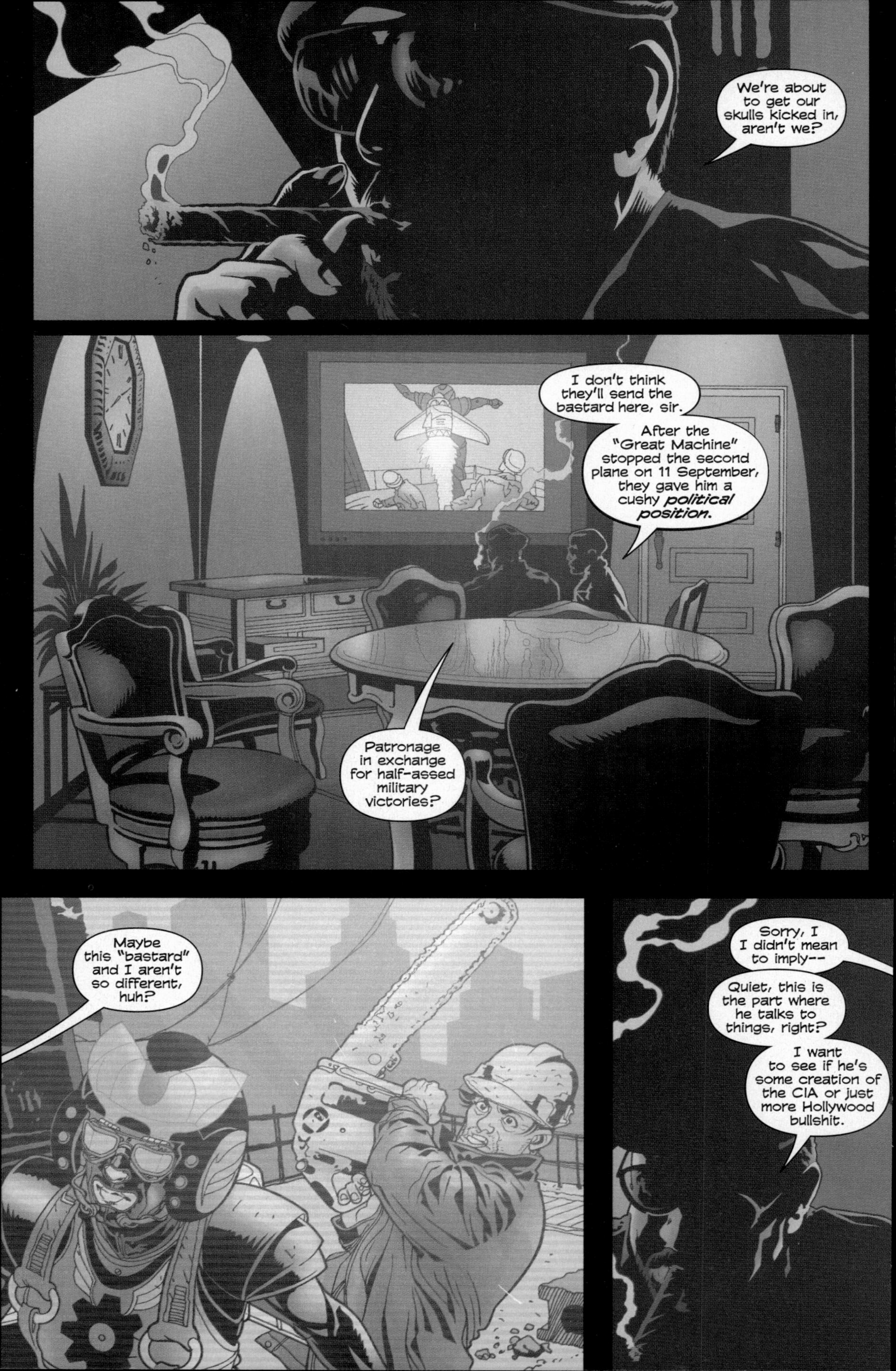

We're about to get our skulls kicked in, aren't we?
I don't think they'll send the bastard here, sir.
After the "Great Machine" stopped the second plane on 11 September, they gave him a cushy *political position.*
Patronage in exchange for half-assed military victories?
Maybe this "bastard" and I aren't so different, huh?
Sorry, I I didn't mean to imply--
Quiet, this is the part where he talks to things, right?
I want to see if he's some creation of the CIA or just more Hollywood bullshit.

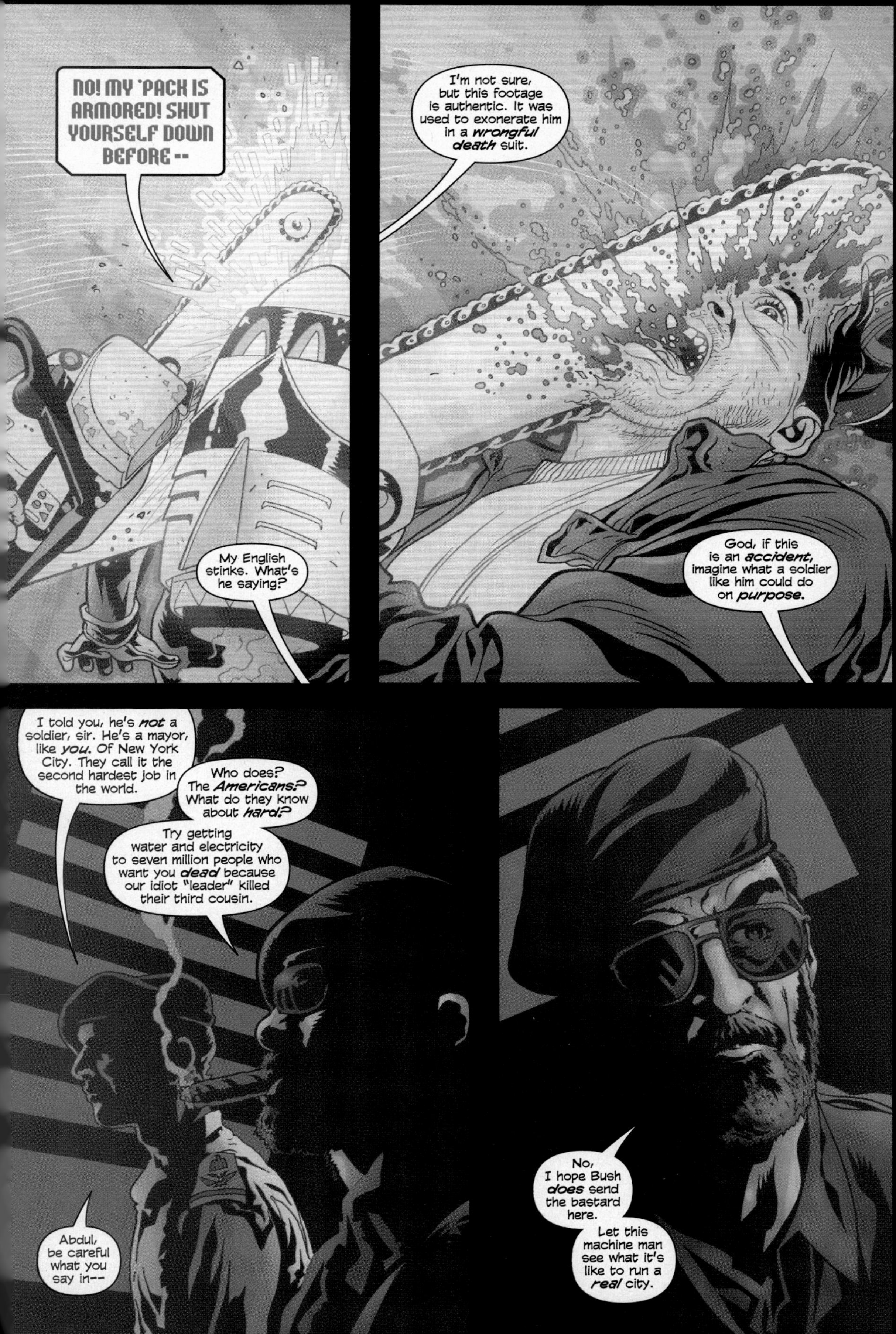

NO! MY 'PACK IS ARMORED! SHUT YOURSELF DOWN BEFORE --
My English stinks. What's he saying?
I'm not sure, but this footage is authentic. It was used to exonerate him in a *wrongful death* suit.
God, if this is an *accident,* imagine what a soldier like him could do on *purpose.*
I told you, he's *not* a soldier, sir. He's a mayor, like *you.* Of New York City. They call it the second hardest job in the world.
Who does? The *Americans?* What do they know about *hard?*
Try getting water and electricity to seven million people who want you *dead* because our idiot "leader" killed their third cousin.
Abdul, be careful what you say in--
No, I hope Bush *does* send the bastard here.
Let this machine man see what it's like to run a *real* city.

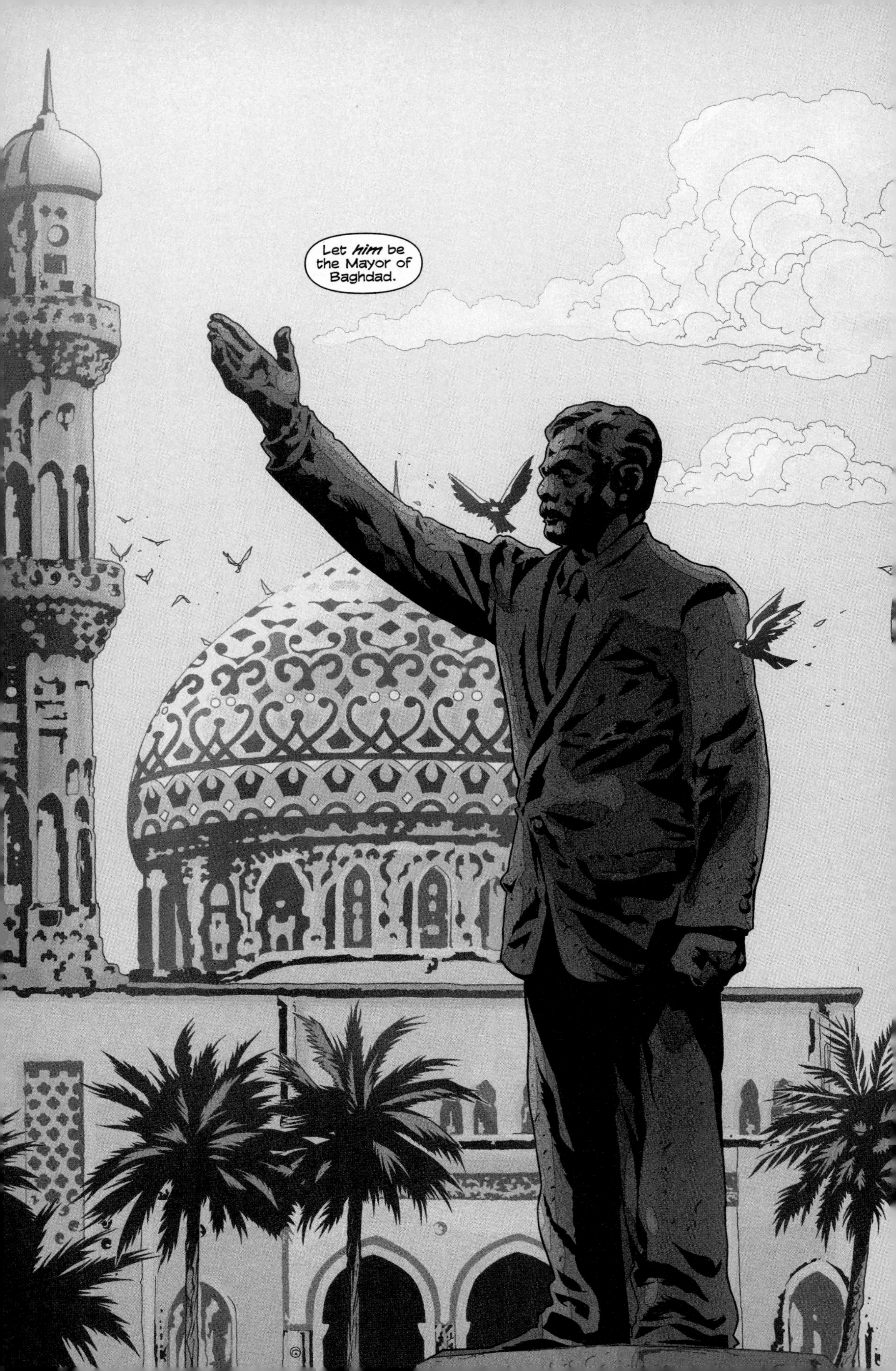
Let *him* be the Mayor of Baghdad.

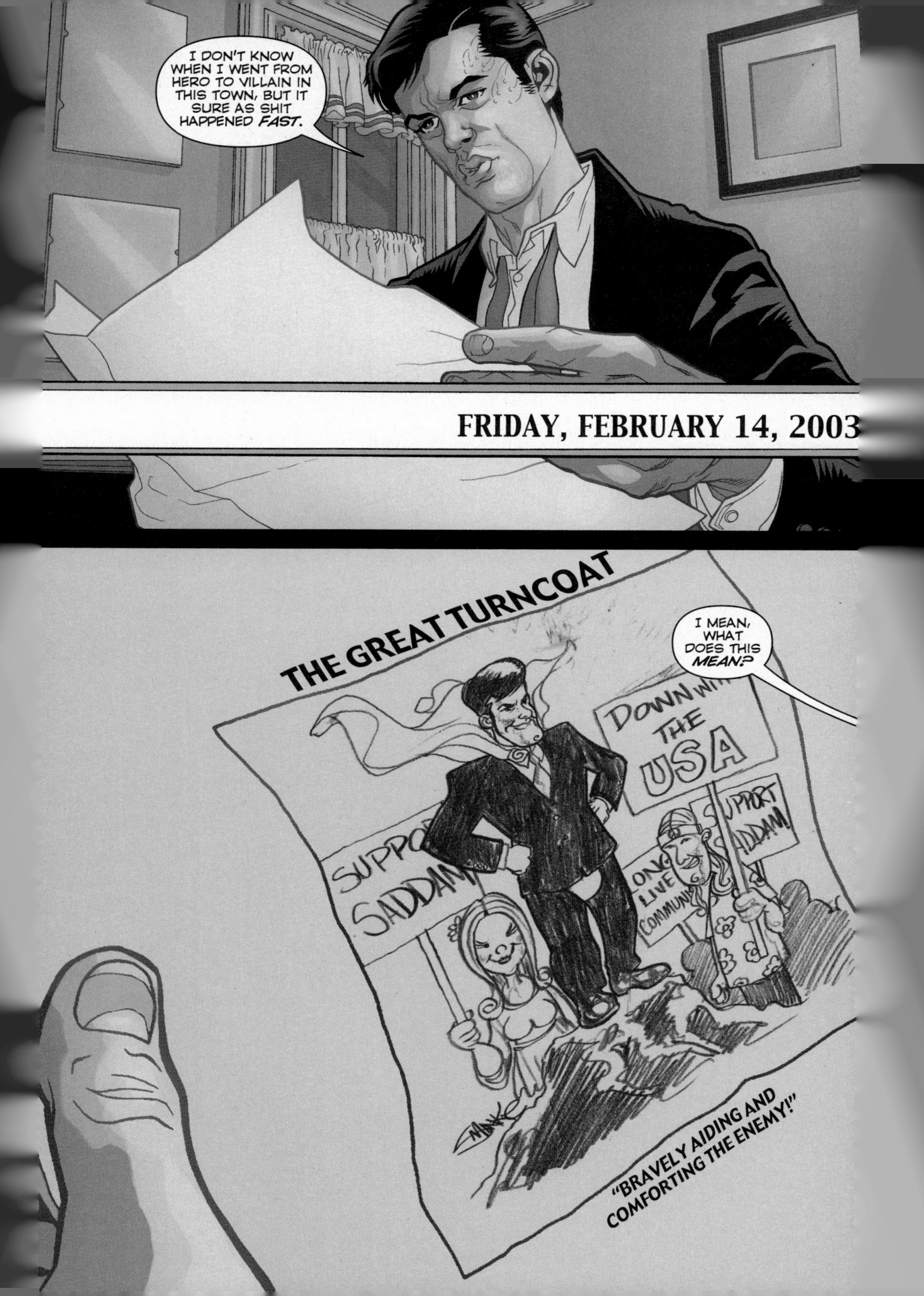
I DON'T KNOW WHEN I WENT FROM HERO TO VILLAIN IN THIS TOWN, BUT IT SURE AS SHIT HAPPENED *FAST*.
FRIDAY, FEBRUARY 14, 2003
THE GREAT TURNCOAT
I MEAN, WHAT DOES THIS *MEAN?*
THE USA
SUPPORT SADDAM!
"BRAVELY AIDING AND COMFORTING THE ENEMY!"

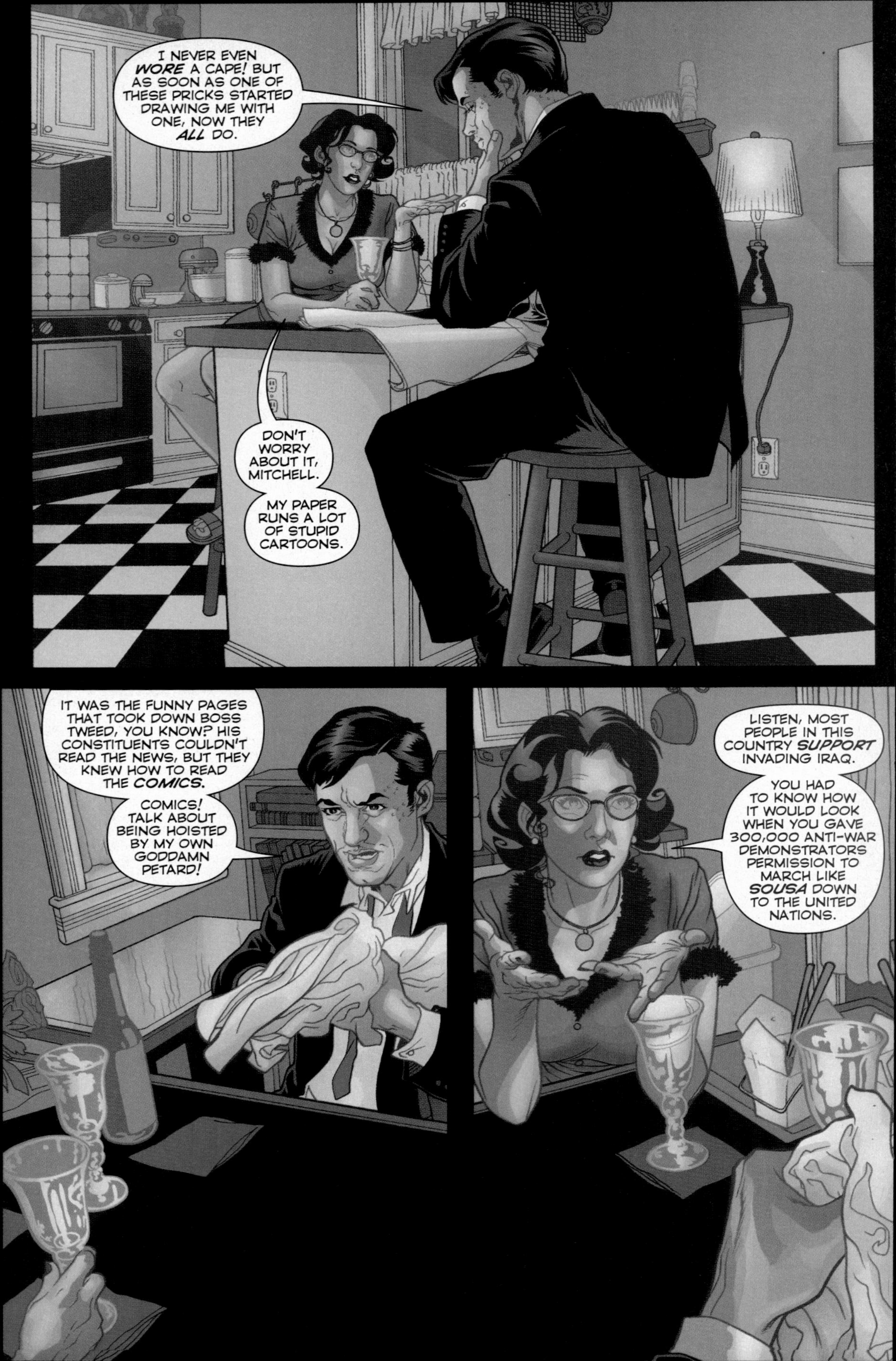
I NEVER EVEN *WORE* A CAPE! BUT AS SOON AS ONE OF THESE PRICKS STARTED DRAWING ME WITH ONE, NOW THEY *ALL* DO.
DON'T WORRY ABOUT IT, MITCHELL.
MY PAPER RUNS A LOT OF STUPID CARTOONS.
IT WAS THE FUNNY PAGES THAT TOOK DOWN BOSS TWEED, YOU KNOW? HIS CONSTITUENTS COULDN'T READ THE NEWS, BUT THEY KNEW HOW TO READ THE *COMICS*.
COMICS! TALK ABOUT BEING HOISTED BY MY OWN GODDAMN PETARD!
LISTEN, MOST PEOPLE IN THIS COUNTRY *SUPPORT* INVADING IRAQ.
YOU HAD TO KNOW HOW IT WOULD LOOK WHEN YOU GAVE 300,000 ANTI-WAR DEMONSTRATORS PERMISSION TO MARCH LIKE *SOUSA* DOWN TO THE UNITED NATIONS.

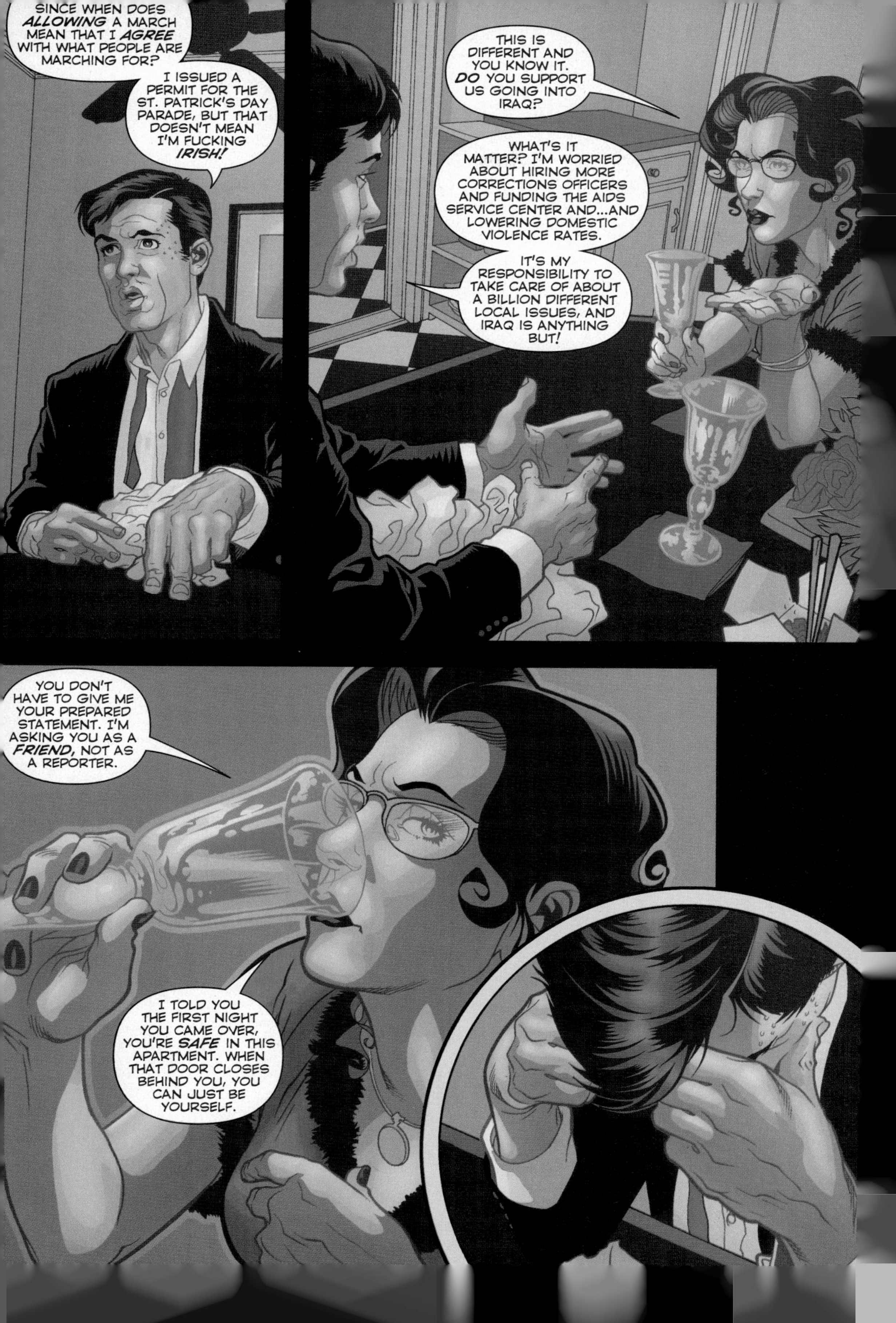

SINCE WHEN DOES *ALLOWING* A MARCH MEAN THAT I *AGREE* WITH WHAT PEOPLE ARE MARCHING FOR?
I ISSUED A PERMIT FOR THE ST. PATRICK'S DAY PARADE, BUT THAT DOESN'T MEAN I'M FUCKING *IRISH!*
THIS IS DIFFERENT AND YOU KNOW IT. *DO* YOU SUPPORT US GOING INTO IRAQ?
WHAT'S IT MATTER? I'M WORRIED ABOUT HIRING MORE CORRECTIONS OFFICERS AND FUNDING THE AIDS SERVICE CENTER AND...AND LOWERING DOMESTIC VIOLENCE RATES.
IT'S MY RESPONSIBILITY TO TAKE CARE OF ABOUT A BILLION DIFFERENT LOCAL ISSUES, AND IRAQ IS ANYTHING BUT!
YOU DON'T HAVE TO GIVE ME YOUR PREPARED STATEMENT. I'M ASKING YOU AS A *FRIEND,* NOT AS A REPORTER.
I TOLD YOU THE FIRST NIGHT YOU CAME OVER, YOU'RE *SAFE* IN THIS APARTMENT. WHEN THAT DOOR CLOSES BEHIND YOU, YOU CAN JUST BE YOURSELF.

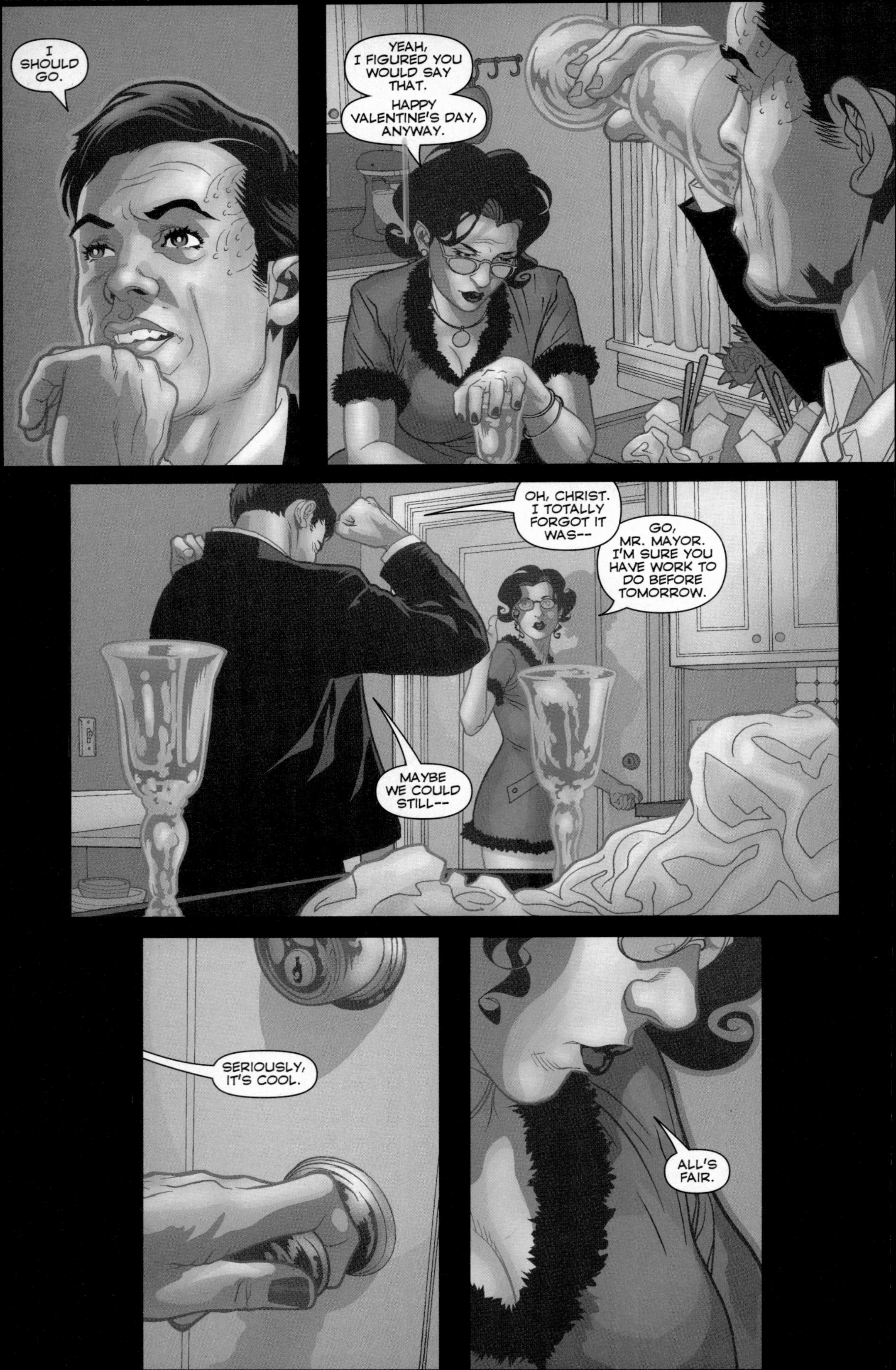

I SHOULD GO.
YEAH, I FIGURED YOU WOULD SAY THAT.
HAPPY VALENTINE'S DAY, ANYWAY.
OH, CHRIST. I TOTALLY FORGOT IT WAS--
GO, MR. MAYOR. I'M SURE YOU HAVE WORK TO DO BEFORE TOMORROW.
MAYBE WE COULD STILL--
SERIOUSLY, IT'S COOL.
ALL'S FAIR.

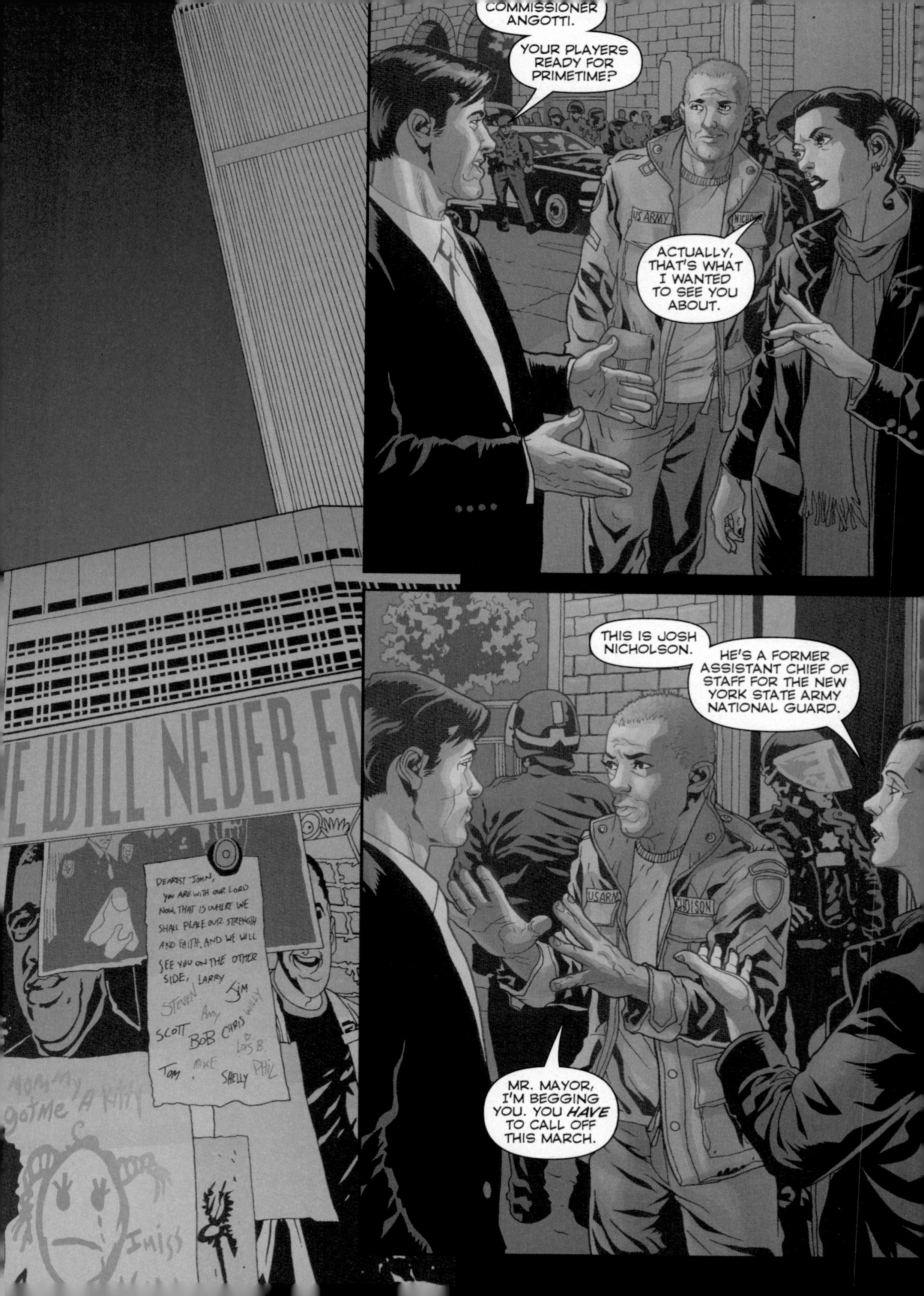
E WILL NEVER FO
DEAREST JOHN, YOU ARE WITH OUR LORD NOW. THAT IS WHERE WE SHALL PLACE OUR STRENGTH AND FAITH. AND WE WILL SEE YOU ON THE OTHER SIDE, LARRY
STEVEN JIM AMY SCOTT BOB CHRIS WILLY LOIS B. TOM MIKE SHELLY PHIL
Mommy got me A kitty
I miss
COMMISSIONER ANGOTTI.
YOUR PLAYERS READY FOR PRIMETIME?
ACTUALLY, THAT'S WHAT I WANTED TO SEE YOU ABOUT.
THIS IS JOSH NICHOLSON.
HE'S A FORMER ASSISTANT CHIEF OF STAFF FOR THE NEW YORK STATE ARMY NATIONAL GUARD.
MR. MAYOR, I'M BEGGING YOU. YOU *HAVE* TO CALL OFF THIS MARCH.

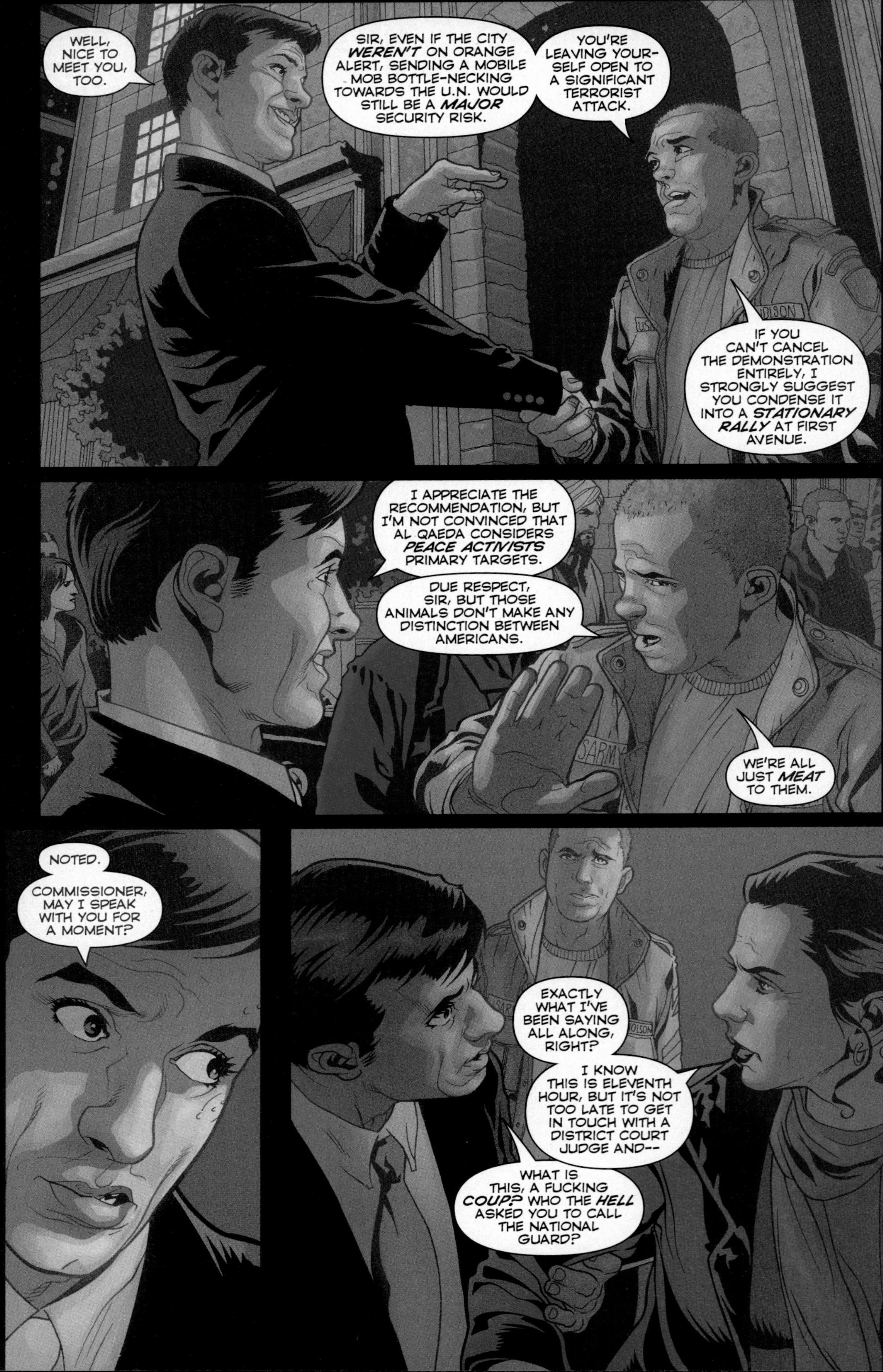
WELL, NICE TO MEET YOU, TOO.
SIR, EVEN IF THE CITY WEREN'T ON ORANGE ALERT, SENDING A MOBILE MOB BOTTLE-NECKING TOWARDS THE U.N. WOULD STILL BE A MAJOR SECURITY RISK.
YOU'RE LEAVING YOUR-SELF OPEN TO A SIGNIFICANT TERRORIST ATTACK.
IF YOU CAN'T CANCEL THE DEMONSTRATION ENTIRELY, I STRONGLY SUGGEST YOU CONDENSE IT INTO A STATIONARY RALLY AT FIRST AVENUE.
I APPRECIATE THE RECOMMENDATION, BUT I'M NOT CONVINCED THAT AL QAEDA CONSIDERS PEACE ACTIVISTS PRIMARY TARGETS.
DUE RESPECT, SIR, BUT THOSE ANIMALS DON'T MAKE ANY DISTINCTION BETWEEN AMERICANS.
WE'RE ALL JUST MEAT TO THEM.
NOTED.
COMMISSIONER, MAY I SPEAK WITH YOU FOR A MOMENT?
EXACTLY WHAT I'VE BEEN SAYING ALL ALONG, RIGHT?
I KNOW THIS IS ELEVENTH HOUR, BUT IT'S NOT TOO LATE TO GET IN TOUCH WITH A DISTRICT COURT JUDGE AND--
WHAT IS THIS, A FUCKING COUP? WHO THE HELL ASKED YOU TO CALL THE NATIONAL GUARD?

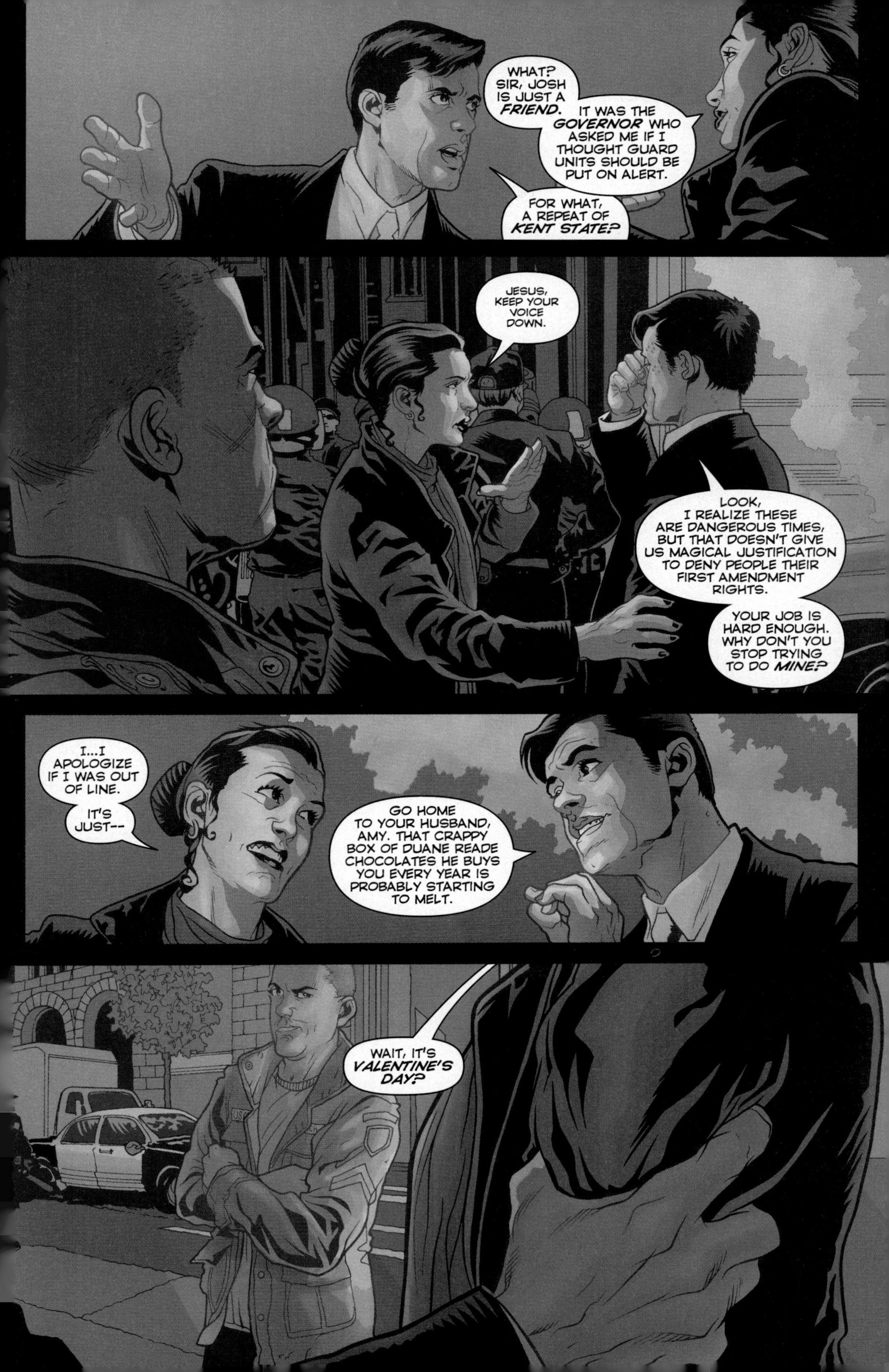
WHAT? SIR, JOSH IS JUST A *FRIEND.*
IT WAS THE *GOVERNOR* WHO ASKED ME IF I THOUGHT GUARD UNITS SHOULD BE PUT ON ALERT.
FOR WHAT, A REPEAT OF *KENT STATE?*
JESUS, KEEP YOUR VOICE DOWN.
LOOK, I REALIZE THESE ARE DANGEROUS TIMES, BUT THAT DOESN'T GIVE US MAGICAL JUSTIFICATION TO DENY PEOPLE THEIR FIRST AMENDMENT RIGHTS.
YOUR JOB IS HARD ENOUGH. WHY DON'T YOU STOP TRYING TO DO *MINE?*
I...I APOLOGIZE IF I WAS OUT OF LINE.
IT'S JUST--
GO HOME TO YOUR HUSBAND, AMY. THAT CRAPPY BOX OF DUANE READE CHOCOLATES HE BUYS YOU EVERY YEAR IS PROBABLY STARTING TO MELT.
WAIT, IT'S *VALENTINE'S DAY?*

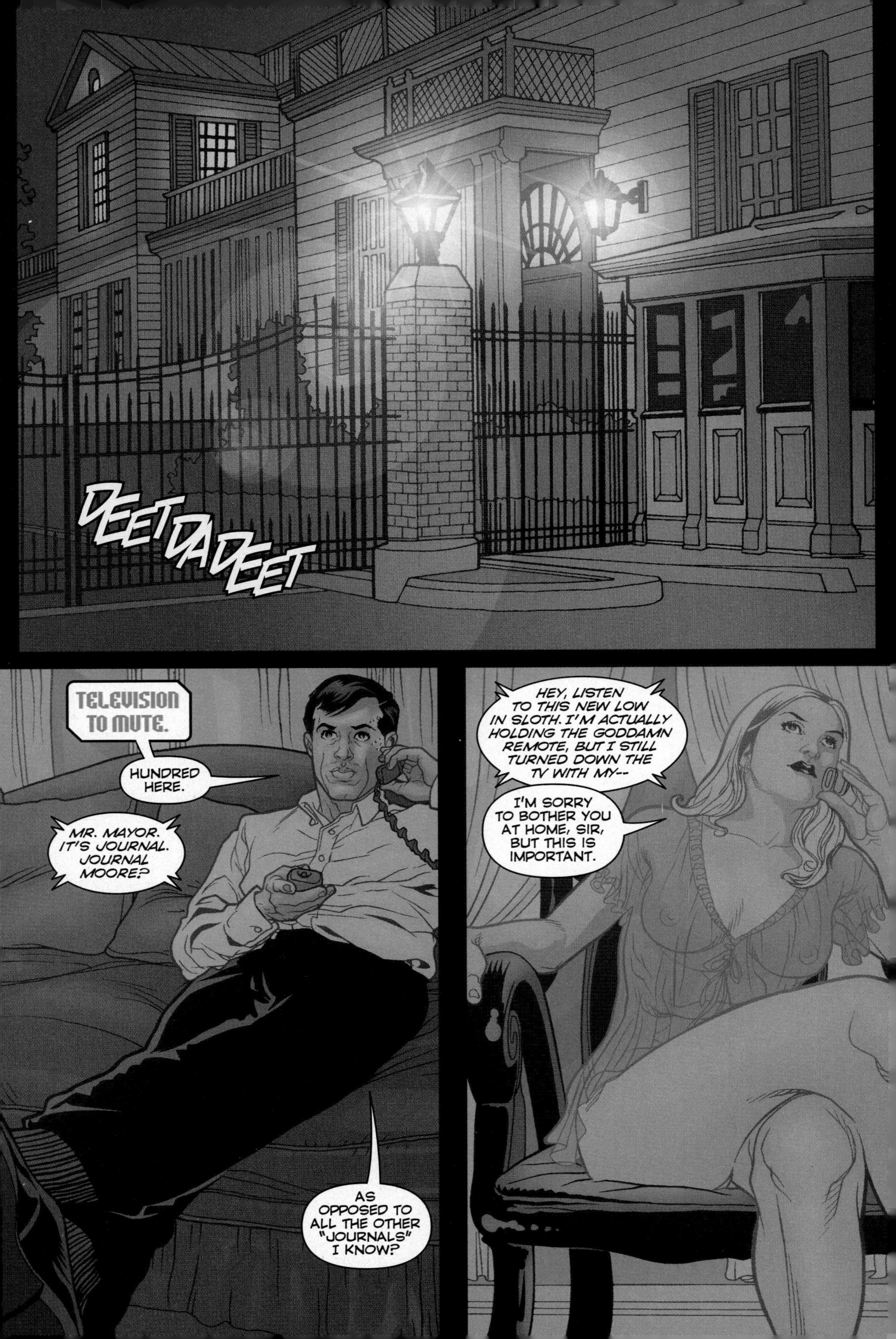
DEET DA DEET
TELEVISION TO MUTE.
HUNDRED HERE.
MR. MAYOR. IT'S JOURNAL. JOURNAL MOORE?
AS OPPOSED TO ALL THE OTHER "JOURNALS" I KNOW?
HEY, LISTEN TO THIS NEW LOW IN SLOTH. I'M ACTUALLY HOLDING THE GODDAMN REMOTE, BUT I STILL TURNED DOWN THE TV WITH MY--
I'M SORRY TO BOTHER YOU AT HOME, SIR, BUT THIS IS IMPORTANT.

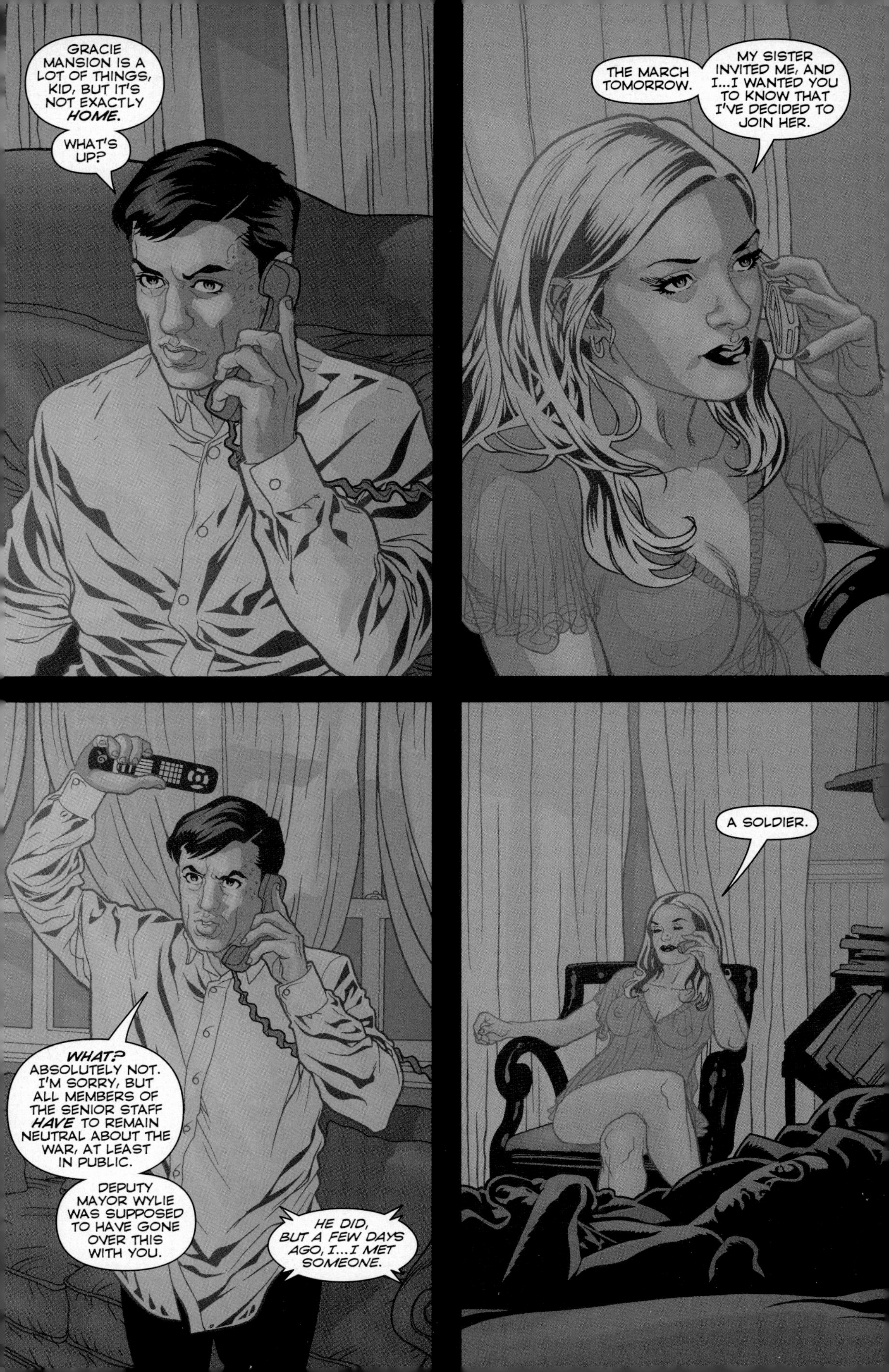
GRACIE MANSION IS A LOT OF THINGS, KID, BUT IT'S NOT EXACTLY *HOME*.
WHAT'S UP?
THE MARCH TOMORROW.
MY SISTER INVITED ME, AND I...I WANTED YOU TO KNOW THAT I'VE DECIDED TO JOIN HER.
WHAT? ABSOLUTELY NOT. I'M SORRY, BUT ALL MEMBERS OF THE SENIOR STAFF *HAVE* TO REMAIN NEUTRAL ABOUT THE WAR, AT LEAST IN PUBLIC.
DEPUTY MAYOR WYLIE WAS SUPPOSED TO HAVE GONE OVER THIS WITH YOU.
HE DID, BUT A FEW DAYS AGO, I...I MET SOMEONE.
A SOLDIER.

OH, NO.

HIS NAME IS SCOTT COOK. HE'S FROM LONG ISLAND. HE'S...HE'S IN THE RESERVES.

IF AMERICA INVADES IRAQ, HE'LL DEFINITELY GET CALLED, SIR. IT WOULD BE ONE THING IF THEY SENT HIM INTO AFGHANISTAN, BUT I DON'T THINK IT'S FAIR THAT--

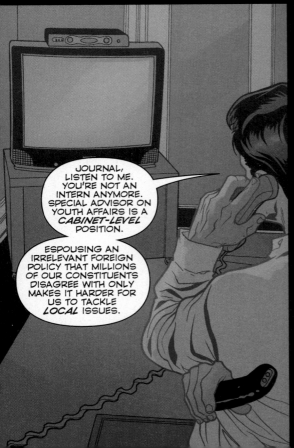

JOURNAL, LISTEN TO ME. YOU'RE NOT AN INTERN ANYMORE. SPECIAL ADVISOR ON YOUTH AFFAIRS IS A CABINET-LEVEL POSITION.

ESPOUSING AN IRRELEVANT FOREIGN POLICY THAT MILLIONS OF OUR CONSTITUENTS DISAGREE WITH ONLY MAKES IT HARDER FOR US TO TACKLE LOCAL ISSUES.

BUT ALL POLITICS ARE LOCAL, SIR. YOU'RE THE ONE WHO TAUGHT ME THAT.

AND WHEN RECRUITERS COME INTO OUR PUBLIC SCHOOLS ENCOURAGING YOUNG PEOPLE TO SIGN UP FOR THE MILITARY, HOW CAN YOU SAY THAT'S NOT RELEVANT TO WHAT WE DO?

I WON'T ARGUE ABOUT THIS, MS. MOORE!

AS LONG AS YOU'RE WORKING FOR ME, YOU *CANNOT* GO ANYWHERE NEAR THAT DEMONSTRATION.

I KNOW, MR. MAYOR.

THAT'S WHY I LEFT MY LETTER OF RESIGNATION ON YOUR DESK.

JOURNAL, DON'T DO THIS! YOU'RE A BRILLIANT YOUNG WOMAN, AND YOU'VE GOT A LONG CAREER IN PUBLIC SERVICE IF YOU WANT IT.

I UNDERSTAND HOW YOU FEEL, BUT COME ON! LAY DOWN YOUR SWORD THIS ONCE, AND LIVE TO FIGHT ANOTHER DAY.

THANK YOU, MAYOR HUNDRED...

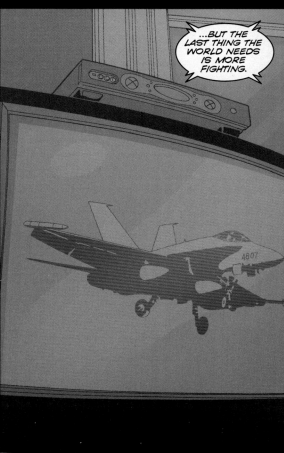

...BUT THE LAST THING THE WORLD NEEDS IS MORE FIGHTING.

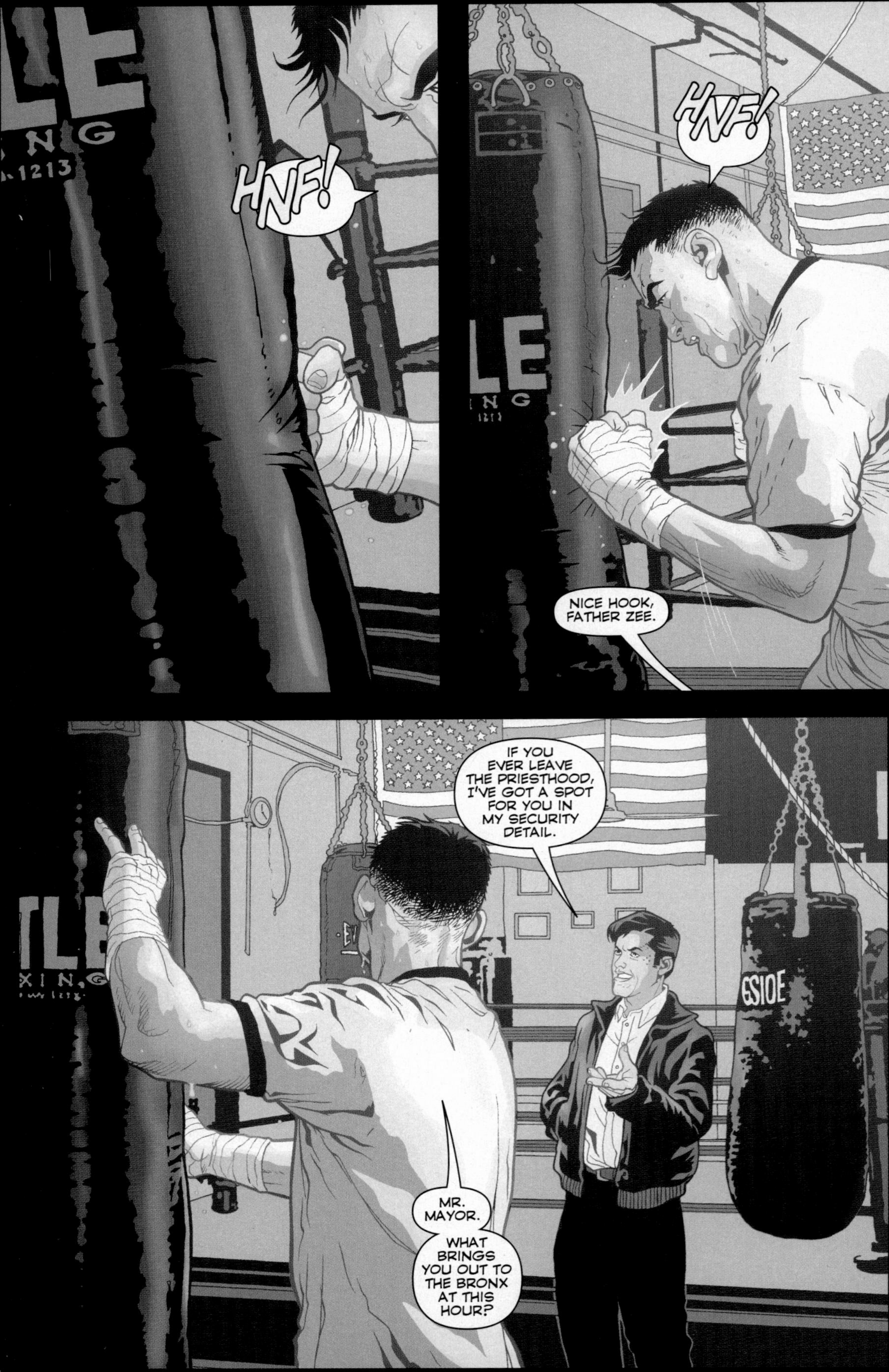
HNF!
HNF!
NICE HOOK, FATHER ZEE.
IF YOU EVER LEAVE THE PRIESTHOOD, I'VE GOT A SPOT FOR YOU IN MY SECURITY DETAIL.
MR. MAYOR.
WHAT BRINGS YOU OUT TO THE BRONX AT THIS HOUR?

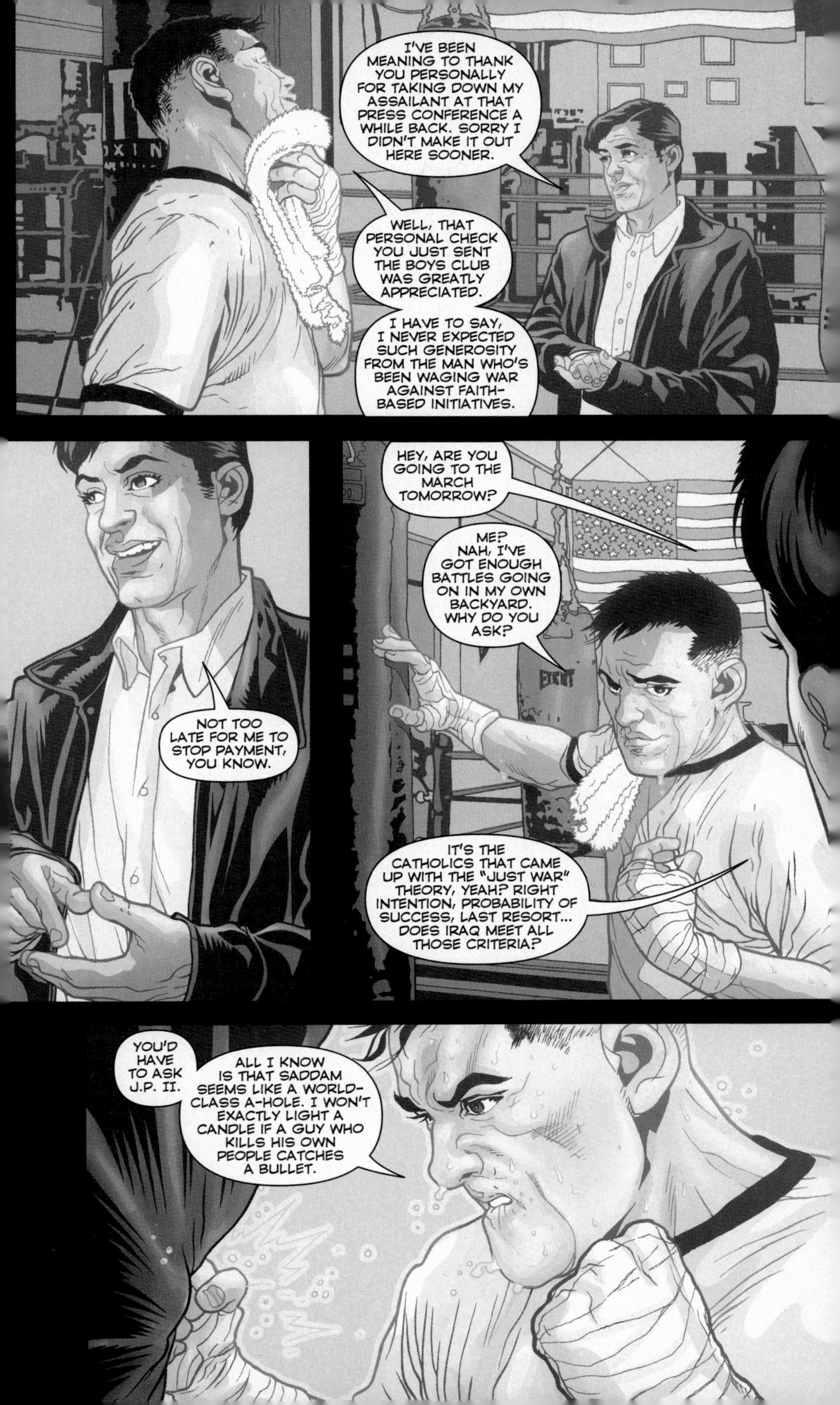

I'VE BEEN MEANING TO THANK YOU PERSONALLY FOR TAKING DOWN MY ASSAILANT AT THAT PRESS CONFERENCE A WHILE BACK. SORRY I DIDN'T MAKE IT OUT HERE SOONER.
WELL, THAT PERSONAL CHECK YOU JUST SENT THE BOYS CLUB WAS GREATLY APPRECIATED.
I HAVE TO SAY, I NEVER EXPECTED SUCH GENEROSITY FROM THE MAN WHO'S BEEN WAGING WAR AGAINST FAITH-BASED INITIATIVES.
NOT TOO LATE FOR ME TO STOP PAYMENT, YOU KNOW.
HEY, ARE YOU GOING TO THE MARCH TOMORROW?
ME? NAH, I'VE GOT ENOUGH BATTLES GOING ON IN MY OWN BACKYARD. WHY DO YOU ASK?
IT'S THE CATHOLICS THAT CAME UP WITH THE "JUST WAR" THEORY, YEAH? RIGHT INTENTION, PROBABILITY OF SUCCESS, LAST RESORT... DOES IRAQ MEET ALL THOSE CRITERIA?
YOU'D HAVE TO ASK J.P. II.
ALL I KNOW IS THAT SADDAM SEEMS LIKE A WORLD-CLASS A-HOLE. I WON'T EXACTLY LIGHT A CANDLE IF A GUY WHO KILLS HIS OWN PEOPLE CATCHES A BULLET.

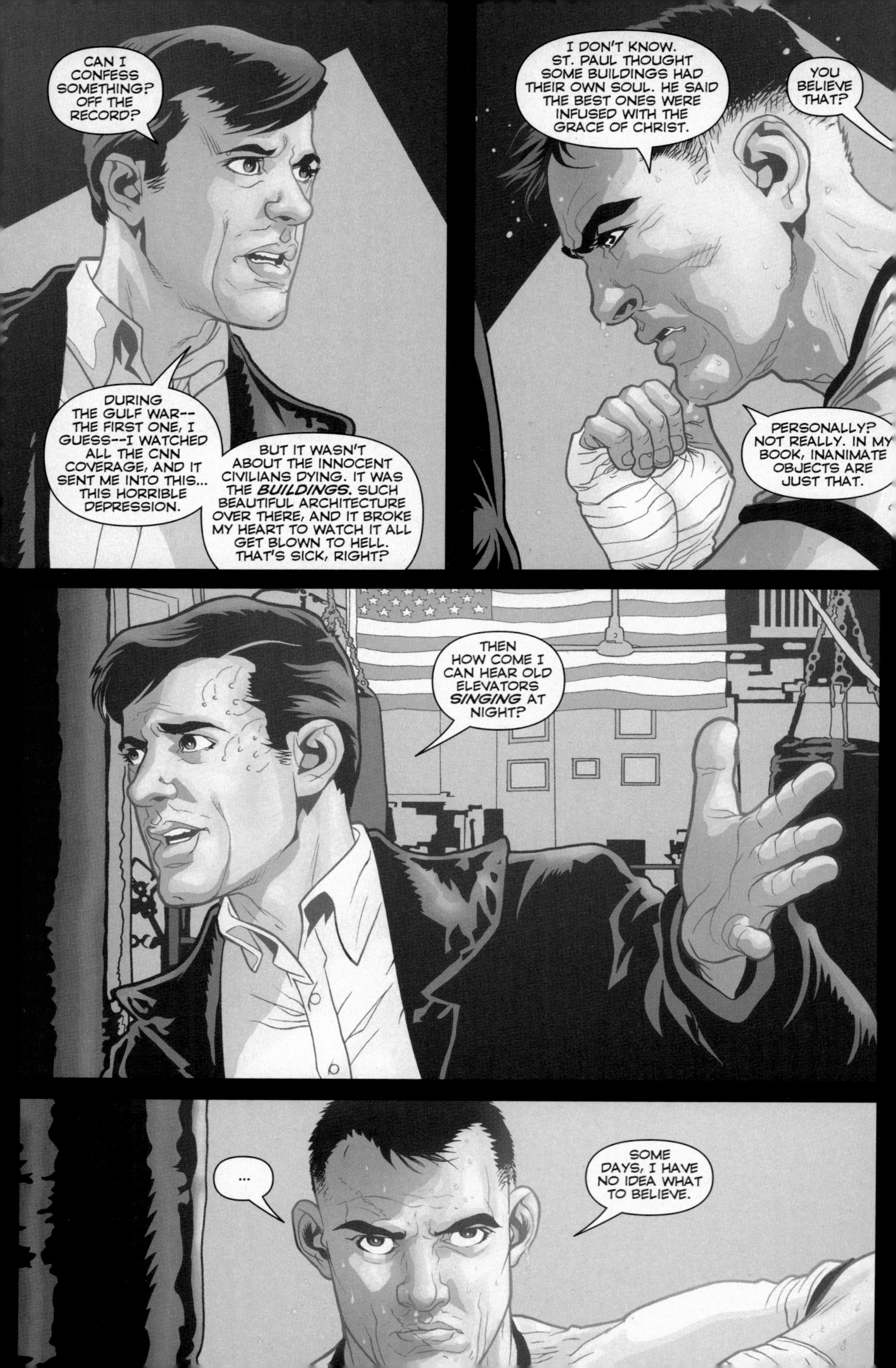
CAN I CONFESS SOMETHING? OFF THE RECORD?
DURING THE GULF WAR-- THE FIRST ONE, I GUESS--I WATCHED ALL THE CNN COVERAGE, AND IT SENT ME INTO THIS... THIS HORRIBLE DEPRESSION.
BUT IT WASN'T ABOUT THE INNOCENT CIVILIANS DYING. IT WAS THE BUILDINGS. SUCH BEAUTIFUL ARCHITECTURE OVER THERE, AND IT BROKE MY HEART TO WATCH IT ALL GET BLOWN TO HELL. THAT'S SICK, RIGHT?
I DON'T KNOW. ST. PAUL THOUGHT SOME BUILDINGS HAD THEIR OWN SOUL. HE SAID THE BEST ONES WERE INFUSED WITH THE GRACE OF CHRIST.
YOU BELIEVE THAT?
PERSONALLY? NOT REALLY. IN MY BOOK, INANIMATE OBJECTS ARE JUST THAT.
THEN HOW COME I CAN HEAR OLD ELEVATORS SINGING AT NIGHT?
...
SOME DAYS, I HAVE NO IDEA WHAT TO BELIEVE.

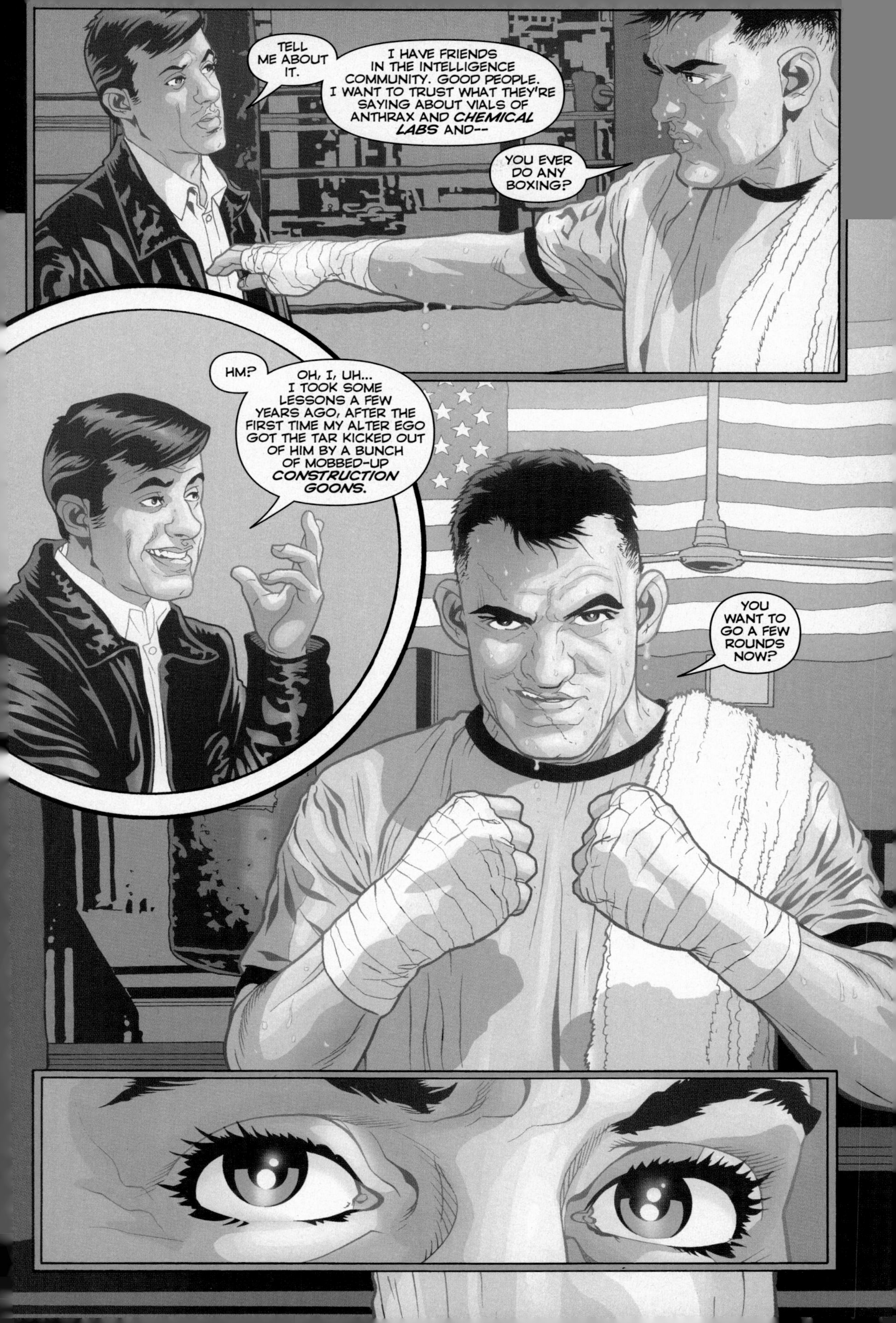
TELL ME ABOUT IT.
I HAVE FRIENDS IN THE INTELLIGENCE COMMUNITY. GOOD PEOPLE. I WANT TO TRUST WHAT THEY'RE SAYING ABOUT VIALS OF ANTHRAX AND *CHEMICAL LABS* AND--
YOU EVER DO ANY BOXING?
HM?
OH, I, UH... I TOOK SOME LESSONS A FEW YEARS AGO, AFTER THE FIRST TIME MY ALTER EGO GOT THE TAR KICKED OUT OF HIM BY A BUNCH OF MOBBED-UP *CONSTRUCTION GOONS.*
YOU WANT TO GO A FEW ROUNDS NOW?

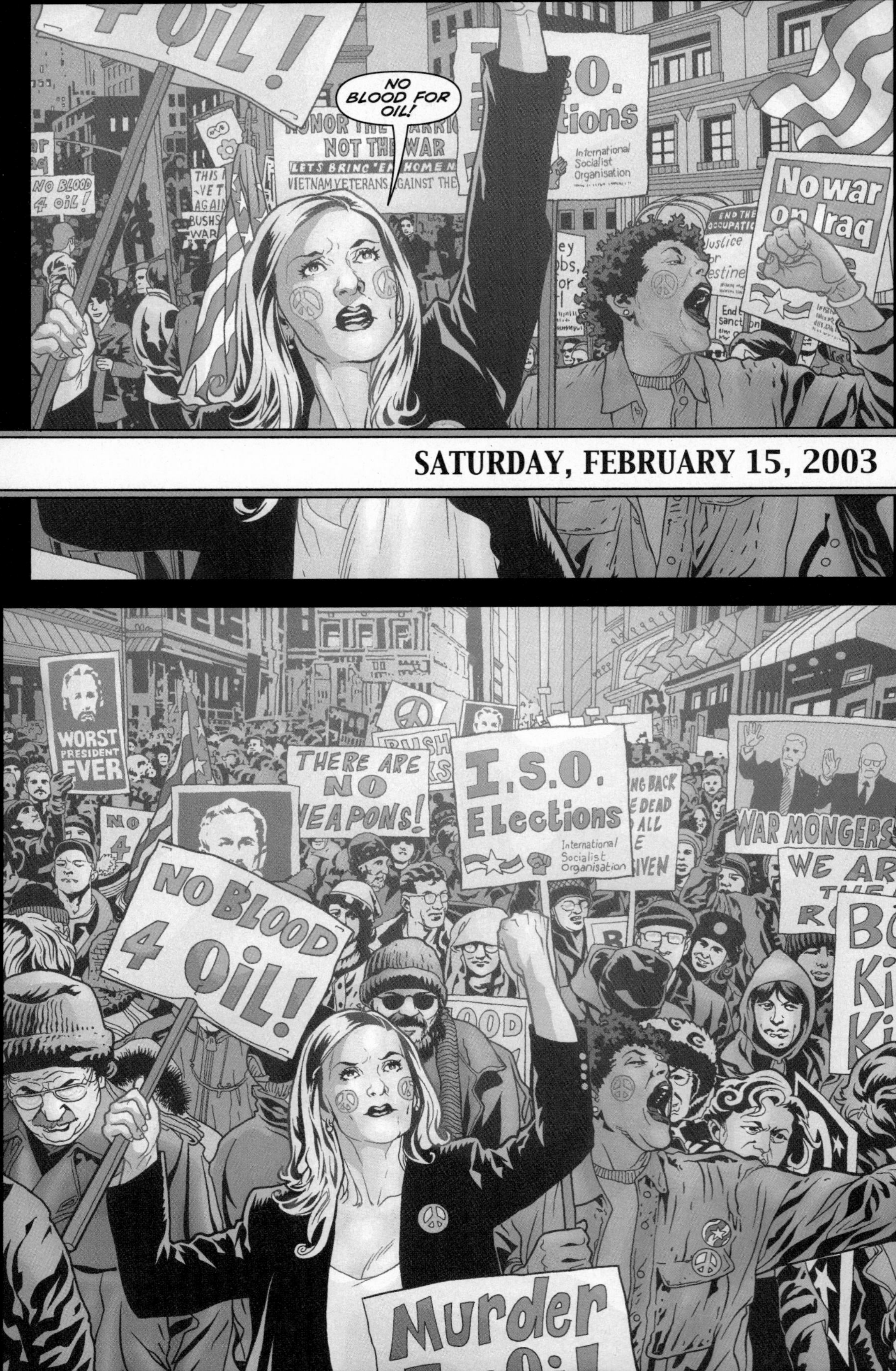
NO BLOOD FOR OIL!
SATURDAY, FEBRUARY 15, 2003
NOT THE WAR
International Socialist Organisation
No war on Iraq
NO BLOOD 4 OIL!
WORST PRESIDENT EVER
THERE ARE NO WEAPONS!
I.S.O. Elections
International Socialist Organisation
WAR MONGERS
NO BLOOD 4 OIL!
Murder

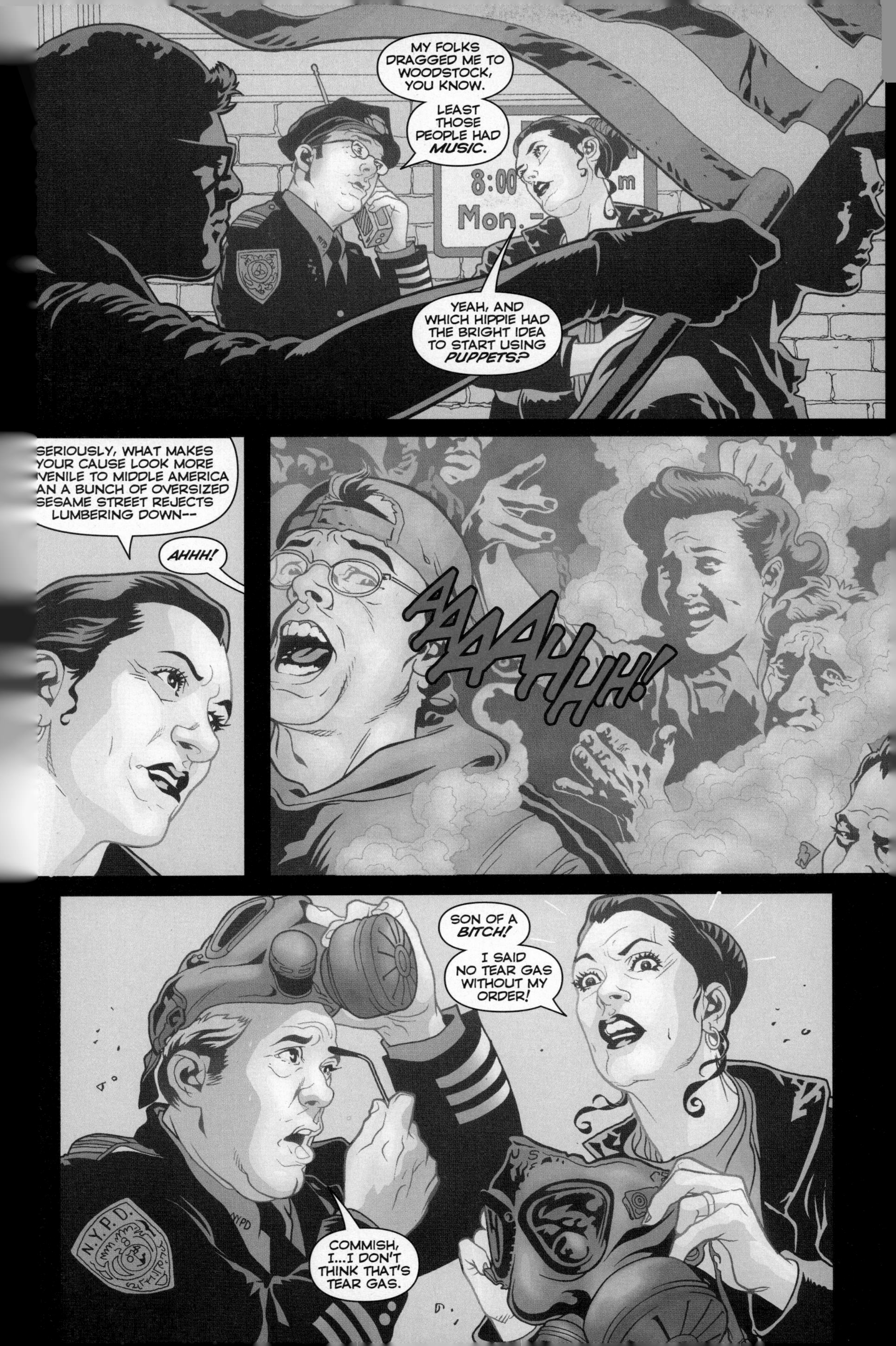

MY FOLKS DRAGGED ME TO WOODSTOCK, YOU KNOW.
LEAST THOSE PEOPLE HAD *MUSIC*.
8:00 m
Mon.
YEAH, AND WHICH HIPPIE HAD THE BRIGHT IDEA TO START USING *PUPPETS?*
SERIOUSLY, WHAT MAKES YOUR CAUSE LOOK MORE VENILE TO MIDDLE AMERICA AN A BUNCH OF OVERSIZED SESAME STREET REJECTS LUMBERING DOWN--
AHHH!
AAAAHHHH!
SON OF A *BITCH!*
I SAID NO TEAR GAS WITHOUT MY *ORDER!*
COMMISH, I...I DON'T THINK THAT'S TEAR GAS.

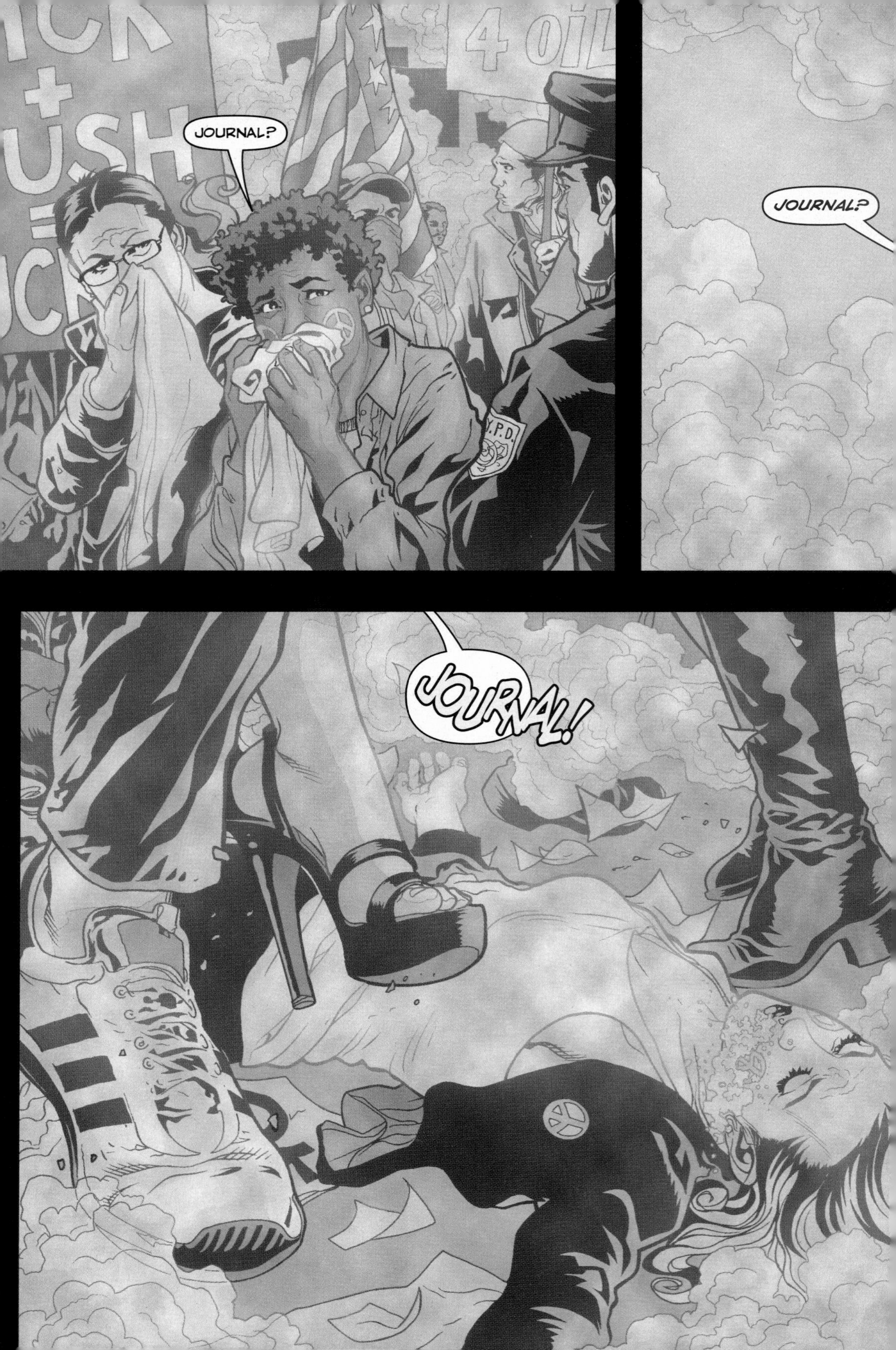
4 oil
JOURNAL?
JOURNAL?
JOURNAL!

CHAPTER 2
March to War

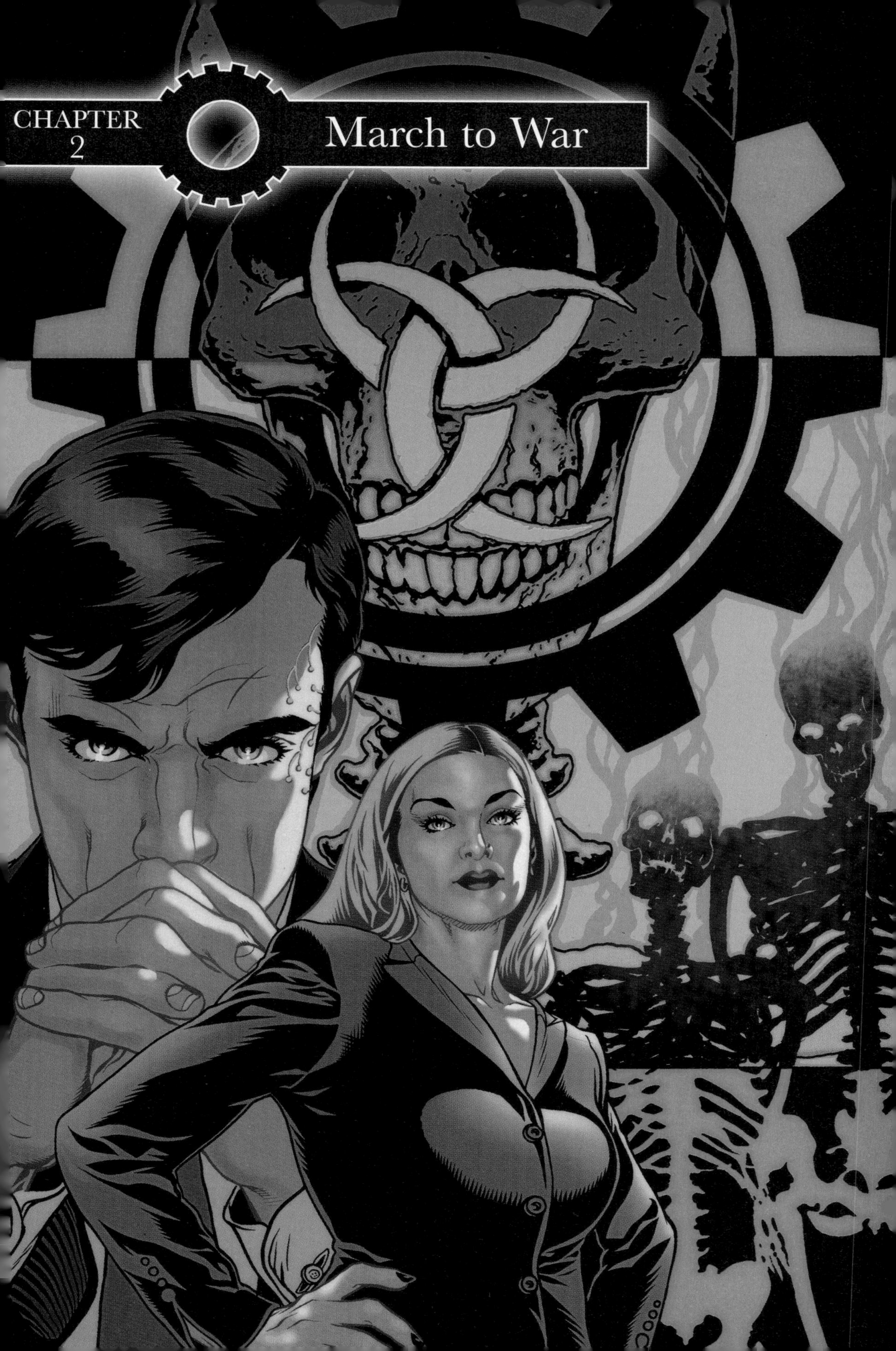

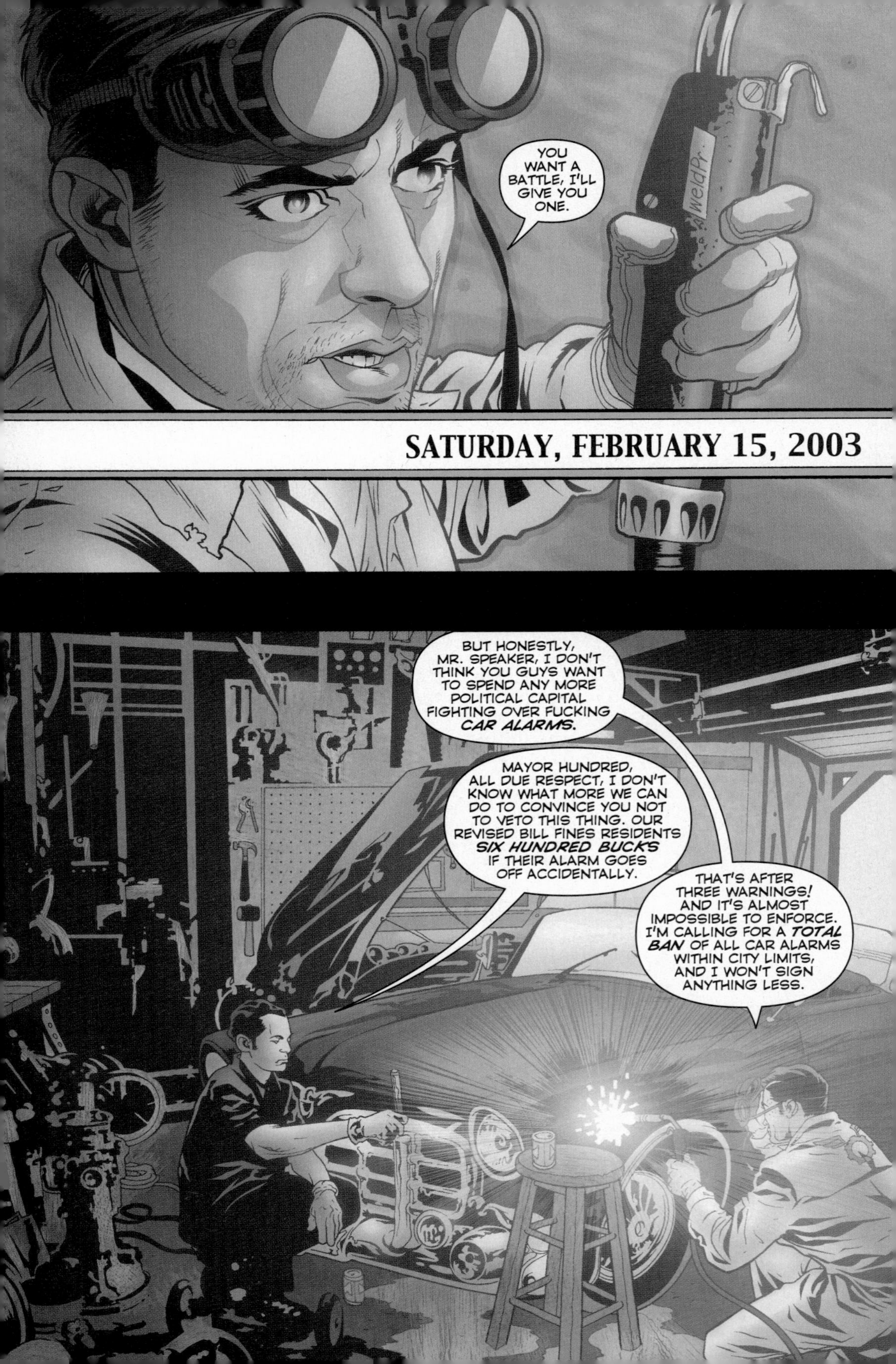
YOU WANT A BATTLE, I'LL GIVE YOU ONE.
SATURDAY, FEBRUARY 15, 2003
BUT HONESTLY, MR. SPEAKER, I DON'T THINK YOU GUYS WANT TO SPEND ANY MORE POLITICAL CAPITAL FIGHTING OVER FUCKING *CAR ALARMS.*
MAYOR HUNDRED, ALL DUE RESPECT, I DON'T KNOW WHAT MORE WE CAN DO TO CONVINCE YOU NOT TO VETO THIS THING. OUR REVISED BILL FINES RESIDENTS ***SIX HUNDRED BUCKS*** IF THEIR ALARM GOES OFF ACCIDENTALLY.
THAT'S AFTER THREE WARNINGS! AND IT'S ALMOST IMPOSSIBLE TO ENFORCE. I'M CALLING FOR A *TOTAL BAN* OF ALL CAR ALARMS WITHIN CITY LIMITS, AND I WON'T SIGN ANYTHING LESS.

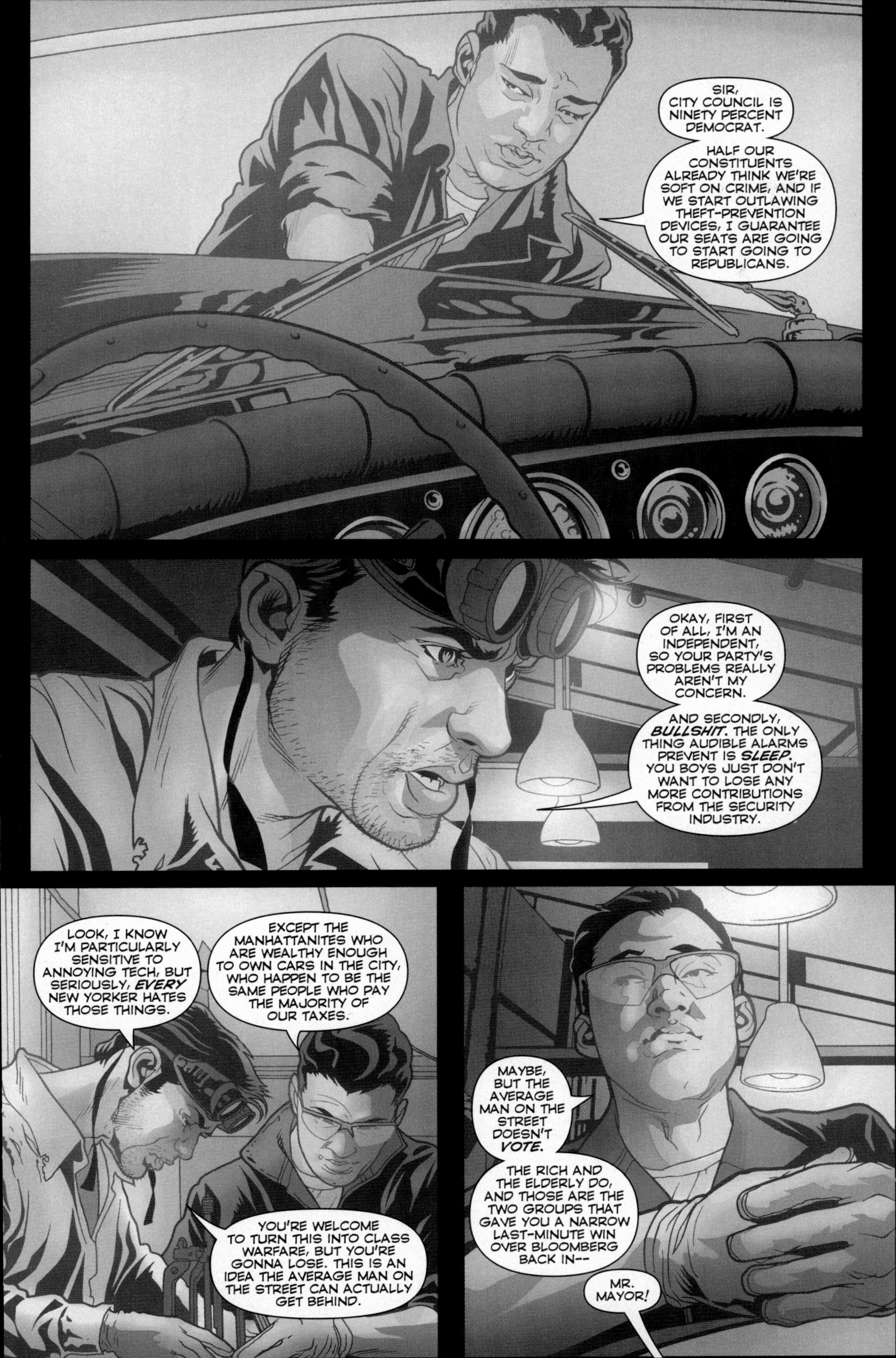
SIR, CITY COUNCIL IS NINETY PERCENT DEMOCRAT.
HALF OUR CONSTITUENTS ALREADY THINK WE'RE SOFT ON CRIME, AND IF WE START OUTLAWING THEFT-PREVENTION DEVICES, I GUARANTEE OUR SEATS ARE GOING TO START GOING TO REPUBLICANS.
OKAY, FIRST OF ALL, I'M AN INDEPENDENT, SO YOUR PARTY'S PROBLEMS REALLY AREN'T MY CONCERN.
AND SECONDLY, ***BULLSHIT***. THE ONLY THING AUDIBLE ALARMS PREVENT IS ***SLEEP***. YOU BOYS JUST DON'T WANT TO LOSE ANY MORE CONTRIBUTIONS FROM THE SECURITY INDUSTRY.
LOOK, I KNOW I'M PARTICULARLY SENSITIVE TO ANNOYING TECH, BUT SERIOUSLY, ***EVERY*** NEW YORKER HATES THOSE THINGS.
EXCEPT THE MANHATTANITES WHO ARE WEALTHY ENOUGH TO OWN CARS IN THE CITY, WHO HAPPEN TO BE THE SAME PEOPLE WHO PAY THE MAJORITY OF OUR TAXES.
YOU'RE WELCOME TO TURN THIS INTO CLASS WARFARE, BUT YOU'RE GONNA LOSE. THIS IS AN IDEA THE AVERAGE MAN ON THE STREET CAN ACTUALLY GET BEHIND.
MAYBE, BUT THE AVERAGE MAN ON THE STREET DOESN'T ***VOTE***.
THE RICH AND THE ELDERLY DO, AND THOSE ARE THE TWO GROUPS THAT GAVE YOU A NARROW LAST-MINUTE WIN OVER BLOOMBERG BACK IN--
MR. MAYOR!

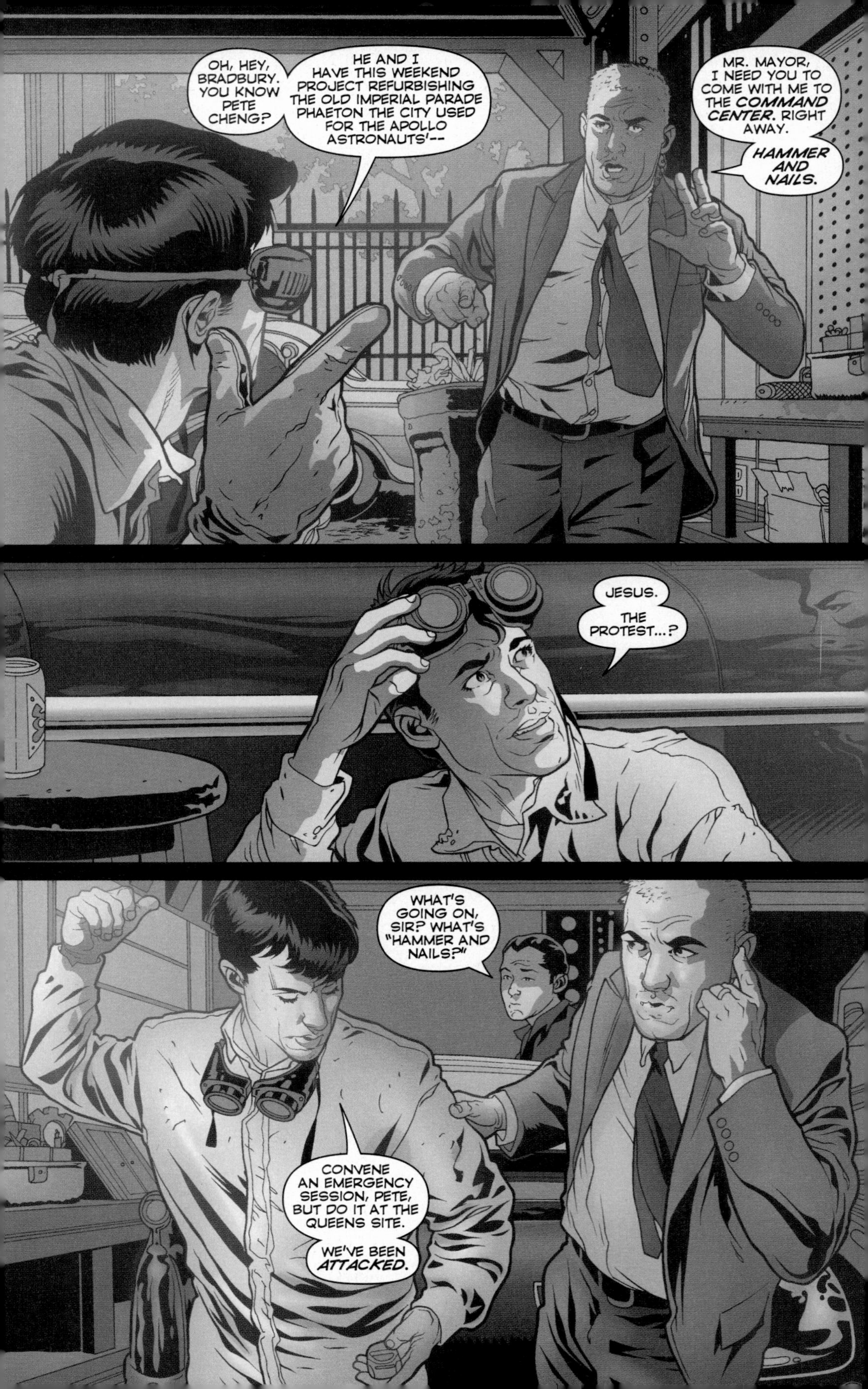
OH, HEY, BRADBURY. YOU KNOW PETE CHENG?
HE AND I HAVE THIS WEEKEND PROJECT REFURBISHING THE OLD IMPERIAL PARADE PHAETON THE CITY USED FOR THE APOLLO ASTRONAUTS'--
MR. MAYOR, I NEED YOU TO COME WITH ME TO THE COMMAND CENTER. RIGHT AWAY.
HAMMER AND NAILS.
JESUS. THE PROTEST...?
WHAT'S GOING ON, SIR? WHAT'S "HAMMER AND NAILS?"
CONVENE AN EMERGENCY SESSION, PETE, BUT DO IT AT THE QUEENS SITE.
WE'VE BEEN ATTACKED.

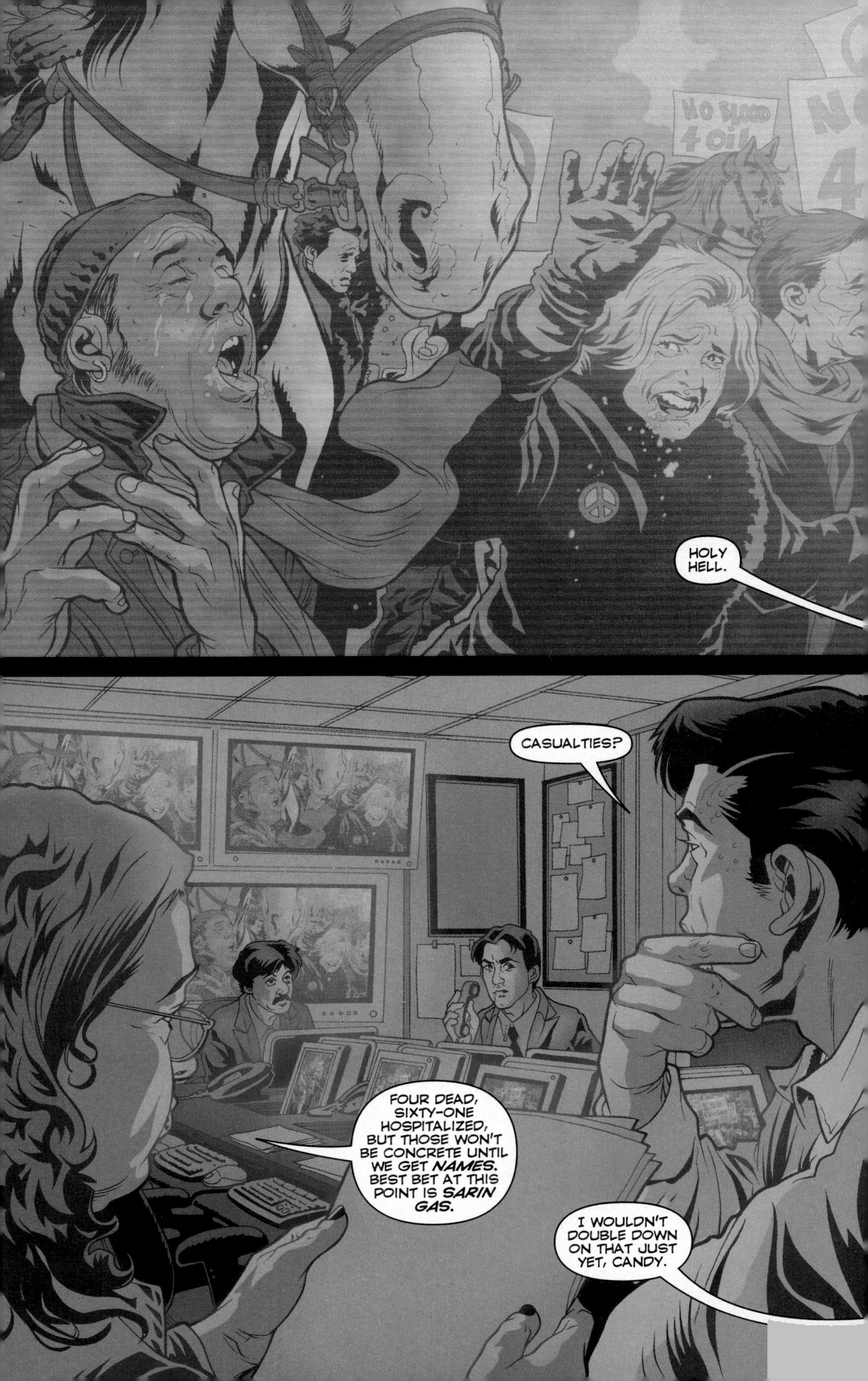
NO BLOOD 4 OIL
HOLY HELL.
CASUALTIES?
FOUR DEAD, SIXTY-ONE HOSPITALIZED, BUT THOSE WON'T BE CONCRETE UNTIL WE GET NAMES. BEST BET AT THIS POINT IS SARIN GAS.
I WOULDN'T DOUBLE DOWN ON THAT JUST YET, CANDY.

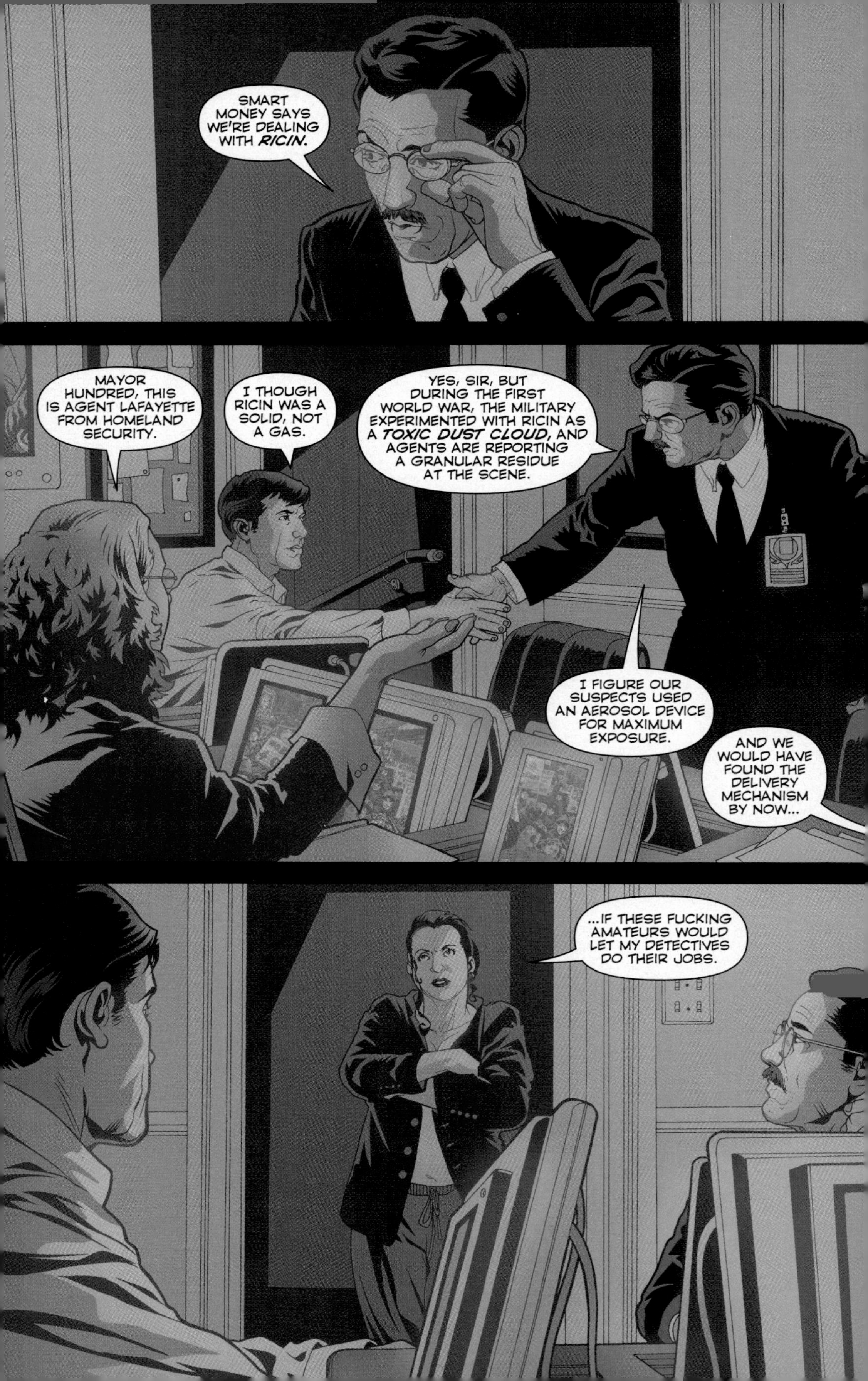
SMART MONEY SAYS WE'RE DEALING WITH *RICIN*.
MAYOR HUNDRED, THIS IS AGENT LAFAYETTE FROM HOMELAND SECURITY.
I THOUGH RICIN WAS A SOLID, NOT A GAS.
YES, SIR, BUT DURING THE FIRST WORLD WAR, THE MILITARY EXPERIMENTED WITH RICIN AS A *TOXIC DUST CLOUD*, AND AGENTS ARE REPORTING A GRANULAR RESIDUE AT THE SCENE.
I FIGURE OUR SUSPECTS USED AN AEROSOL DEVICE FOR MAXIMUM EXPOSURE.
AND WE WOULD HAVE FOUND THE DELIVERY MECHANISM BY NOW...
...IF THESE FUCKING AMATEURS WOULD LET MY DETECTIVES DO THEIR JOBS.

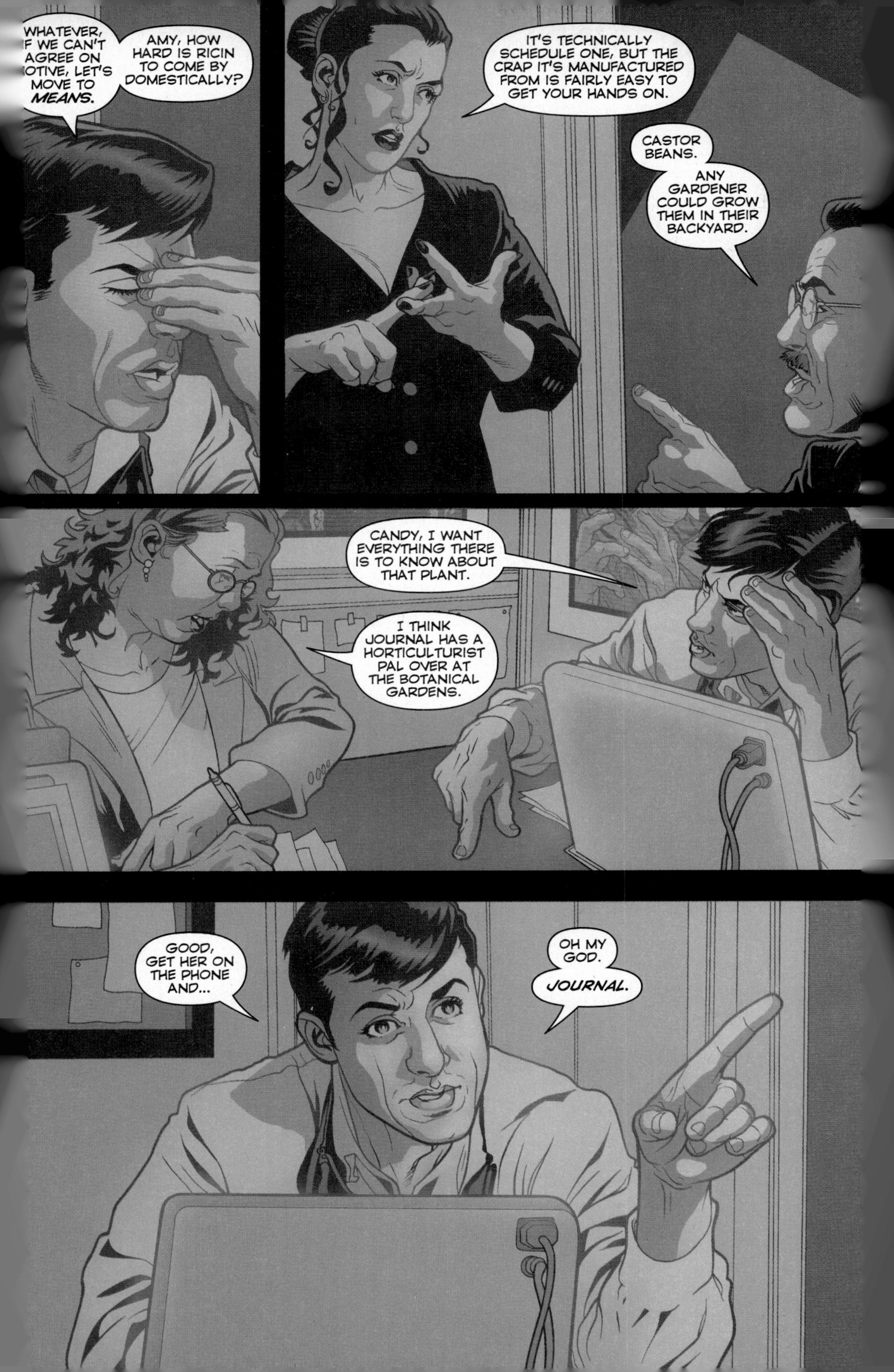
WHATEVER, IF WE CAN'T AGREE ON MOTIVE, LET'S MOVE TO *MEANS*.
AMY, HOW HARD IS RICIN TO COME BY DOMESTICALLY?
IT'S TECHNICALLY SCHEDULE ONE, BUT THE CRAP IT'S MANUFACTURED FROM IS FAIRLY EASY TO GET YOUR HANDS ON.
CASTOR BEANS.
ANY GARDENER COULD GROW THEM IN THEIR BACKYARD.
CANDY, I WANT EVERYTHING THERE IS TO KNOW ABOUT THAT PLANT.
I THINK JOURNAL HAS A HORTICULTURIST PAL OVER AT THE BOTANICAL GARDENS.
GOOD, GET HER ON THE PHONE AND...
OH MY GOD.
JOURNAL.

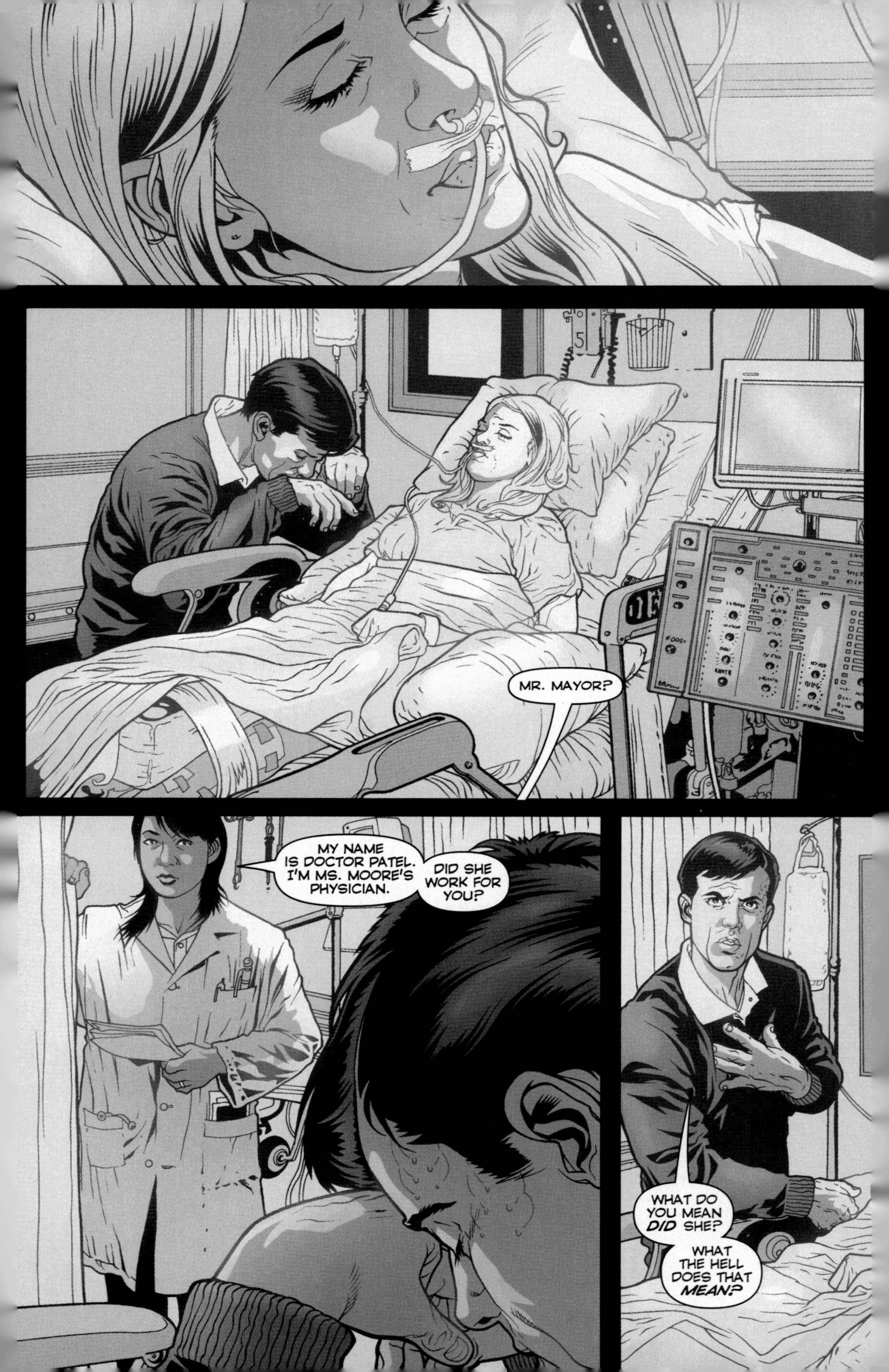
MR. MAYOR?
MY NAME IS DOCTOR PATEL. I'M MS. MOORE'S PHYSICIAN.
DID SHE WORK FOR YOU?
WHAT DO YOU MEAN *DID* SHE?
WHAT THE HELL DOES THAT *MEAN?*

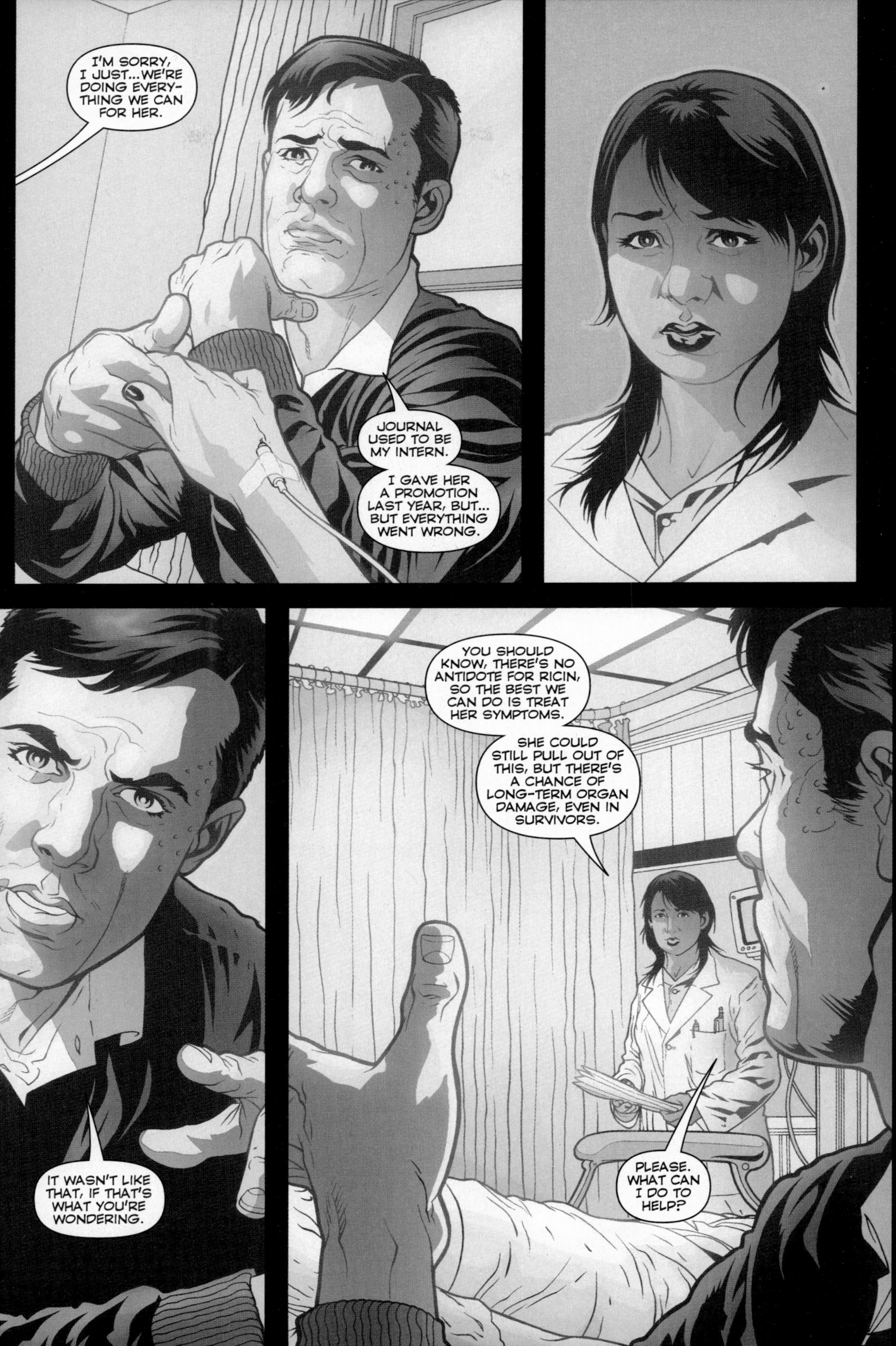
I'M SORRY, I JUST...WE'RE DOING EVERYTHING WE CAN FOR HER.
JOURNAL USED TO BE MY INTERN.
I GAVE HER A PROMOTION LAST YEAR, BUT... BUT EVERYTHING WENT WRONG.
IT WASN'T LIKE THAT, IF THAT'S WHAT YOU'RE WONDERING.
YOU SHOULD KNOW, THERE'S NO ANTIDOTE FOR RICIN, SO THE BEST WE CAN DO IS TREAT HER SYMPTOMS.
SHE COULD STILL PULL OUT OF THIS, BUT THERE'S A CHANCE OF LONG-TERM ORGAN DAMAGE, EVEN IN SURVIVORS.
PLEASE. WHAT CAN I DO TO HELP?

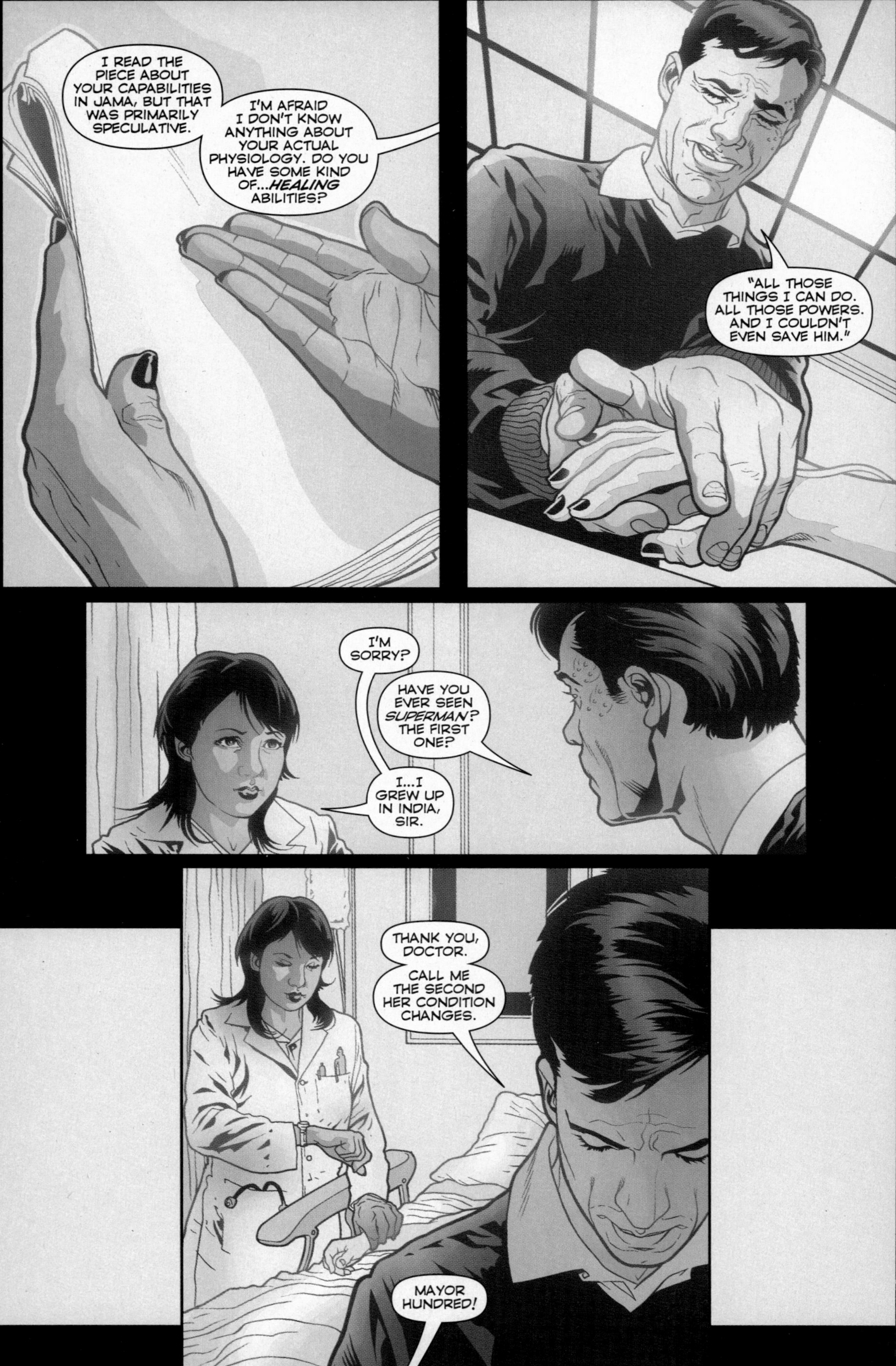
I READ THE PIECE ABOUT YOUR CAPABILITIES IN JAMA, BUT THAT WAS PRIMARILY SPECULATIVE.
I'M AFRAID I DON'T KNOW ANYTHING ABOUT YOUR ACTUAL PHYSIOLOGY. DO YOU HAVE SOME KIND OF...*HEALING* ABILITIES?
"ALL THOSE THINGS I CAN DO. ALL THOSE POWERS. AND I COULDN'T EVEN SAVE HIM."
I'M SORRY?
HAVE YOU EVER SEEN *SUPERMAN*? THE FIRST ONE?
I...I GREW UP IN INDIA, SIR.
THANK YOU, DOCTOR.
CALL ME THE SECOND HER CONDITION CHANGES.
MAYOR HUNDRED!

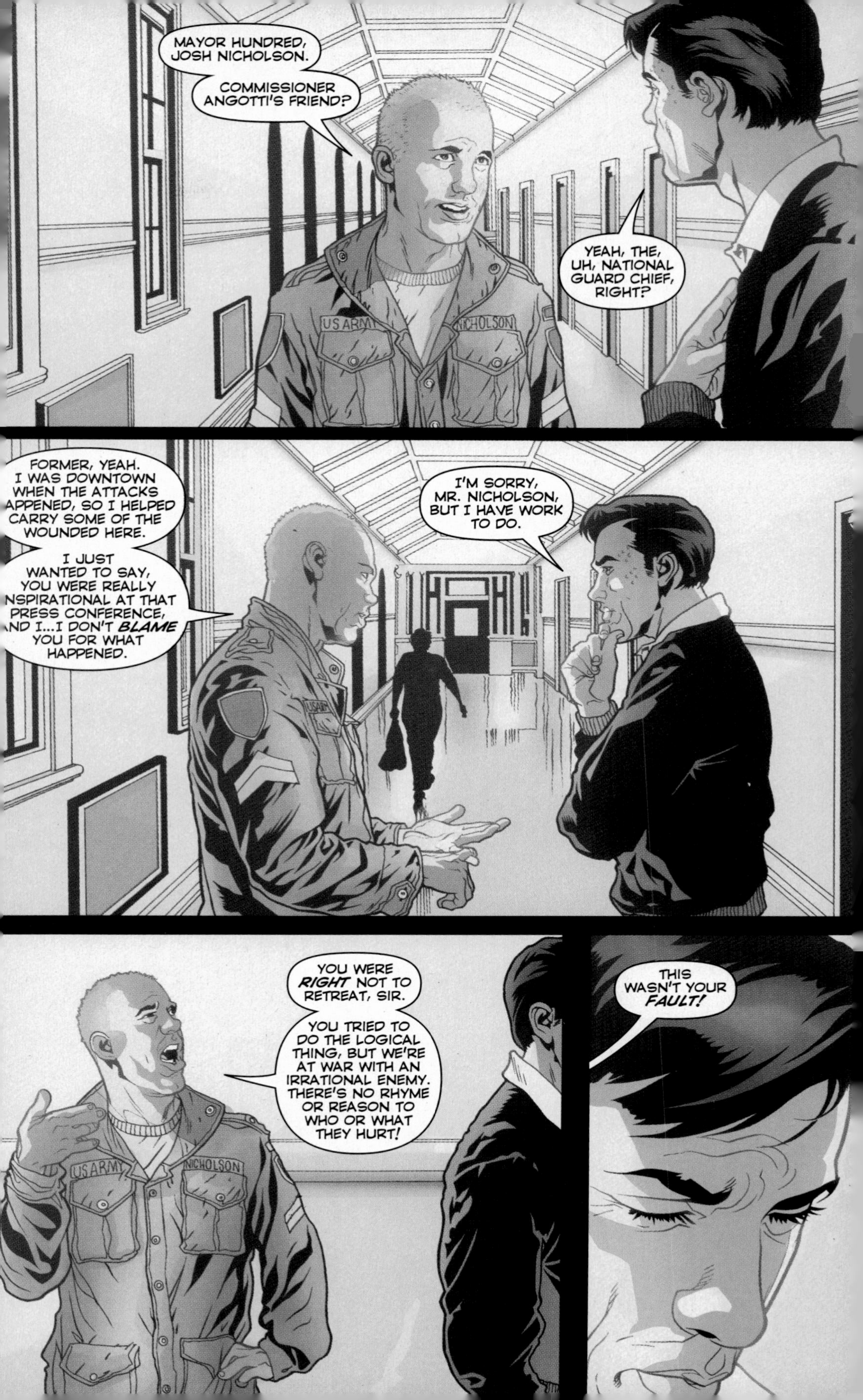
MAYOR HUNDRED, JOSH NICHOLSON.
COMMISSIONER ANGOTTI'S FRIEND?
YEAH, THE, UH, NATIONAL GUARD CHIEF, RIGHT?
FORMER, YEAH. I WAS DOWNTOWN WHEN THE ATTACKS APPENED, SO I HELPED CARRY SOME OF THE WOUNDED HERE.
I JUST WANTED TO SAY, YOU WERE REALLY NSPIRATIONAL AT THAT PRESS CONFERENCE, ND I...I DON'T *BLAME* YOU FOR WHAT HAPPENED.
I'M SORRY, MR. NICHOLSON, BUT I HAVE WORK TO DO.
YOU WERE *RIGHT* NOT TO RETREAT, SIR.
YOU TRIED TO DO THE LOGICAL THING, BUT WE'RE AT WAR WITH AN IRRATIONAL ENEMY. THERE'S NO RHYME OR REASON TO WHO OR WHAT THEY HURT!
THIS WASN'T YOUR *FAULT!*

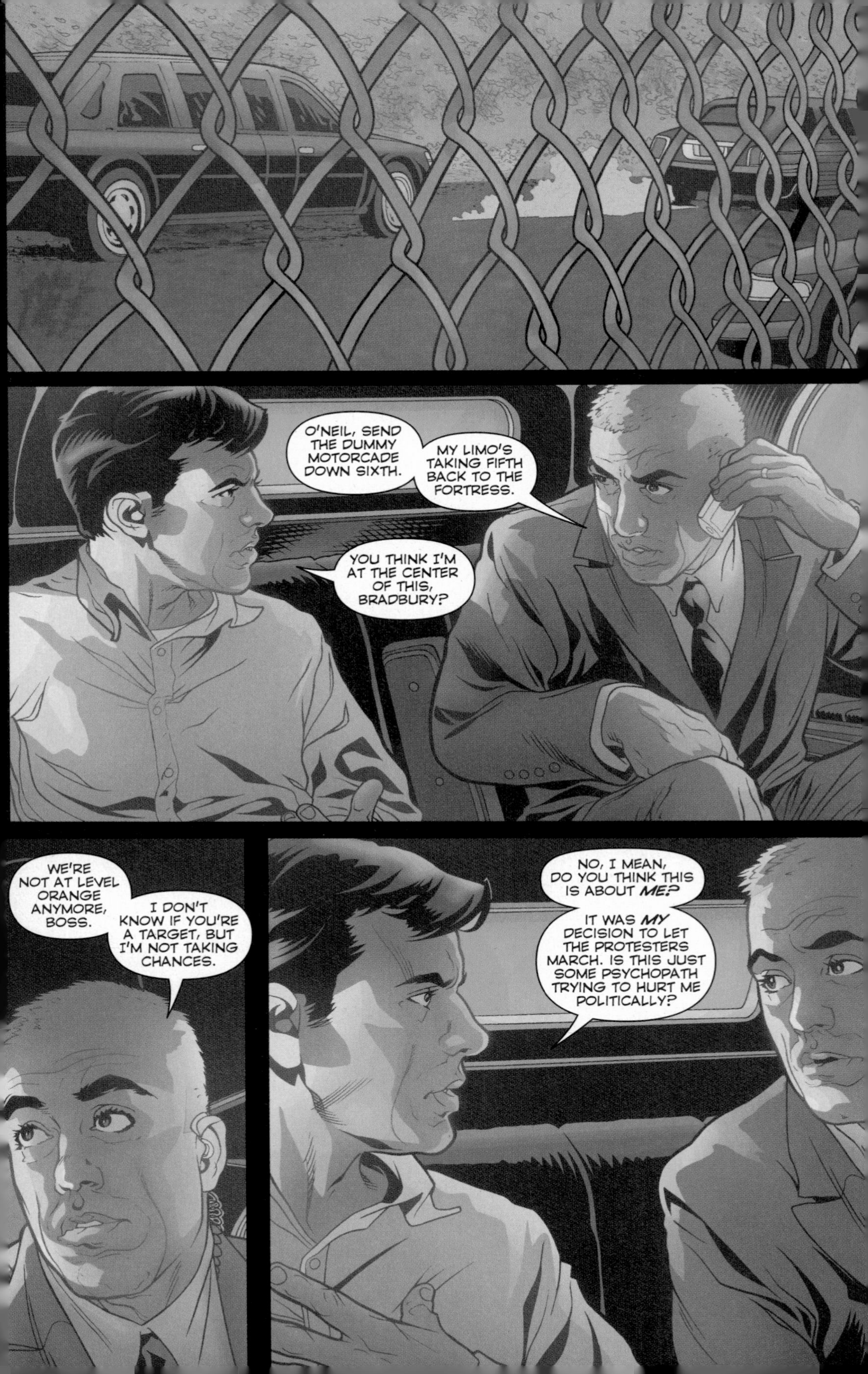
O'NEIL, SEND THE DUMMY MOTORCADE DOWN SIXTH.
MY LIMO'S TAKING FIFTH BACK TO THE FORTRESS.
YOU THINK I'M AT THE CENTER OF THIS, BRADBURY?
WE'RE NOT AT LEVEL ORANGE ANYMORE, BOSS.
I DON'T KNOW IF YOU'RE A TARGET, BUT I'M NOT TAKING CHANCES.
NO, I MEAN, DO YOU THINK THIS IS ABOUT *ME?*
IT WAS *MY* DECISION TO LET THE PROTESTERS MARCH. IS THIS JUST SOME PSYCHOPATH TRYING TO HURT ME POLITICALLY?

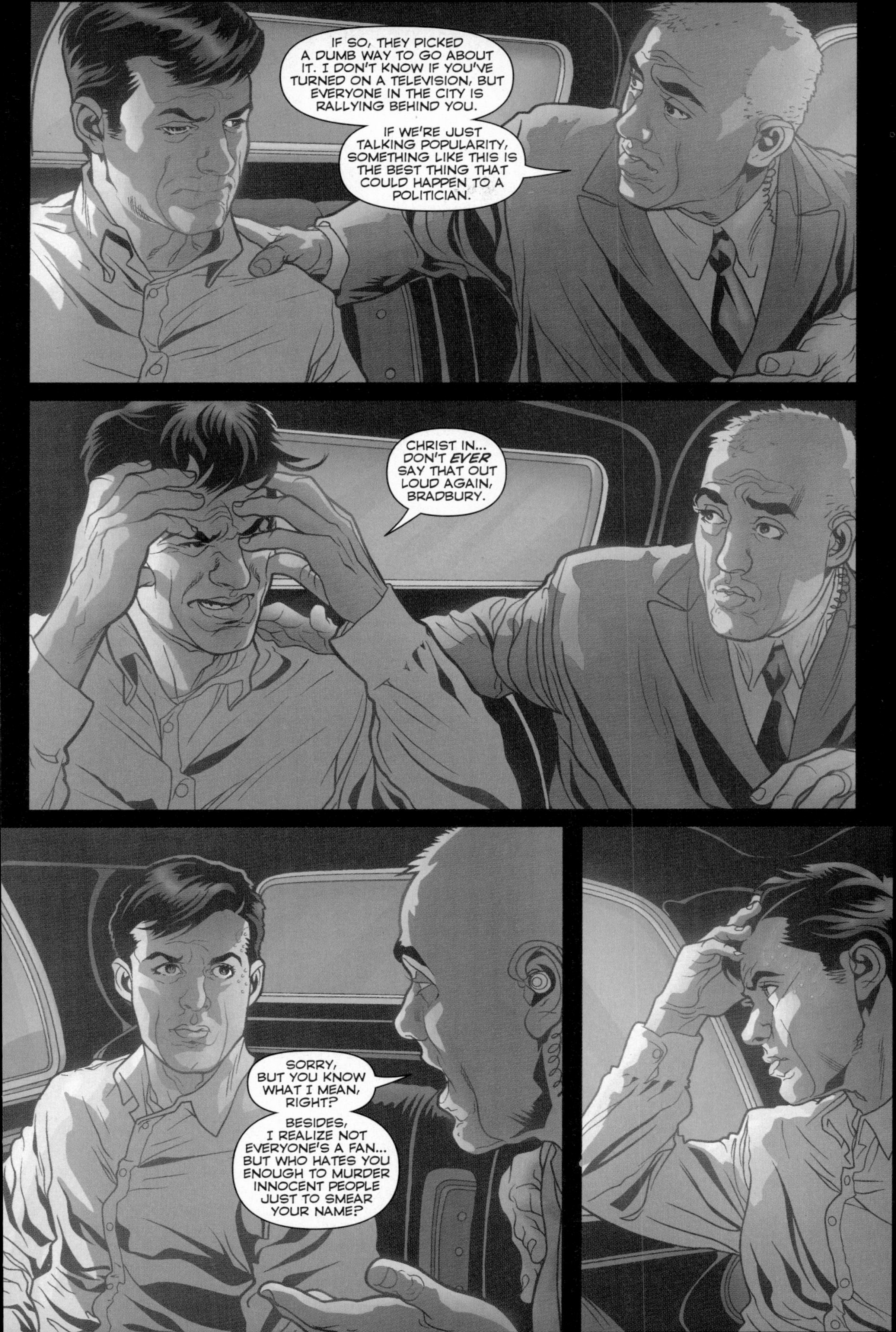
IF SO, THEY PICKED A DUMB WAY TO GO ABOUT IT. I DON'T KNOW IF YOU'VE TURNED ON A TELEVISION, BUT EVERYONE IN THE CITY IS RALLYING BEHIND YOU.
IF WE'RE JUST TALKING POPULARITY, SOMETHING LIKE THIS IS THE BEST THING THAT COULD HAPPEN TO A POLITICIAN.
CHRIST IN... DON'T *EVER* SAY THAT OUT LOUD AGAIN, BRADBURY.
SORRY, BUT YOU KNOW WHAT I MEAN, RIGHT?
BESIDES, I REALIZE NOT EVERYONE'S A FAN... BUT WHO HATES YOU ENOUGH TO MURDER INNOCENT PEOPLE JUST TO SMEAR YOUR NAME?

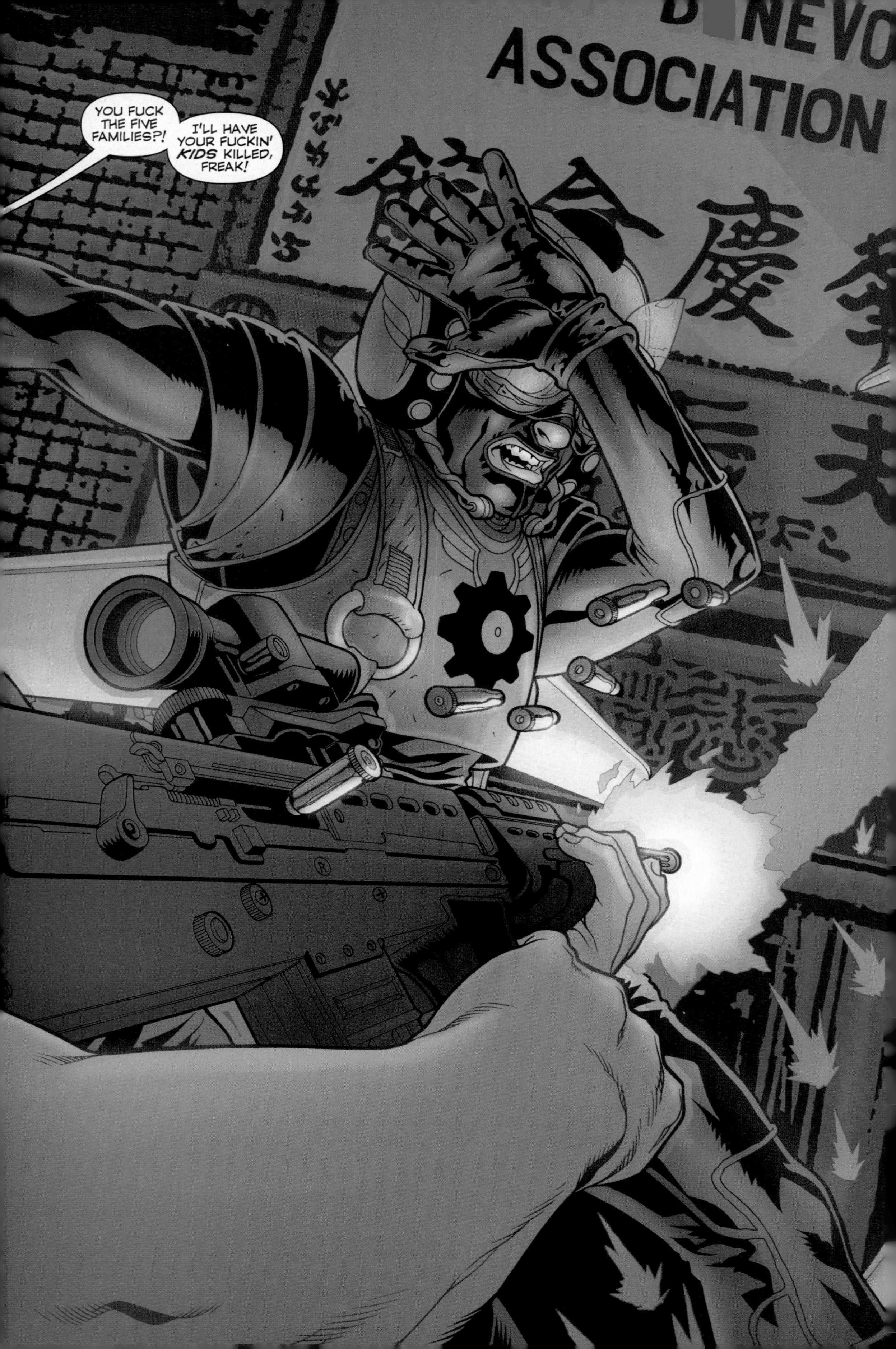
ASSOCIATION
YOU FUCK THE FIVE FAMILIES?!
I'LL HAVE YOUR FUCKIN' *KIDS* KILLED, FREAK!

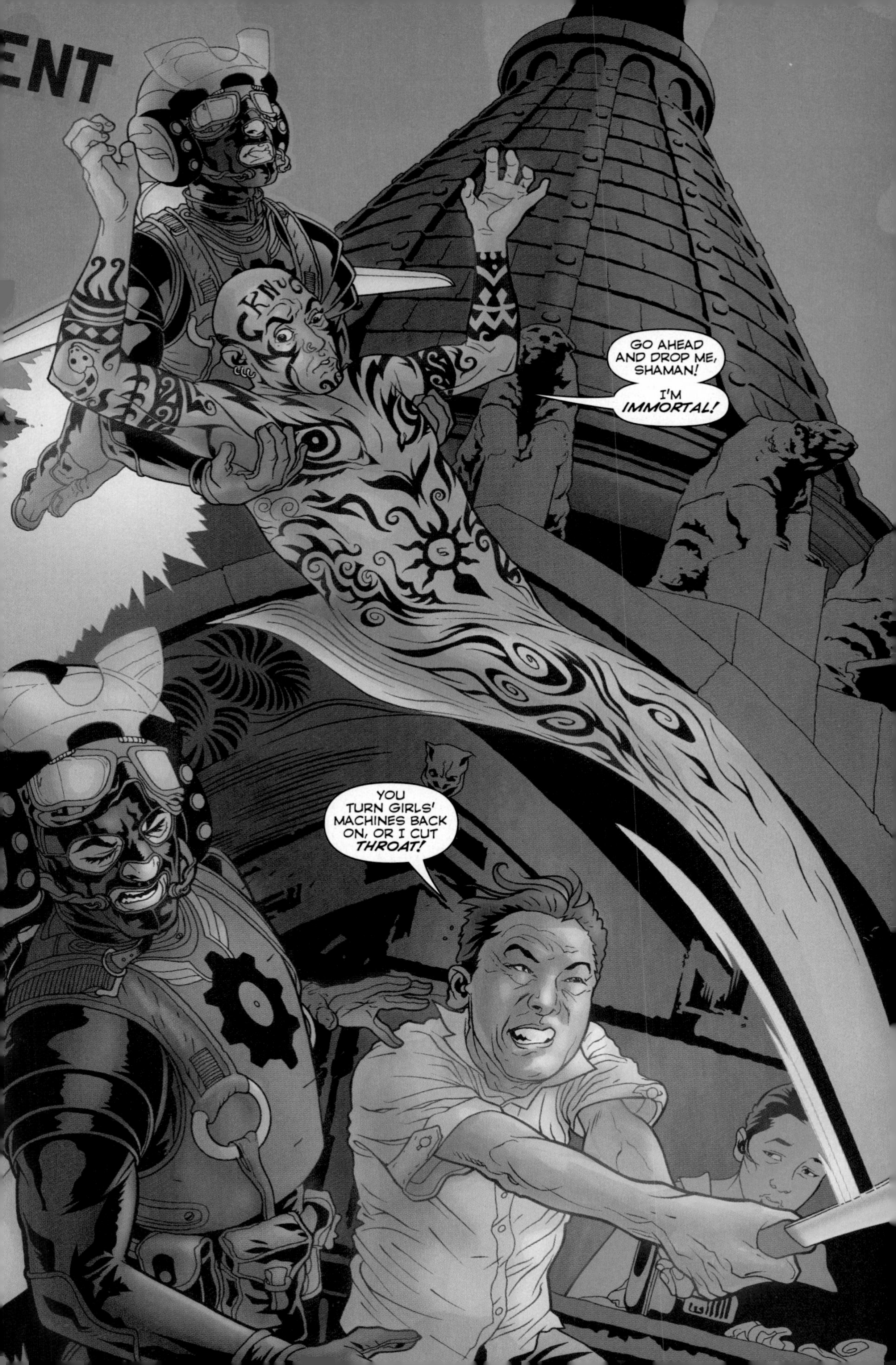
ENT
GO AHEAD AND DROP ME, SHAMAN!
I'M IMMORTAL!
YOU TURN GIRLS' MACHINES BACK ON, OR I CUT THROAT!

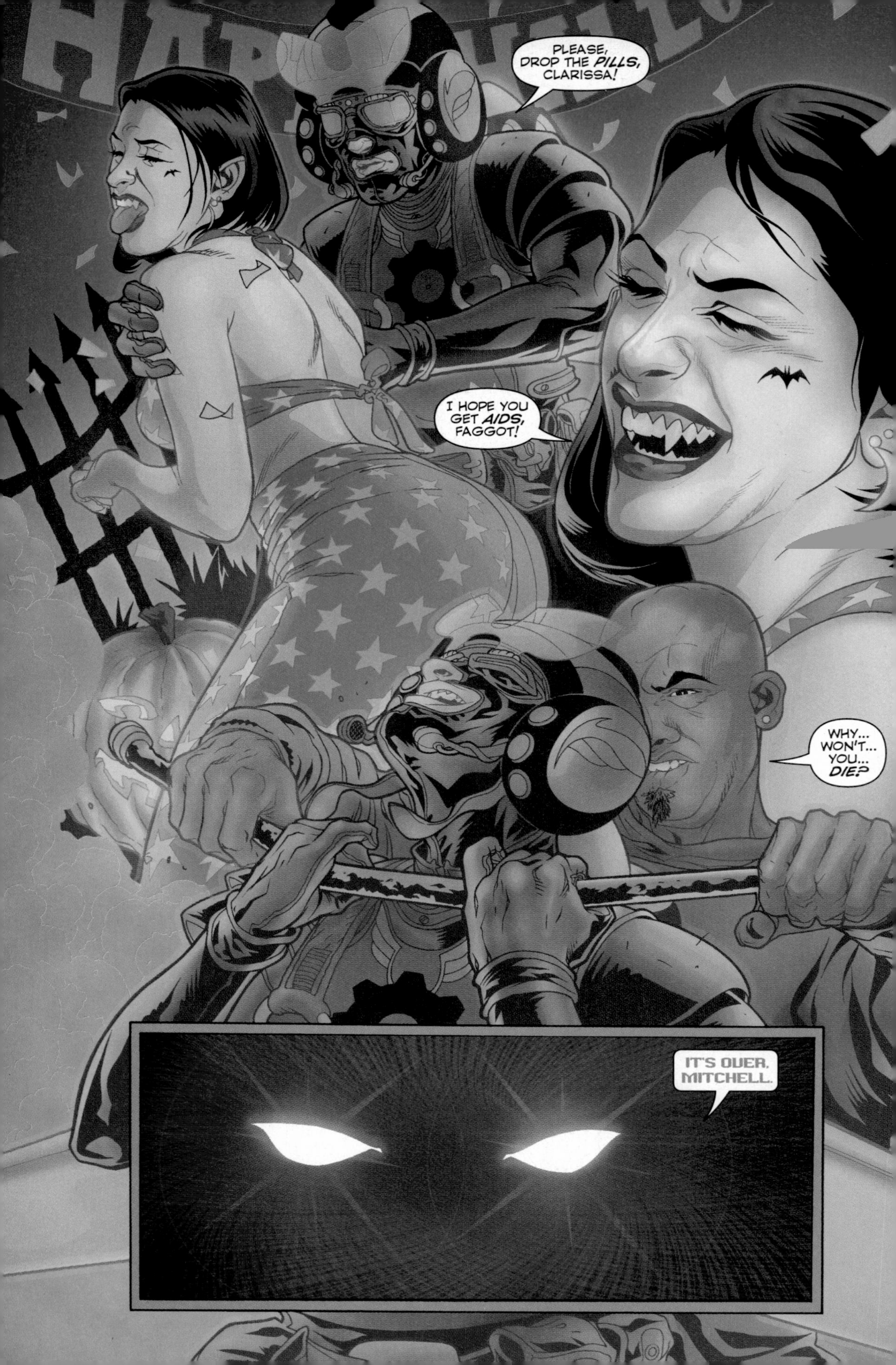
PLEASE, DROP THE PILLS, CLARISSA!
I HOPE YOU GET AIDS, FAGGOT!
WHY... WON'T... YOU... DIE?
IT'S OVER, MITCHELL.

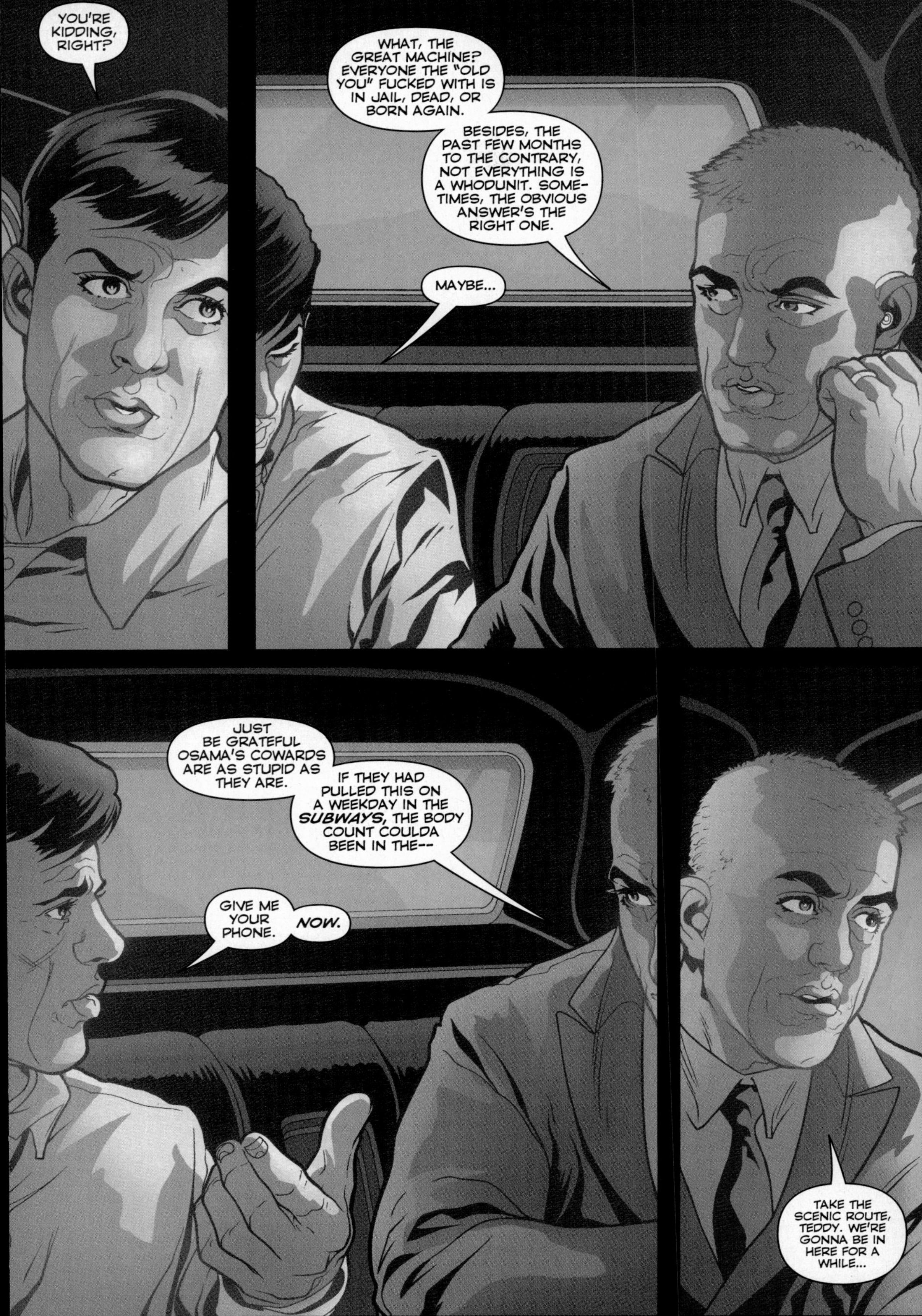
YOU'RE KIDDING, RIGHT?
WHAT, THE GREAT MACHINE? EVERYONE THE "OLD YOU" FUCKED WITH IS IN JAIL, DEAD, OR BORN AGAIN.
BESIDES, THE PAST FEW MONTHS TO THE CONTRARY, NOT EVERYTHING IS A WHODUNIT. SOME-TIMES, THE OBVIOUS ANSWER'S THE RIGHT ONE.
MAYBE...
JUST BE GRATEFUL OSAMA'S COWARDS ARE AS STUPID AS THEY ARE.
IF THEY HAD PULLED THIS ON A WEEKDAY IN THE *SUBWAYS,* THE BODY COUNT COULDA BEEN IN THE--
GIVE ME YOUR PHONE. ***NOW.***
TAKE THE SCENIC ROUTE, TEDDY. WE'RE GONNA BE IN HERE FOR A WHILE...

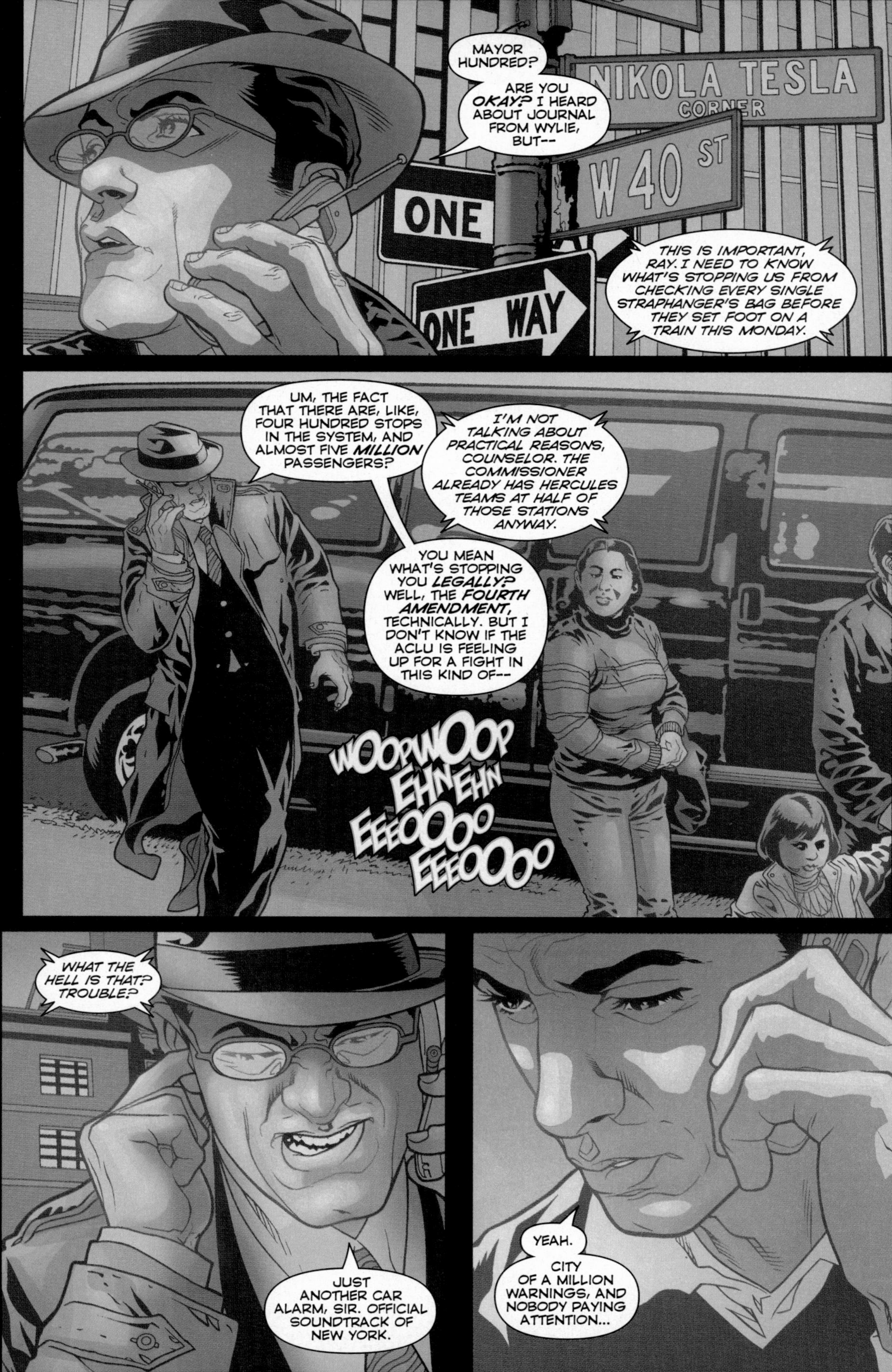
NIKOLA TESLA CORNER
W 40 ST
ONE
ONE WAY
MAYOR HUNDRED?
ARE YOU *OKAY?* I HEARD ABOUT JOURNAL FROM WYLIE, BUT--
THIS IS IMPORTANT, RAY. I NEED TO KNOW WHAT'S STOPPING US FROM CHECKING EVERY SINGLE STRAPHANGER'S BAG BEFORE THEY SET FOOT ON A TRAIN THIS MONDAY.
UM, THE FACT THAT THERE ARE, LIKE, FOUR HUNDRED STOPS IN THE SYSTEM, AND ALMOST FIVE ***MILLION*** PASSENGERS?
I'M NOT TALKING ABOUT PRACTICAL REASONS, COUNSELOR. THE COMMISSIONER ALREADY HAS HERCULES TEAMS AT HALF OF THOSE STATIONS ANYWAY.
YOU MEAN WHAT'S STOPPING YOU ***LEGALLY?*** WELL, THE ***FOURTH AMENDMENT,*** TECHNICALLY. BUT I DON'T KNOW IF THE ACLU IS FEELING UP FOR A FIGHT IN THIS KIND OF--
WOOPWOOP EHNEHN EEEOOoo EEEOOOoo
WHAT THE HELL IS THAT? TROUBLE?
JUST ANOTHER CAR ALARM, SIR. OFFICIAL SOUNDTRACK OF NEW YORK.
YEAH.
CITY OF A MILLION WARNINGS, AND NOBODY PAYING ATTENTION...

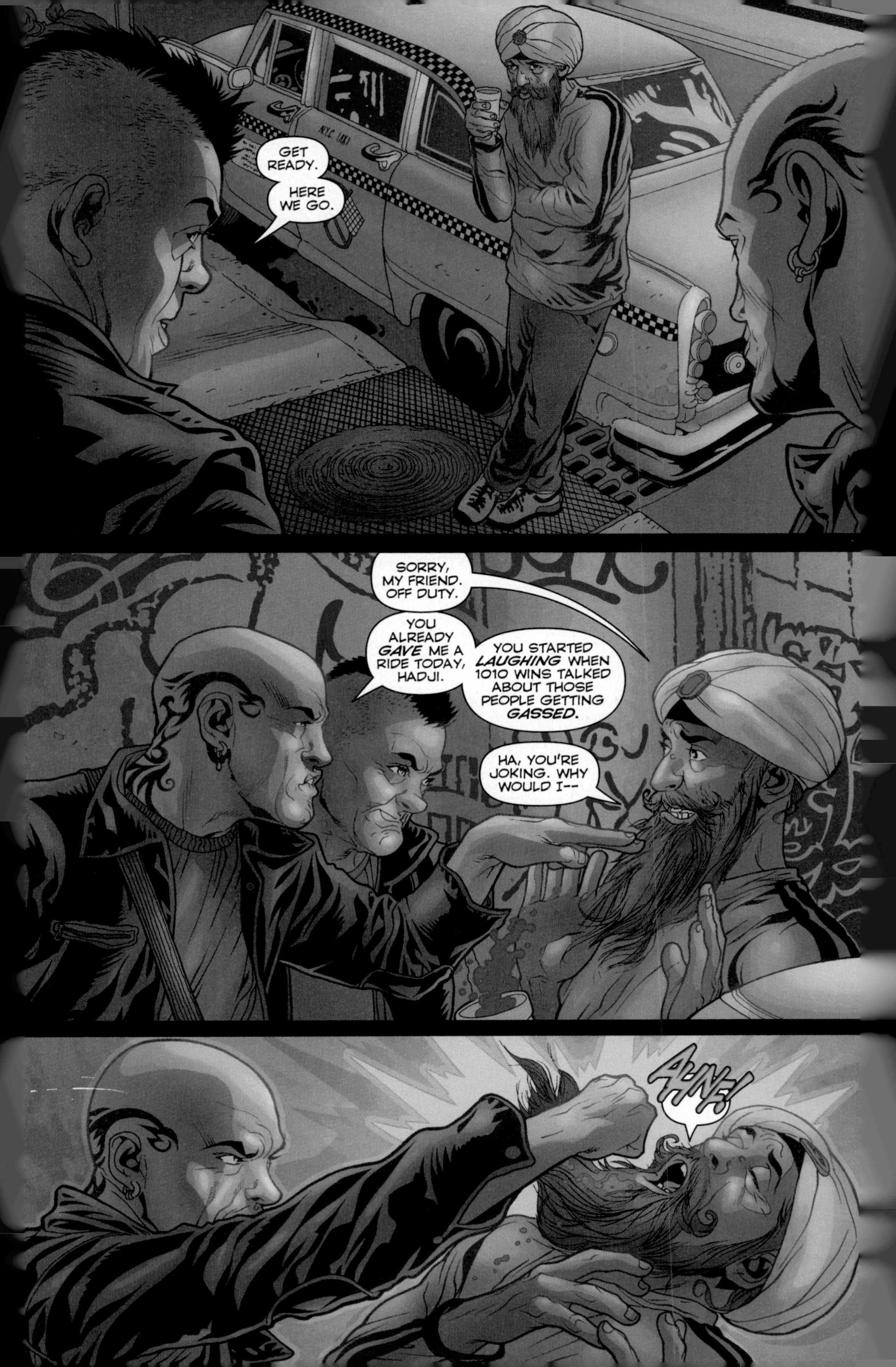
GET READY.
HERE WE GO.
SORRY, MY FRIEND. OFF DUTY.
YOU ALREADY *GAVE* ME A RIDE TODAY, HADJI.
YOU STARTED *LAUGHING* WHEN 1010 WINS TALKED ABOUT THOSE PEOPLE GETTING *GASSED*.
HA, YOU'RE JOKING. WHY WOULD I--
AHNE!

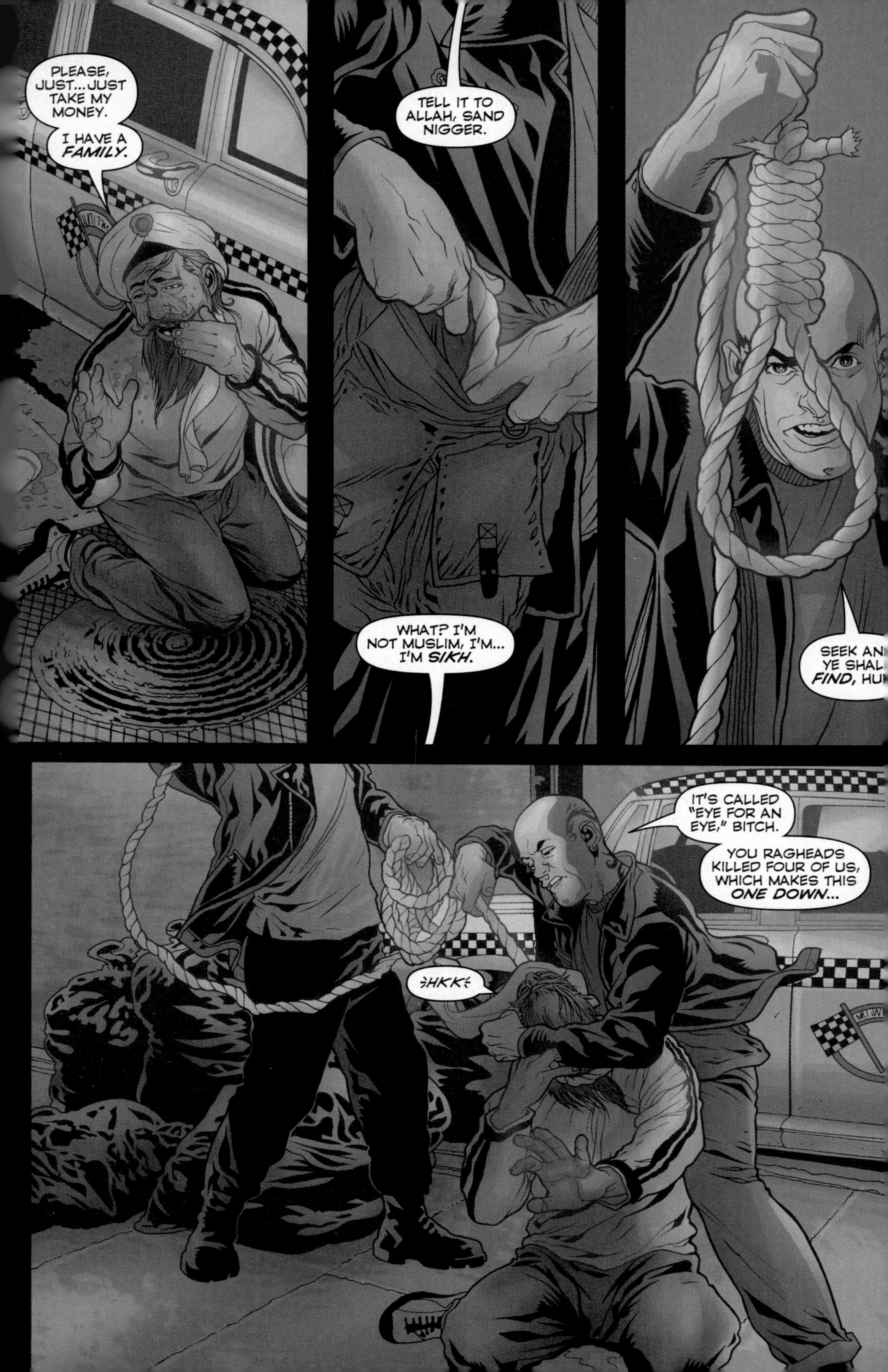
PLEASE, JUST...JUST TAKE MY MONEY.
I HAVE A *FAMILY.*
TELL IT TO ALLAH, SAND NIGGER.
WHAT? I'M NOT MUSLIM, I'M... I'M *SIKH.*
SEEK AN YE SHAL *FIND,* HU
IT'S CALLED "EYE FOR AN EYE," BITCH.
YOU RAGHEADS KILLED FOUR OF US, WHICH MAKES THIS *ONE DOWN...*
HKK

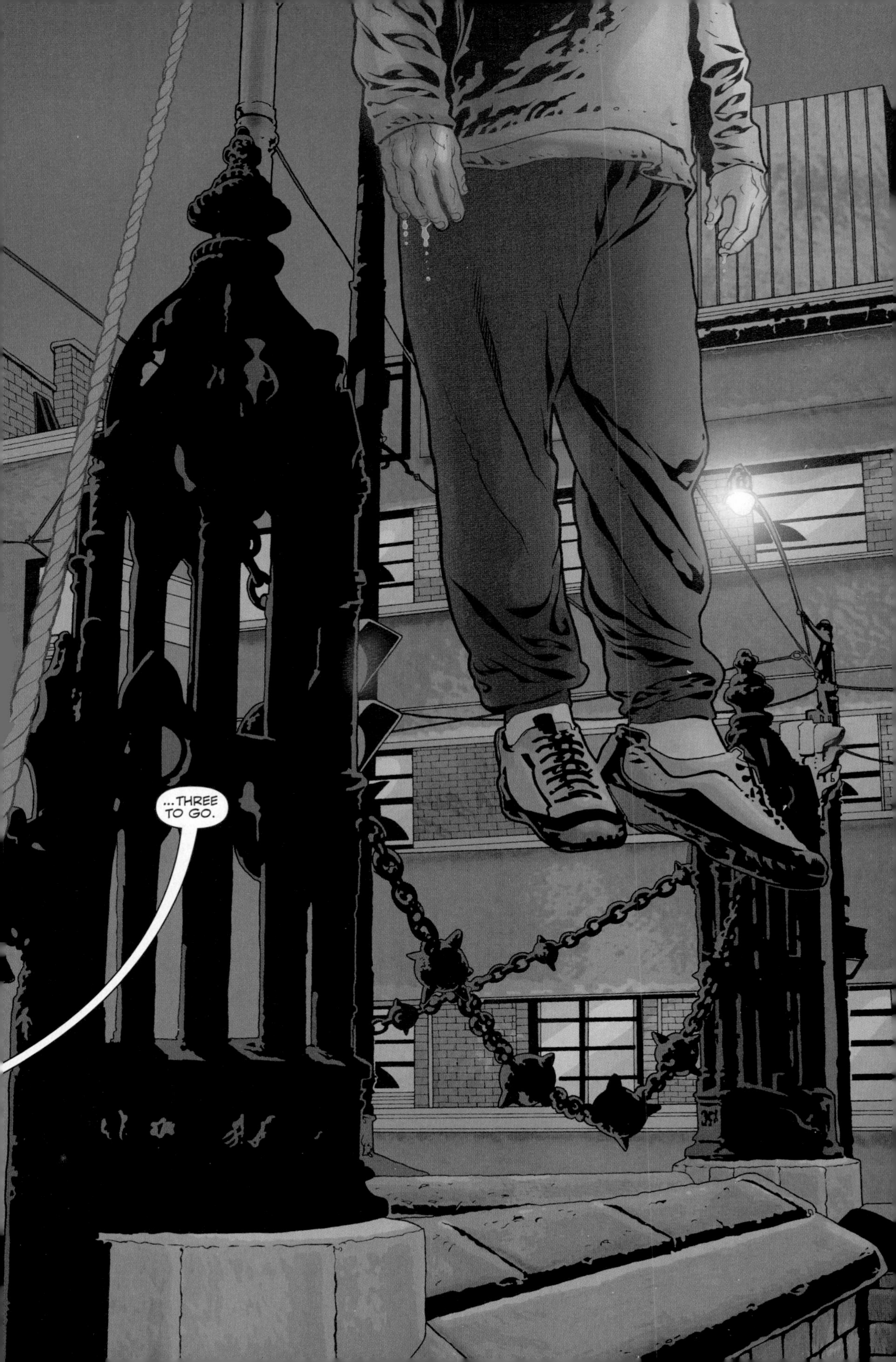
...THREE TO GO.

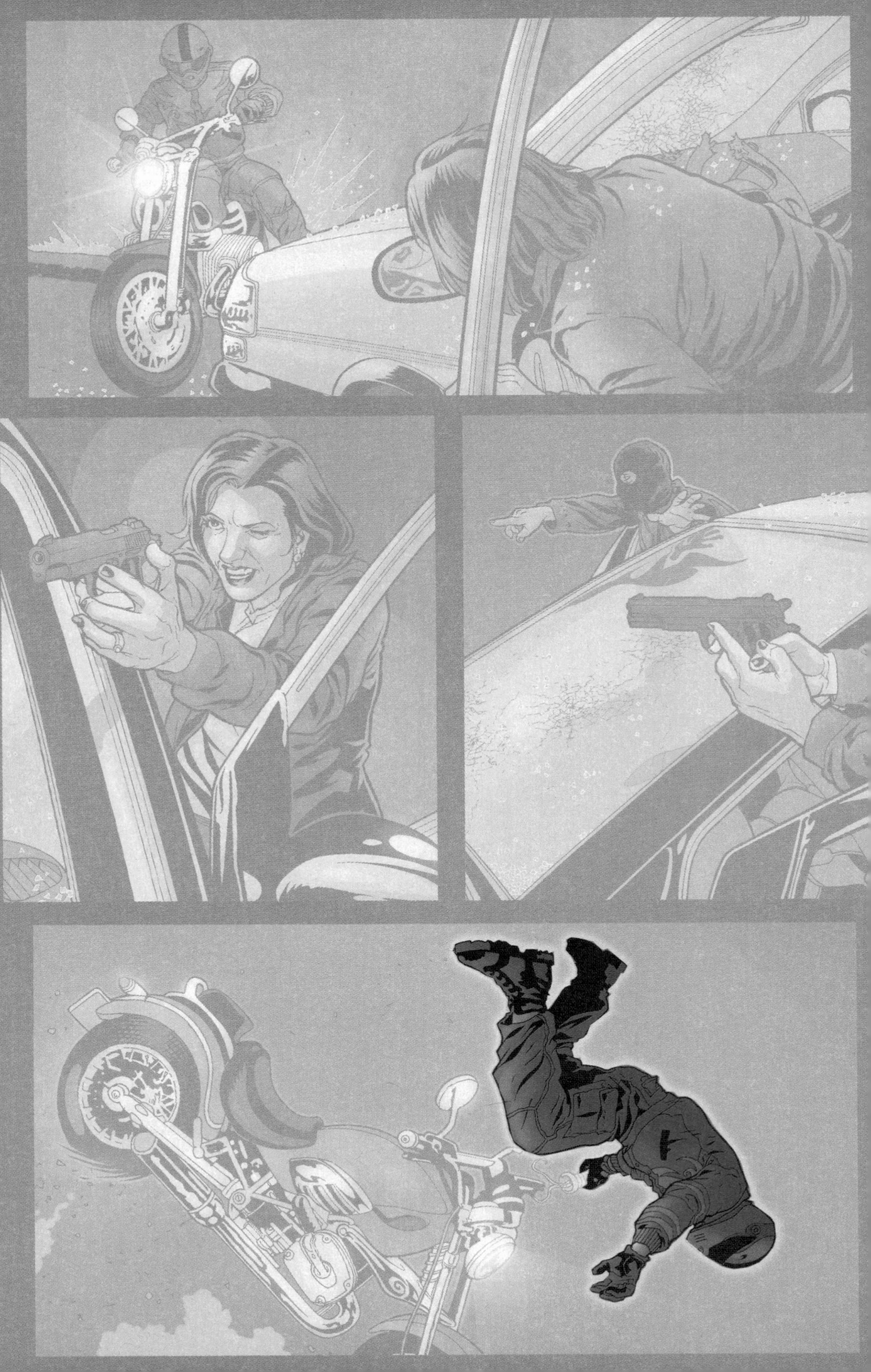

CHAPTER 3 March to War

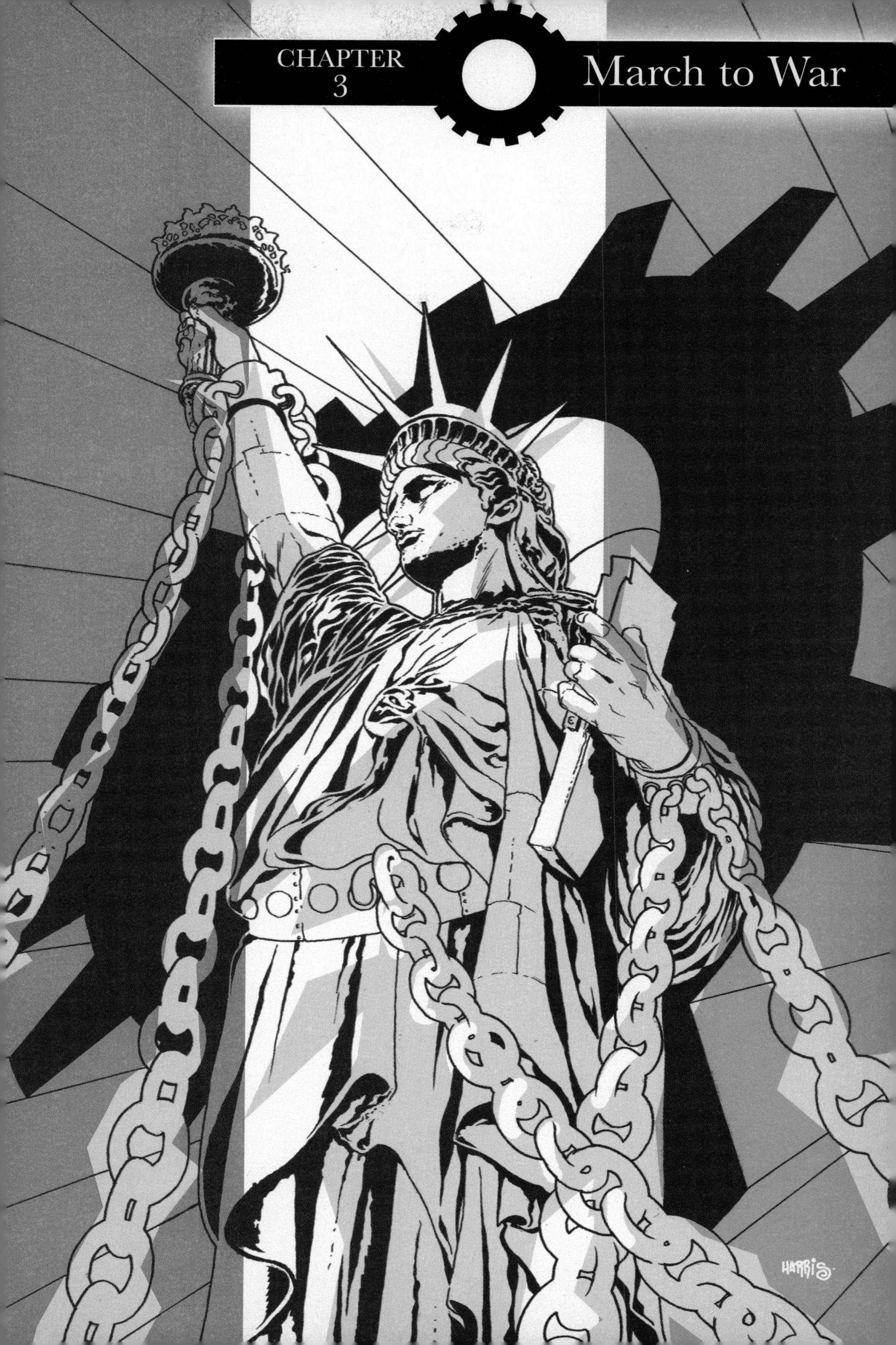
HARRIS

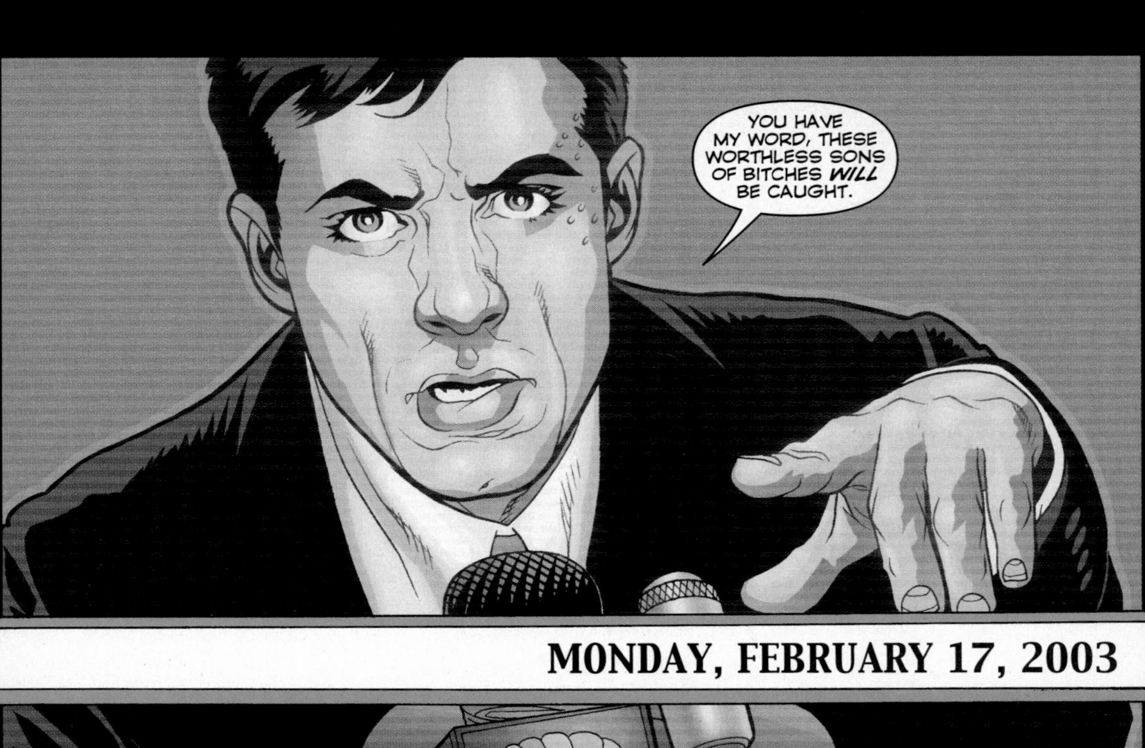
YOU HAVE MY WORD, THESE WORTHLESS SONS OF BITCHES *WILL* BE CAUGHT.

MONDAY, FEBRUARY 17, 2003

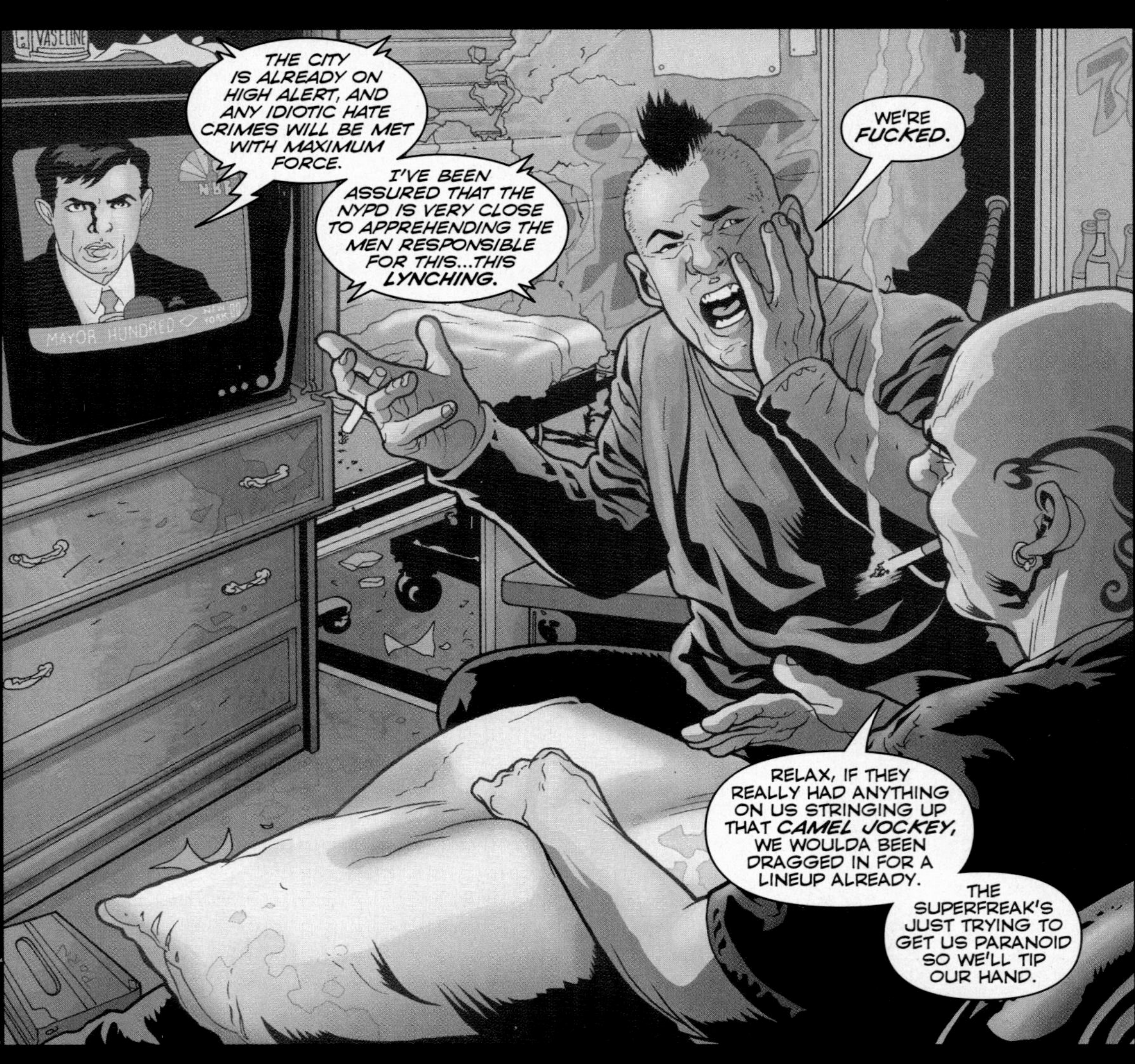
VASELINE
THE CITY IS ALREADY ON HIGH ALERT, AND ANY IDIOTIC HATE CRIMES WILL BE MET WITH MAXIMUM FORCE.
I'VE BEEN ASSURED THAT THE NYPD IS VERY CLOSE TO APPREHENDING THE MEN RESPONSIBLE FOR THIS...THIS *LYNCHING.*
MAYOR HUNDRED
WE'RE *FUCKED.*
RELAX, IF THEY REALLY HAD ANYTHING ON US STRINGING UP THAT *CAMEL JOCKEY,* WE WOULDA BEEN DRAGGED IN FOR A LINEUP ALREADY.
THE SUPERFREAK'S JUST TRYING TO GET US PARANOID SO WE'LL TIP OUR HAND.

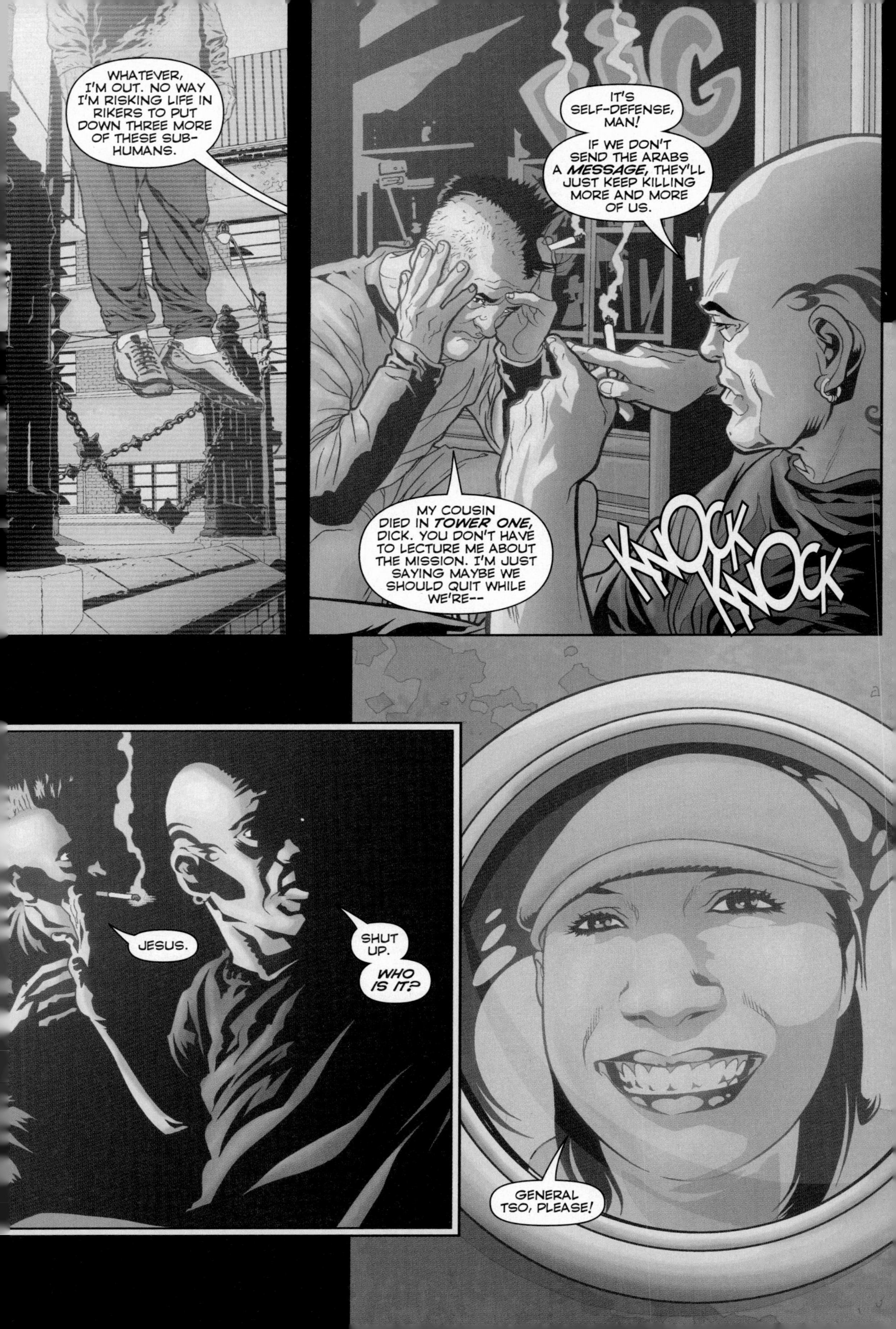
WHATEVER, I'M OUT. NO WAY I'M RISKING LIFE IN RIKERS TO PUT DOWN THREE MORE OF THESE SUB-HUMANS.
IT'S SELF-DEFENSE, MAN!
IF WE DON'T SEND THE ARABS A *MESSAGE,* THEY'LL JUST KEEP KILLING MORE AND MORE OF US.
MY COUSIN DIED IN *TOWER ONE,* DICK. YOU DON'T HAVE TO LECTURE ME ABOUT THE MISSION. I'M JUST SAYING MAYBE WE SHOULD QUIT WHILE WE'RE--
KNOCK KNOCK
JESUS.
SHUT UP.
WHO IS IT?
GENERAL TSO, PLEASE!

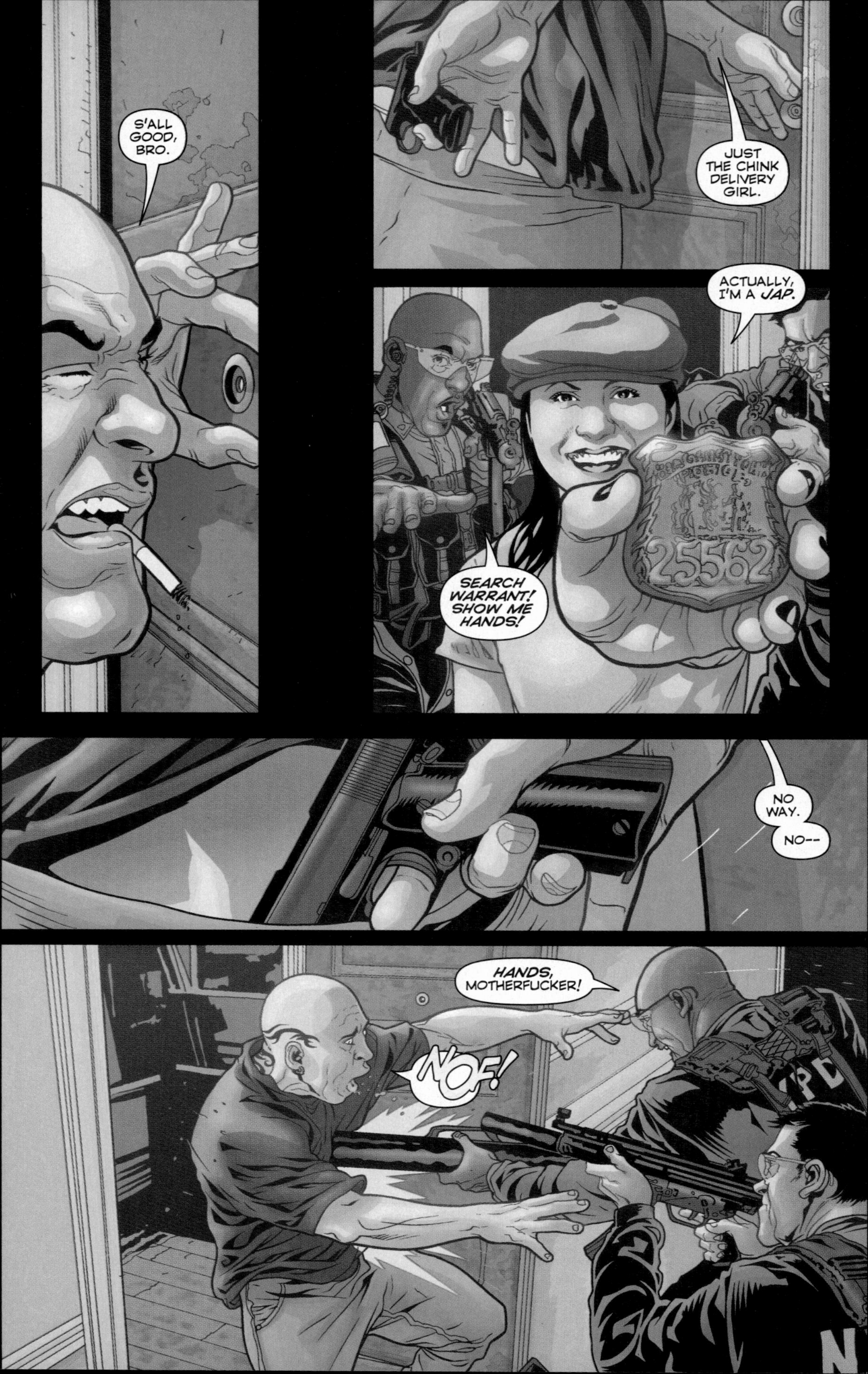
S'ALL GOOD, BRO.
JUST THE CHINK DELIVERY GIRL.
ACTUALLY, I'M A *JAP*.
SEARCH WARRANT! SHOW ME HANDS!
25562
NO WAY.
NO--
HANDS, MOTHERFUCKER!
NOF!

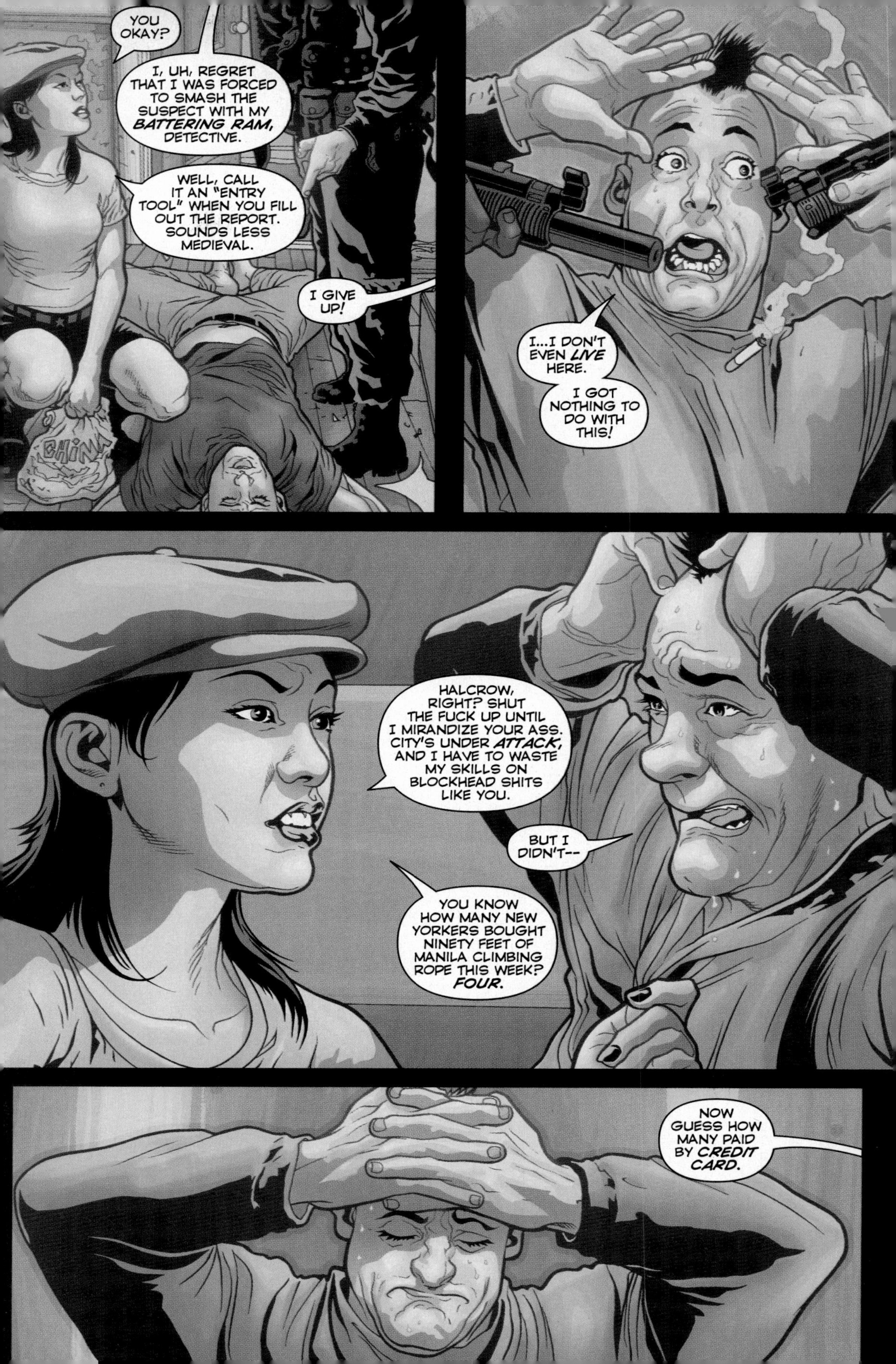
YOU OKAY?
I, UH, REGRET THAT I WAS FORCED TO SMASH THE SUSPECT WITH MY *BATTERING RAM,* DETECTIVE.
WELL, CALL IT AN "ENTRY TOOL" WHEN YOU FILL OUT THE REPORT. SOUNDS LESS MEDIEVAL.
I GIVE UP!
I...I DON'T EVEN *LIVE* HERE.
I GOT NOTHING TO DO WITH THIS!
HALCROW, RIGHT? SHUT THE FUCK UP UNTIL I MIRANDIZE YOUR ASS. CITY'S UNDER *ATTACK,* AND I HAVE TO WASTE MY SKILLS ON BLOCKHEAD SHITS LIKE YOU.
BUT I DIDN'T--
YOU KNOW HOW MANY NEW YORKERS BOUGHT NINETY FEET OF MANILA CLIMBING ROPE THIS WEEK? *FOUR.*
NOW GUESS HOW MANY PAID BY *CREDIT CARD.*

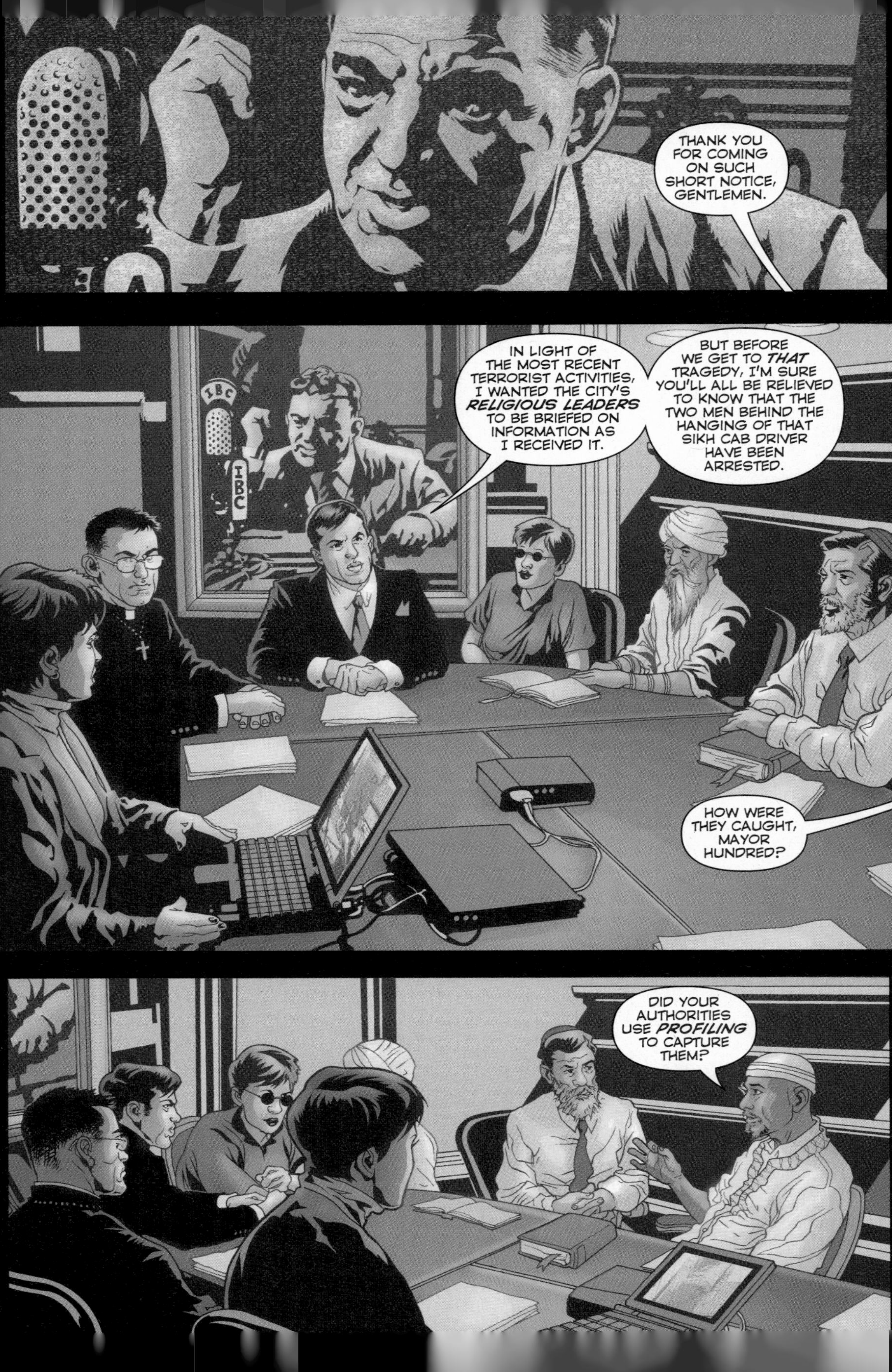
THANK YOU FOR COMING ON SUCH SHORT NOTICE, GENTLEMEN.
IBC
IBC
IN LIGHT OF THE MOST RECENT TERRORIST ACTIVITIES, I WANTED THE CITY'S *RELIGIOUS LEADERS* TO BE BRIEFED ON INFORMATION AS I RECEIVED IT.
BUT BEFORE WE GET TO *THAT* TRAGEDY, I'M SURE YOU'LL ALL BE RELIEVED TO KNOW THAT THE TWO MEN BEHIND THE HANGING OF THAT SIKH CAB DRIVER HAVE BEEN ARRESTED.
HOW WERE THEY CAUGHT, MAYOR HUNDRED?
DID YOUR AUTHORITIES USE *PROFILING* TO CAPTURE THEM?

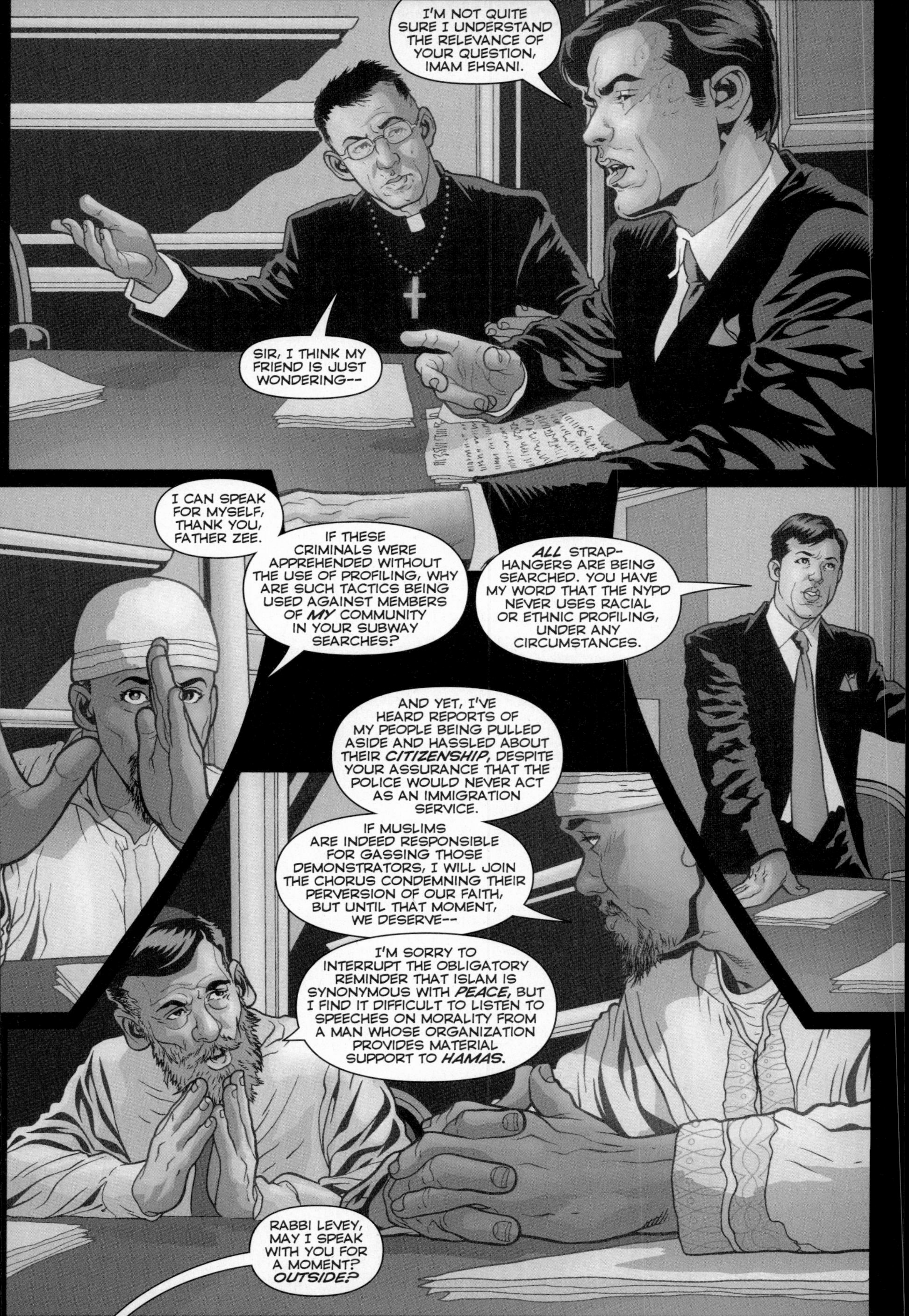
I'M NOT QUITE SURE I UNDERSTAND THE RELEVANCE OF YOUR QUESTION, IMAM EHSANI.
SIR, I THINK MY FRIEND IS JUST WONDERING--
I CAN SPEAK FOR MYSELF, THANK YOU, FATHER ZEE.
IF THESE CRIMINALS WERE APPREHENDED WITHOUT THE USE OF PROFILING, WHY ARE SUCH TACTICS BEING USED AGAINST MEMBERS OF MY COMMUNITY IN YOUR SUBWAY SEARCHES?
ALL STRAP-HANGERS ARE BEING SEARCHED. YOU HAVE MY WORD THAT THE NYPD NEVER USES RACIAL OR ETHNIC PROFILING, UNDER ANY CIRCUMSTANCES.
AND YET, I'VE HEARD REPORTS OF MY PEOPLE BEING PULLED ASIDE AND HASSLED ABOUT THEIR CITIZENSHIP, DESPITE YOUR ASSURANCE THAT THE POLICE WOULD NEVER ACT AS AN IMMIGRATION SERVICE.
IF MUSLIMS ARE INDEED RESPONSIBLE FOR GASSING THOSE DEMONSTRATORS, I WILL JOIN THE CHORUS CONDEMNING THEIR PERVERSION OF OUR FAITH, BUT UNTIL THAT MOMENT, WE DESERVE--
I'M SORRY TO INTERRUPT THE OBLIGATORY REMINDER THAT ISLAM IS SYNONYMOUS WITH PEACE, BUT I FIND IT DIFFICULT TO LISTEN TO SPEECHES ON MORALITY FROM A MAN WHOSE ORGANIZATION PROVIDES MATERIAL SUPPORT TO HAMAS.
RABBI LEVEY, MAY I SPEAK WITH YOU FOR A MOMENT? OUTSIDE?

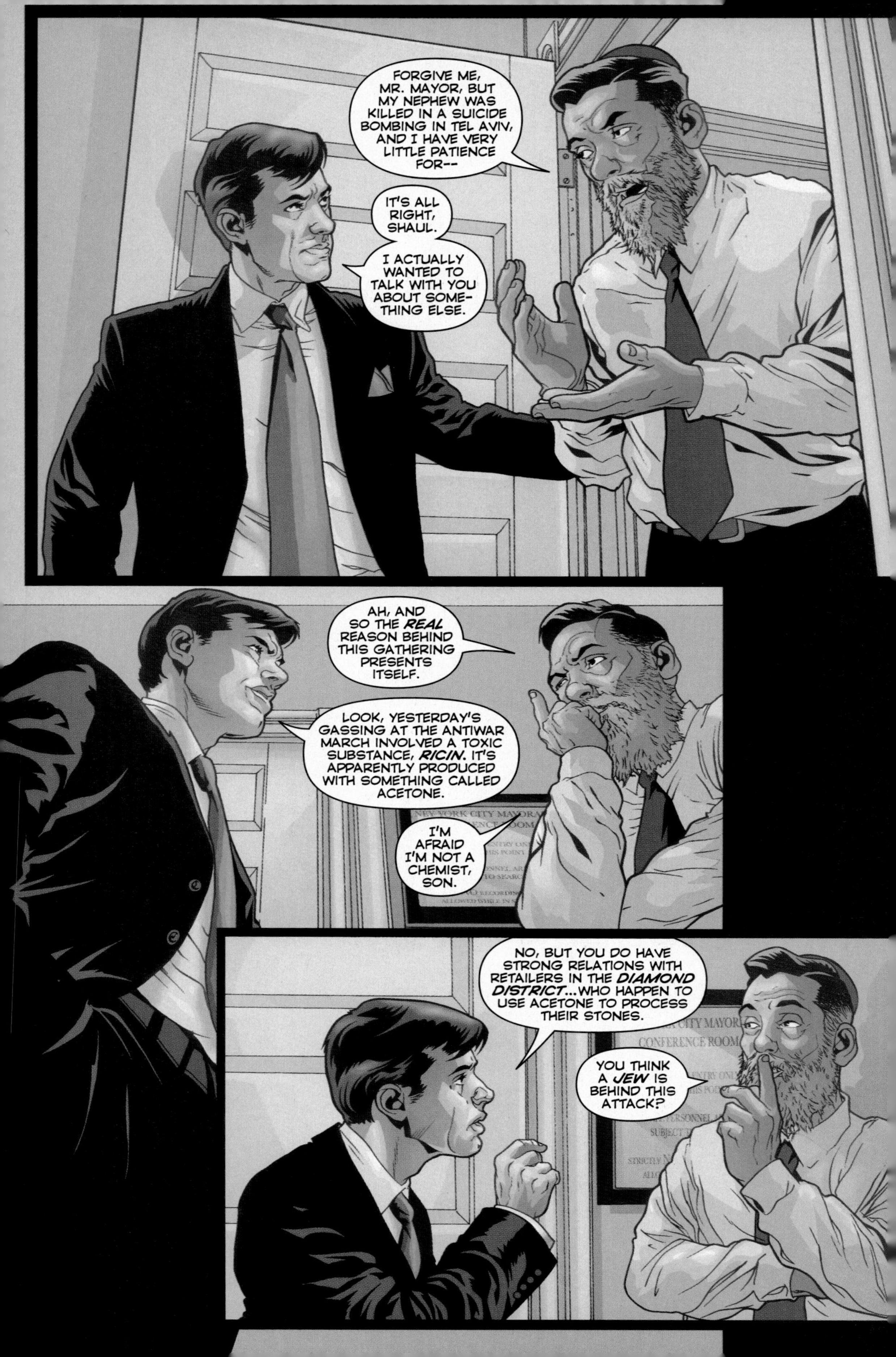
FORGIVE ME, MR. MAYOR, BUT MY NEPHEW WAS KILLED IN A SUICIDE BOMBING IN TEL AVIV, AND I HAVE VERY LITTLE PATIENCE FOR--
IT'S ALL RIGHT, SHAUL.
I ACTUALLY WANTED TO TALK WITH YOU ABOUT SOME-THING ELSE.
AH, AND SO THE *REAL* REASON BEHIND THIS GATHERING PRESENTS ITSELF.
LOOK, YESTERDAY'S GASSING AT THE ANTIWAR MARCH INVOLVED A TOXIC SUBSTANCE, ***RICIN***. IT'S APPARENTLY PRODUCED WITH SOMETHING CALLED ACETONE.
I'M AFRAID I'M NOT A CHEMIST, SON.
NO, BUT YOU DO HAVE STRONG RELATIONS WITH RETAILERS IN THE *DIAMOND DISTRICT*...WHO HAPPEN TO USE ACETONE TO PROCESS THEIR STONES.
YOU THINK A *JEW* IS BEHIND THIS ATTACK?

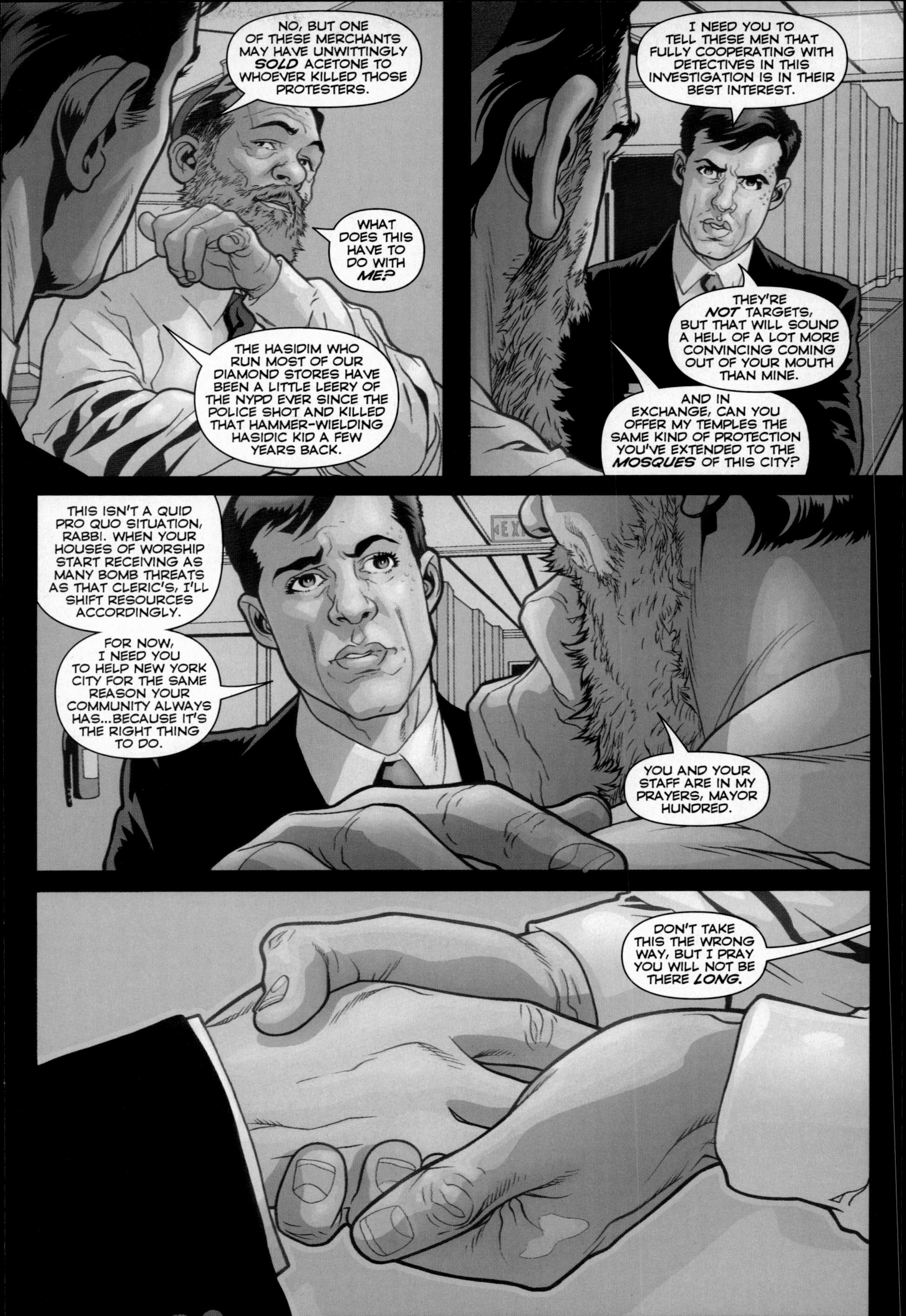
NO, BUT ONE OF THESE MERCHANTS MAY HAVE UNWITTINGLY SOLD ACETONE TO WHOEVER KILLED THOSE PROTESTERS.
WHAT DOES THIS HAVE TO DO WITH ME?
THE HASIDIM WHO RUN MOST OF OUR DIAMOND STORES HAVE BEEN A LITTLE LEERY OF THE NYPD EVER SINCE THE POLICE SHOT AND KILLED THAT HAMMER-WIELDING HASIDIC KID A FEW YEARS BACK.
I NEED YOU TO TELL THESE MEN THAT FULLY COOPERATING WITH DETECTIVES IN THIS INVESTIGATION IS IN THEIR BEST INTEREST.
THEY'RE NOT TARGETS, BUT THAT WILL SOUND A HELL OF A LOT MORE CONVINCING COMING OUT OF YOUR MOUTH THAN MINE.
AND IN EXCHANGE, CAN YOU OFFER MY TEMPLES THE SAME KIND OF PROTECTION YOU'VE EXTENDED TO THE MOSQUES OF THIS CITY?
THIS ISN'T A QUID PRO QUO SITUATION, RABBI. WHEN YOUR HOUSES OF WORSHIP START RECEIVING AS MANY BOMB THREATS AS THAT CLERIC'S, I'LL SHIFT RESOURCES ACCORDINGLY.
FOR NOW, I NEED YOU TO HELP NEW YORK CITY FOR THE SAME REASON YOUR COMMUNITY ALWAYS HAS...BECAUSE IT'S THE RIGHT THING TO DO.
YOU AND YOUR STAFF ARE IN MY PRAYERS, MAYOR HUNDRED.
DON'T TAKE THIS THE WRONG WAY, BUT I PRAY YOU WILL NOT BE THERE LONG.

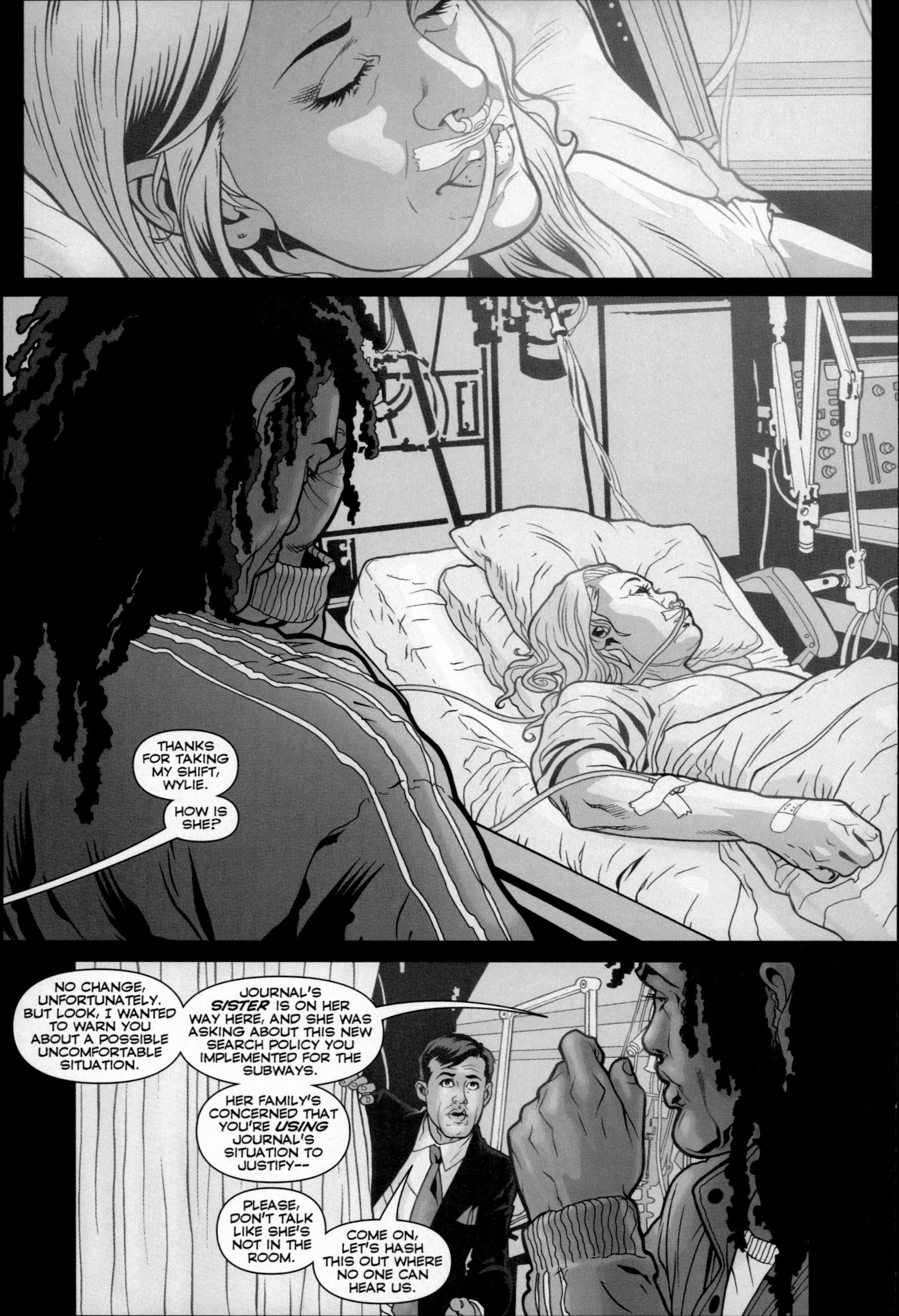
THANKS FOR TAKING MY SHIFT, WYLIE.
HOW IS SHE?
NO CHANGE, UNFORTUNATELY. BUT LOOK, I WANTED TO WARN YOU ABOUT A POSSIBLE UNCOMFORTABLE SITUATION.
JOURNAL'S SISTER IS ON HER WAY HERE, AND SHE WAS ASKING ABOUT THIS NEW SEARCH POLICY YOU IMPLEMENTED FOR THE SUBWAYS.
HER FAMILY'S CONCERNED THAT YOU'RE USING JOURNAL'S SITUATION TO JUSTIFY--
PLEASE, DON'T TALK LIKE SHE'S NOT IN THE ROOM.
COME ON, LET'S HASH THIS OUT WHERE NO ONE CAN HEAR US.

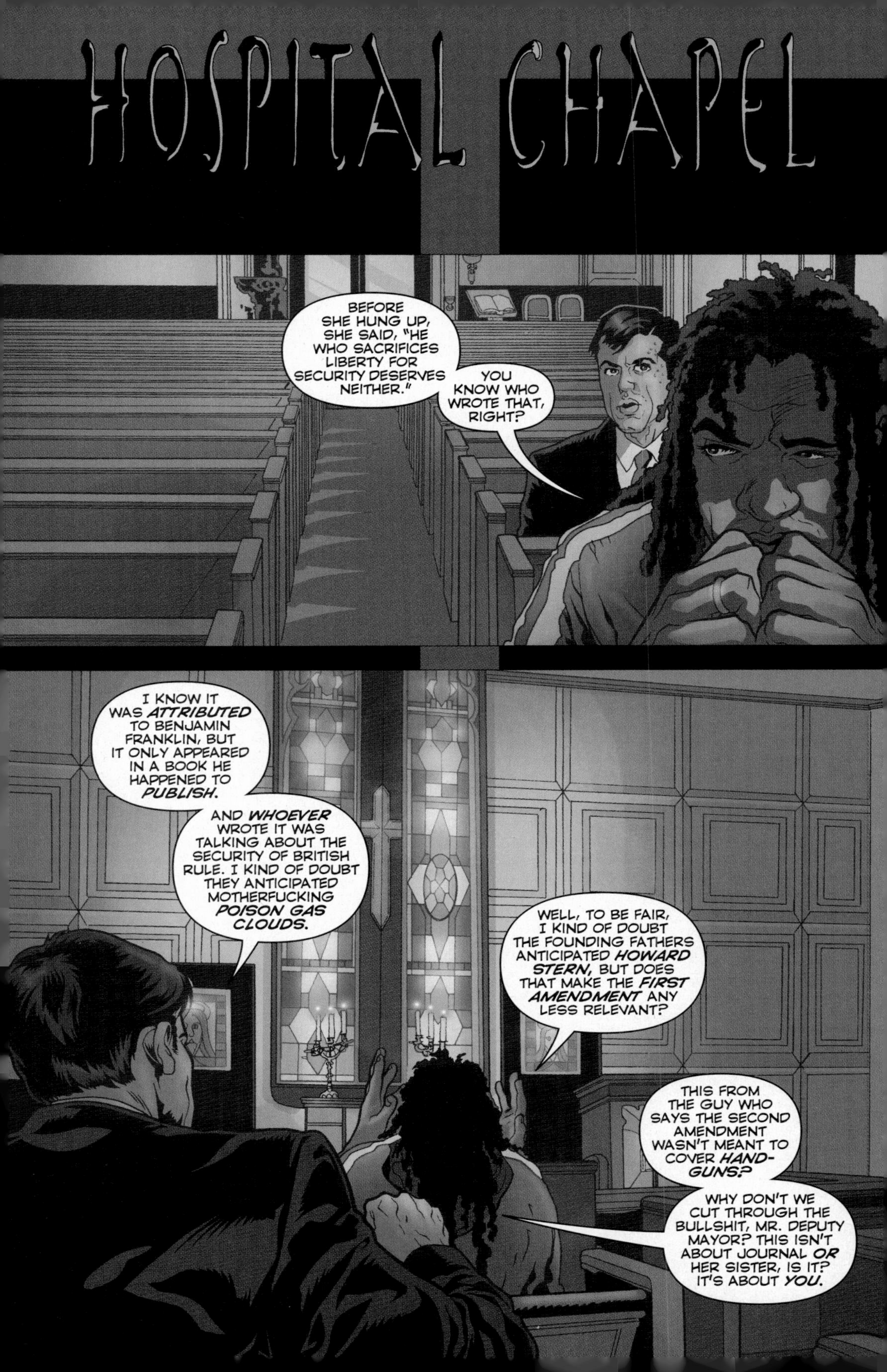
HOSPITAL CHAPEL
BEFORE SHE HUNG UP, SHE SAID, "HE WHO SACRIFICES LIBERTY FOR SECURITY DESERVES NEITHER."
YOU KNOW WHO WROTE THAT, RIGHT?
I KNOW IT WAS ATTRIBUTED TO BENJAMIN FRANKLIN, BUT IT ONLY APPEARED IN A BOOK HE HAPPENED TO PUBLISH.
AND WHOEVER WROTE IT WAS TALKING ABOUT THE SECURITY OF BRITISH RULE. I KIND OF DOUBT THEY ANTICIPATED MOTHERFUCKING POISON GAS CLOUDS.
WELL, TO BE FAIR, I KIND OF DOUBT THE FOUNDING FATHERS ANTICIPATED HOWARD STERN, BUT DOES THAT MAKE THE FIRST AMENDMENT ANY LESS RELEVANT?
THIS FROM THE GUY WHO SAYS THE SECOND AMENDMENT WASN'T MEANT TO COVER HAND-GUNS?
WHY DON'T WE CUT THROUGH THE BULLSHIT, MR. DEPUTY MAYOR? THIS ISN'T ABOUT JOURNAL OR HER SISTER, IS IT? IT'S ABOUT YOU.

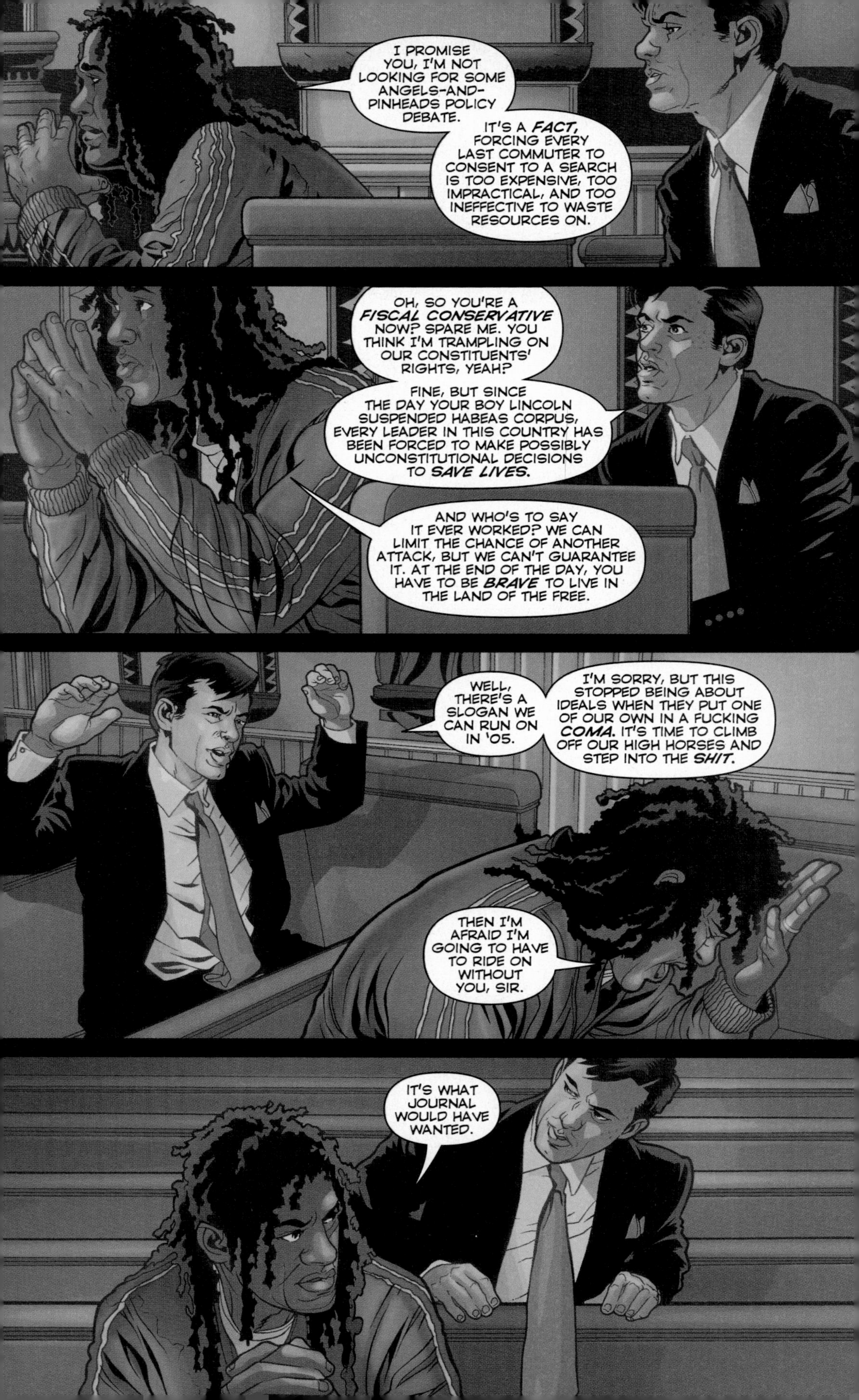
I PROMISE YOU, I'M NOT LOOKING FOR SOME ANGELS-AND-PINHEADS POLICY DEBATE.
IT'S A FACT, FORCING EVERY LAST COMMUTER TO CONSENT TO A SEARCH IS TOO EXPENSIVE, TOO IMPRACTICAL, AND TOO INEFFECTIVE TO WASTE RESOURCES ON.
OH, SO YOU'RE A FISCAL CONSERVATIVE NOW? SPARE ME. YOU THINK I'M TRAMPLING ON OUR CONSTITUENTS' RIGHTS, YEAH?
FINE, BUT SINCE THE DAY YOUR BOY LINCOLN SUSPENDED HABEAS CORPUS, EVERY LEADER IN THIS COUNTRY HAS BEEN FORCED TO MAKE POSSIBLY UNCONSTITUTIONAL DECISIONS TO SAVE LIVES.
AND WHO'S TO SAY IT EVER WORKED? WE CAN LIMIT THE CHANCE OF ANOTHER ATTACK, BUT WE CAN'T GUARANTEE IT. AT THE END OF THE DAY, YOU HAVE TO BE BRAVE TO LIVE IN THE LAND OF THE FREE.
WELL, THERE'S A SLOGAN WE CAN RUN ON IN '05.
I'M SORRY, BUT THIS STOPPED BEING ABOUT IDEALS WHEN THEY PUT ONE OF OUR OWN IN A FUCKING COMA. IT'S TIME TO CLIMB OFF OUR HIGH HORSES AND STEP INTO THE SHIT.
THEN I'M AFRAID I'M GOING TO HAVE TO RIDE ON WITHOUT YOU, SIR.
IT'S WHAT JOURNAL WOULD HAVE WANTED.

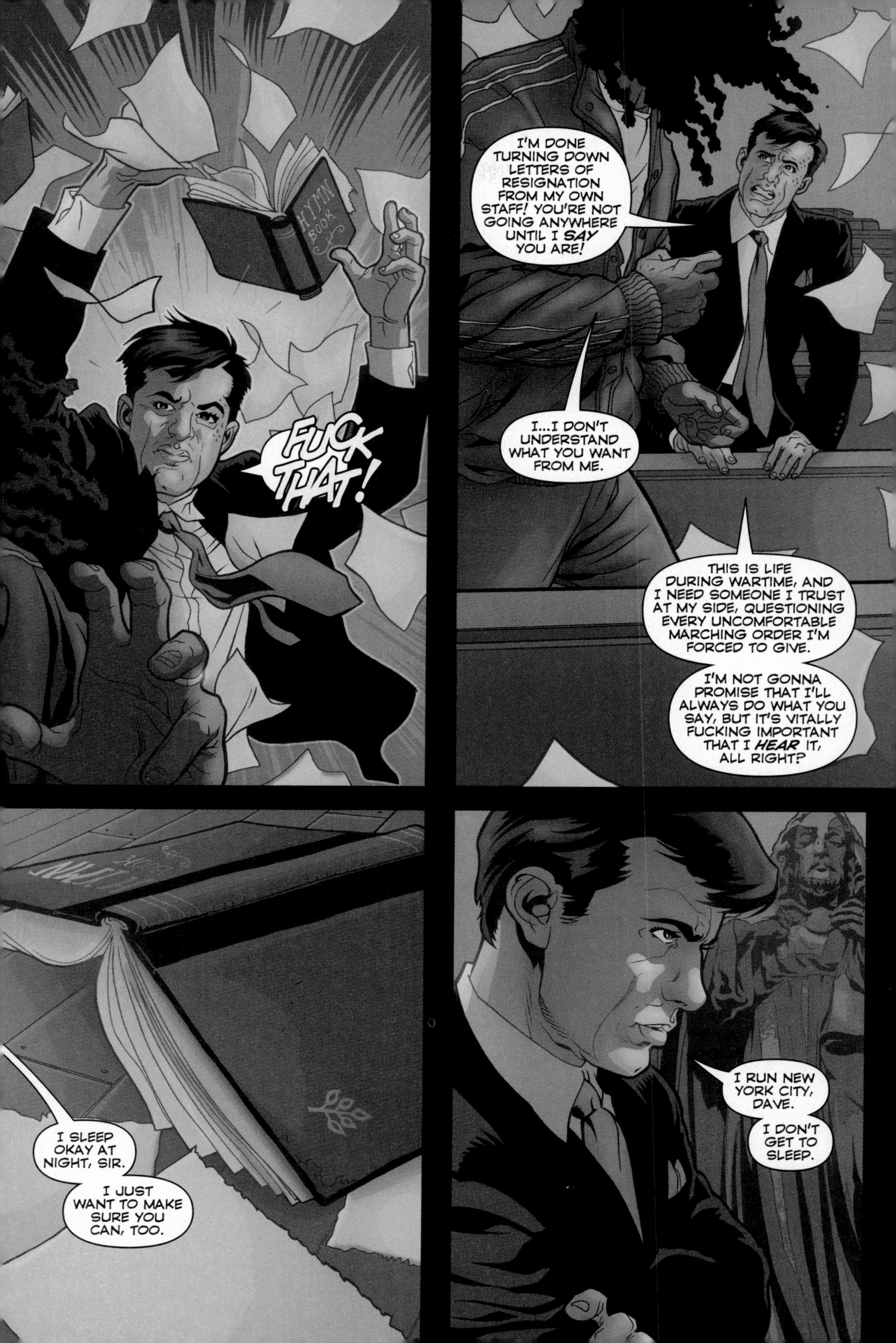
FUCK THAT!
I'M DONE TURNING DOWN LETTERS OF RESIGNATION FROM MY OWN STAFF! YOU'RE NOT GOING ANYWHERE UNTIL I SAY YOU ARE!
I...I DON'T UNDERSTAND WHAT YOU WANT FROM ME.
THIS IS LIFE DURING WARTIME, AND I NEED SOMEONE I TRUST AT MY SIDE, QUESTIONING EVERY UNCOMFORTABLE MARCHING ORDER I'M FORCED TO GIVE.
I'M NOT GONNA PROMISE THAT I'LL ALWAYS DO WHAT YOU SAY, BUT IT'S VITALLY FUCKING IMPORTANT THAT I HEAR IT, ALL RIGHT?
I SLEEP OKAY AT NIGHT, SIR.
I JUST WANT TO MAKE SURE YOU CAN, TOO.
I RUN NEW YORK CITY, DAVE.
I DON'T GET TO SLEEP.

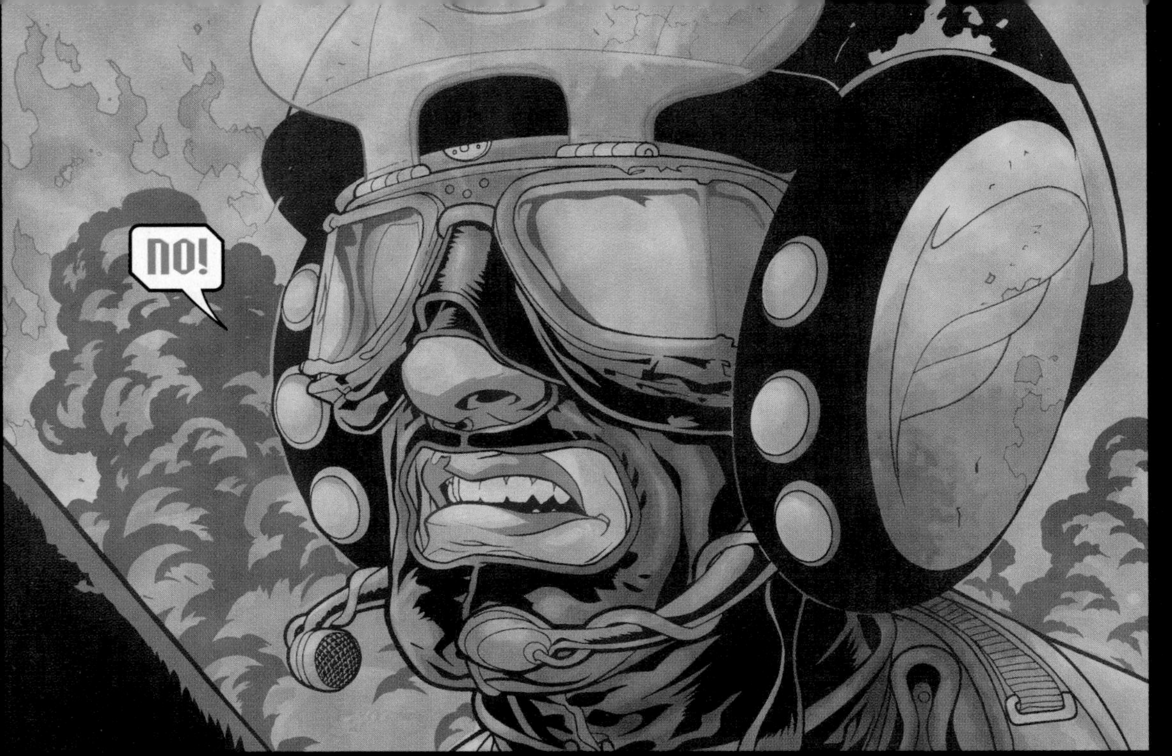
NO!

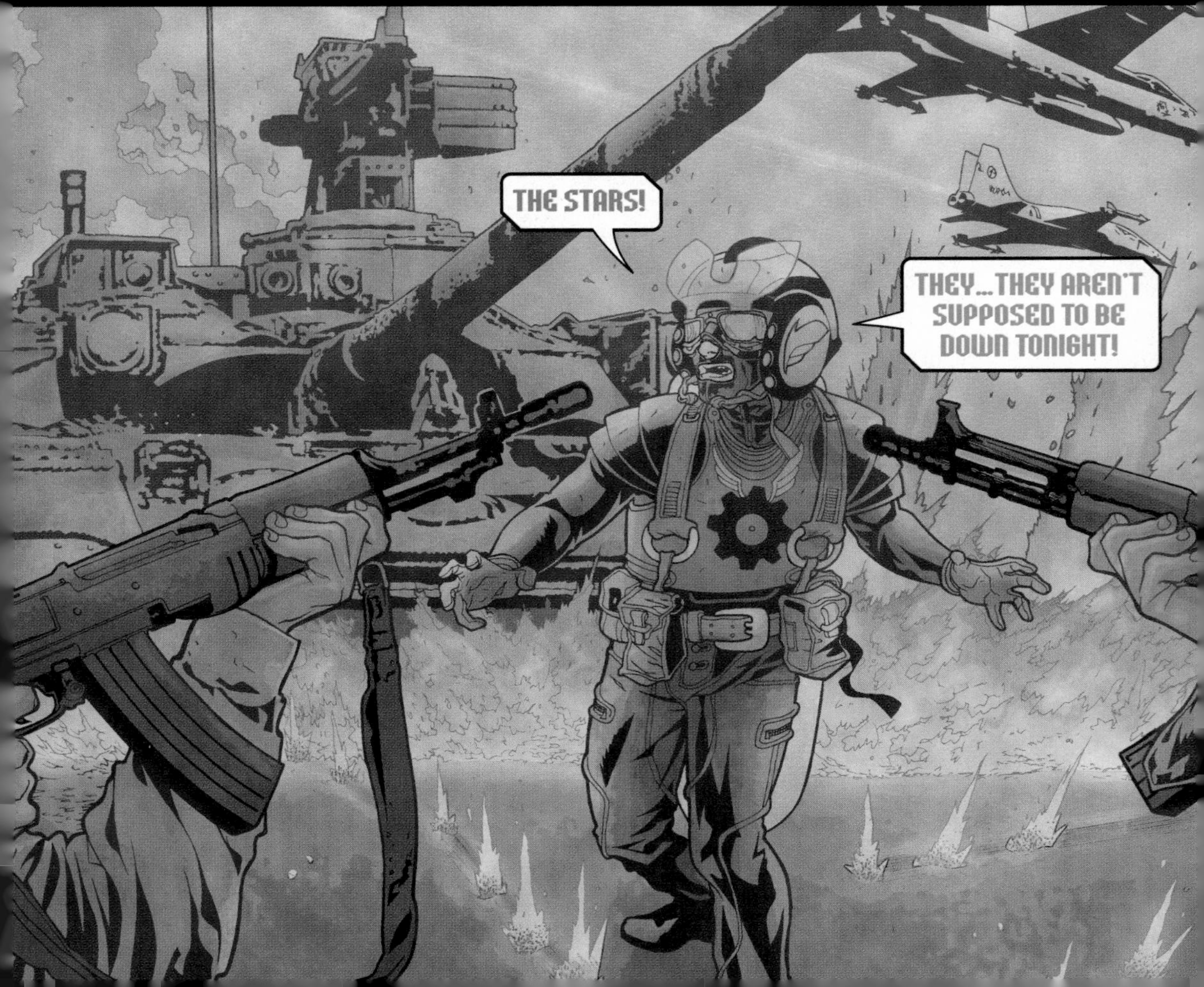
THE STARS!
THEY...THEY AREN'T SUPPOSED TO BE DOWN TONIGHT!

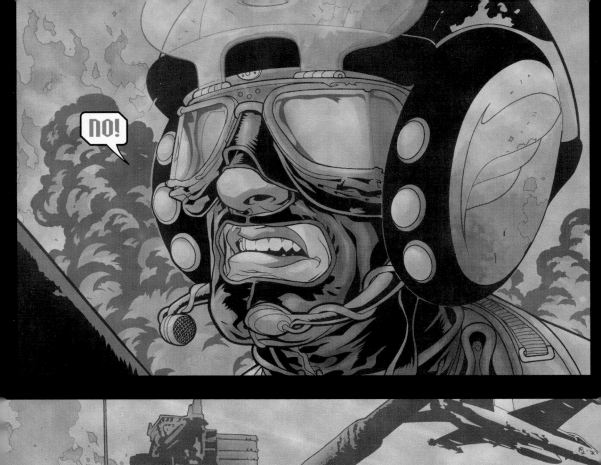

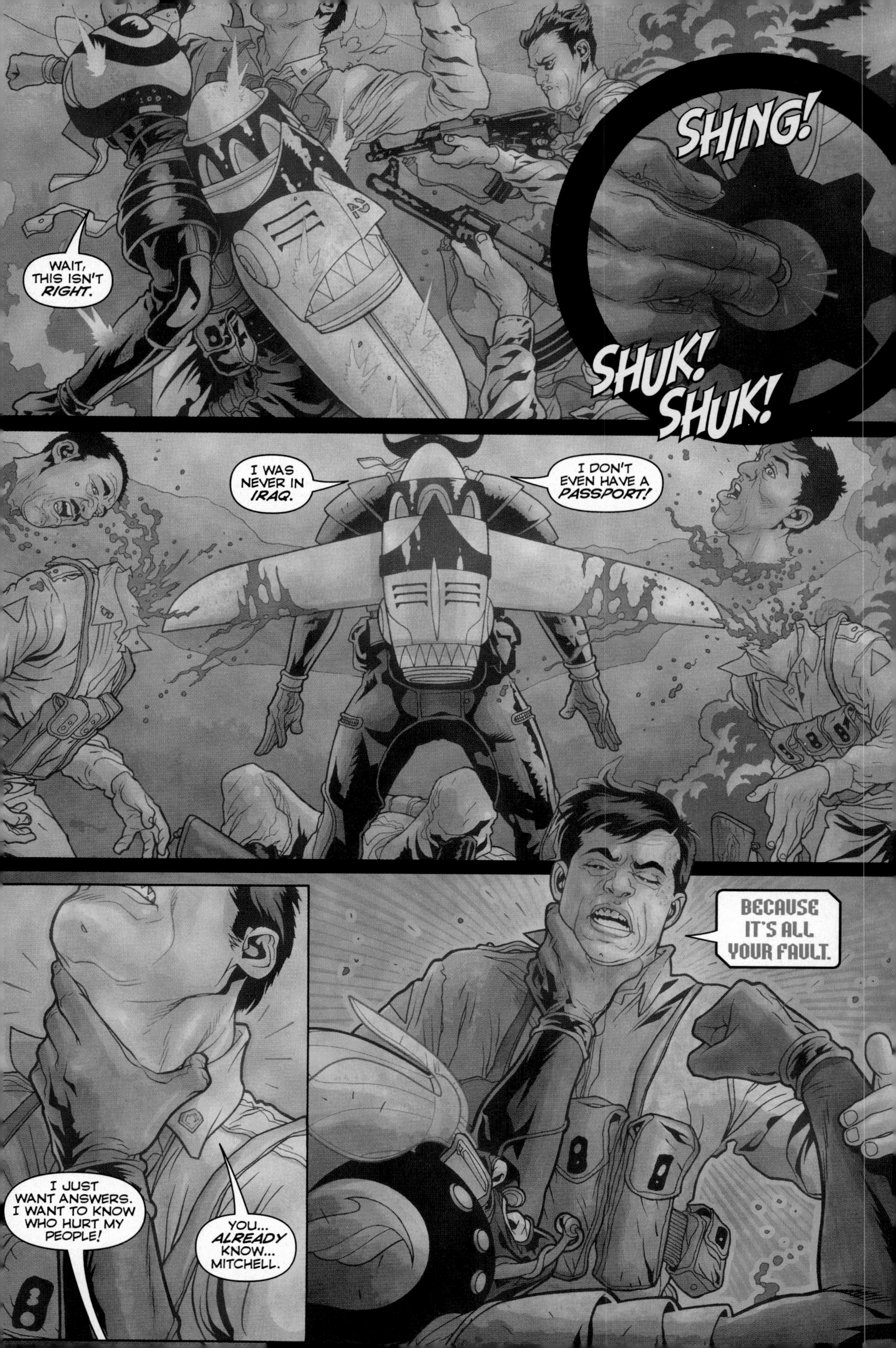
WAIT, THIS ISN'T RIGHT.
SHING!
SHUK! SHUK!
I WAS NEVER IN IRAQ.
I DON'T EVEN HAVE A PASSPORT!
BECAUSE IT'S ALL YOUR FAULT.
I JUST WANT ANSWERS. I WANT TO KNOW WHO HURT MY PEOPLE!
YOU... ALREADY KNOW... MITCHELL.

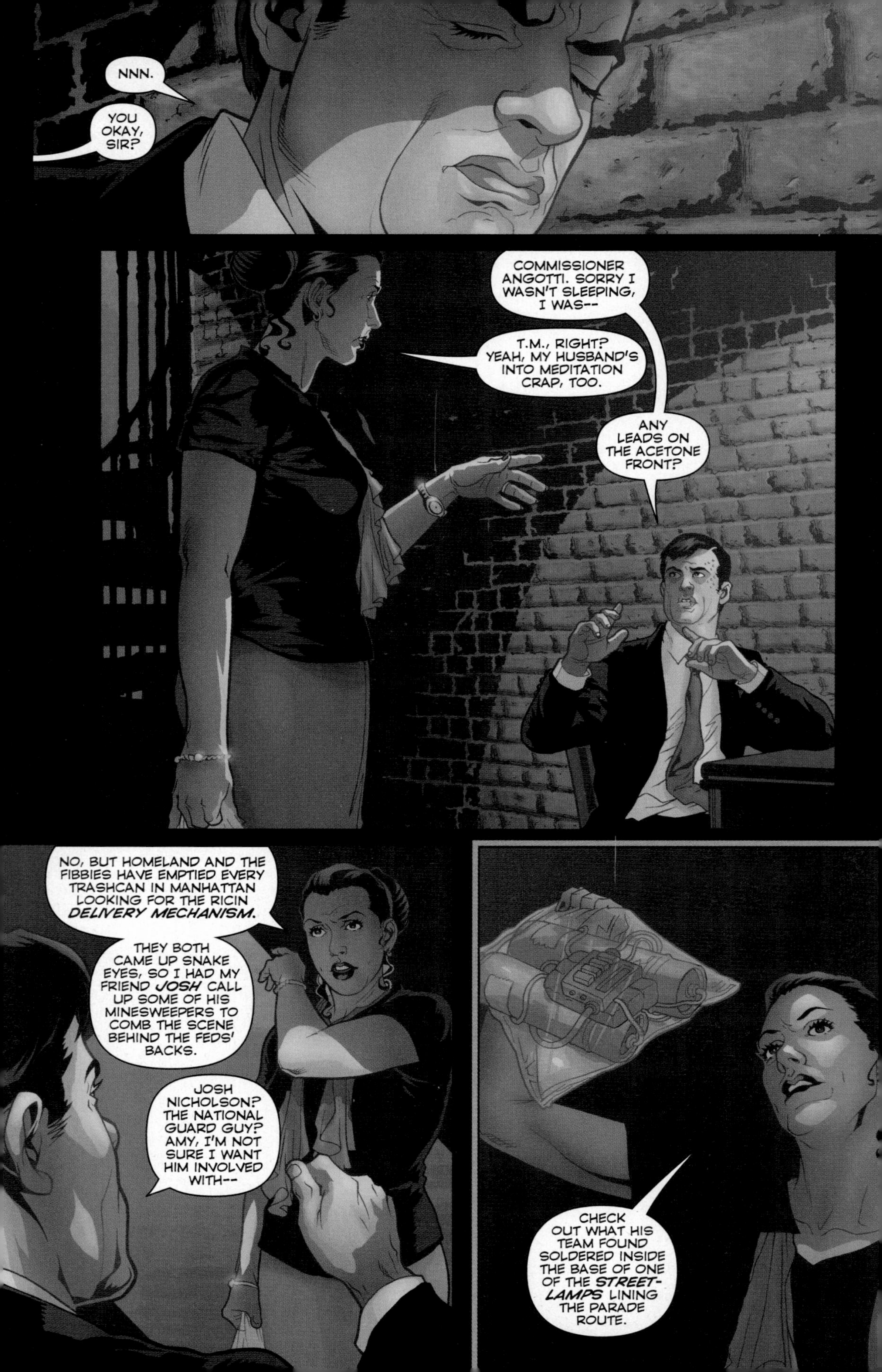
NNN.
YOU OKAY, SIR?
COMMISSIONER ANGOTTI. SORRY I WASN'T SLEEPING, I WAS--
T.M., RIGHT? YEAH, MY HUSBAND'S INTO MEDITATION CRAP, TOO.
ANY LEADS ON THE ACETONE FRONT?
NO, BUT HOMELAND AND THE FIBBIES HAVE EMPTIED EVERY TRASHCAN IN MANHATTAN LOOKING FOR THE RICIN *DELIVERY MECHANISM*.
THEY BOTH CAME UP SNAKE EYES, SO I HAD MY FRIEND *JOSH* CALL UP SOME OF HIS MINESWEEPERS TO COMB THE SCENE BEHIND THE FEDS' BACKS.
JOSH NICHOLSON? THE NATIONAL GUARD GUY? AMY, I'M NOT SURE I WANT HIM INVOLVED WITH--
CHECK OUT WHAT HIS TEAM FOUND SOLDERED INSIDE THE BASE OF ONE OF THE *STREET-LAMPS* LINING THE PARADE ROUTE.

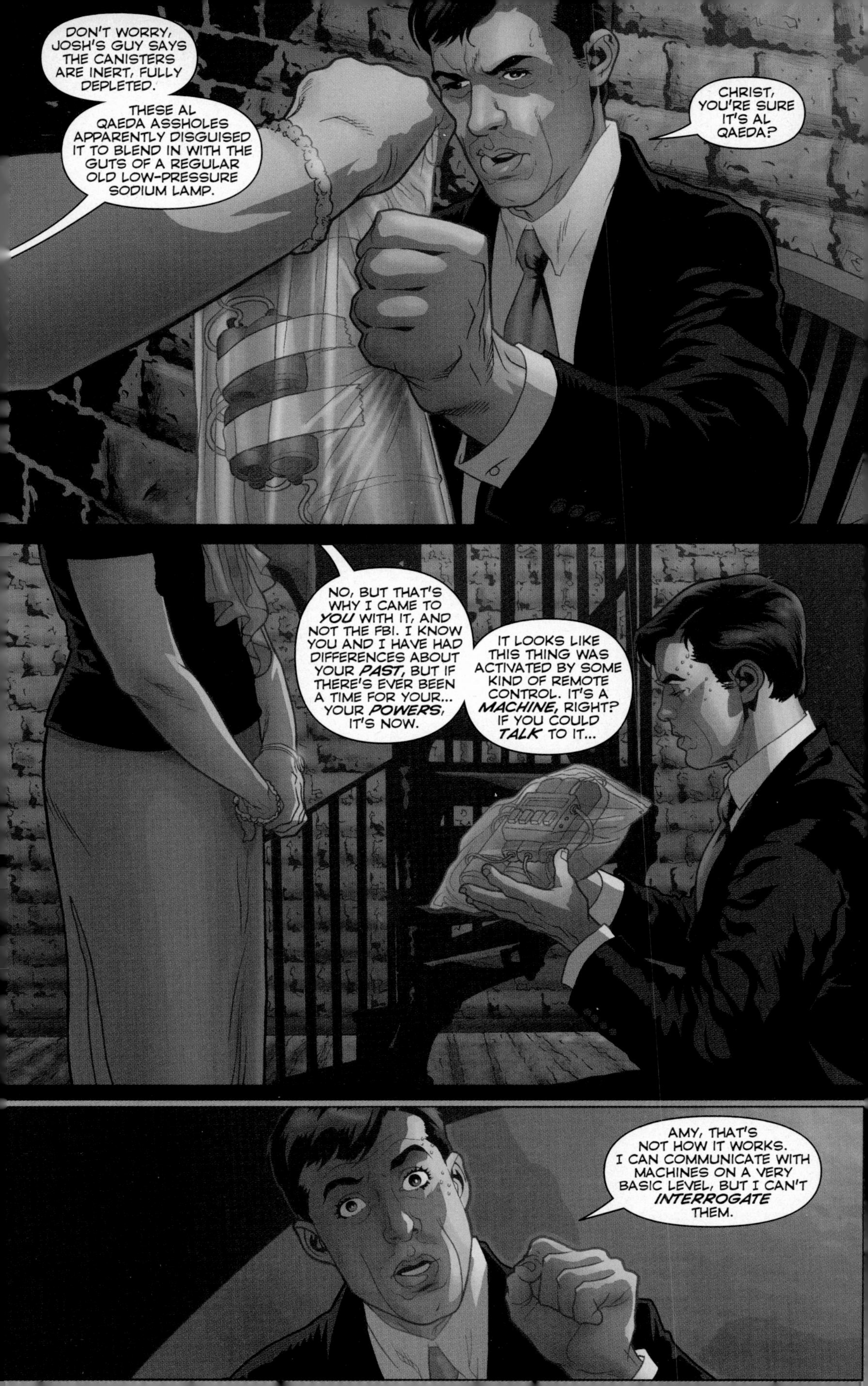
DON'T WORRY, JOSH'S GUY SAYS THE CANISTERS ARE INERT, FULLY DEPLETED.
THESE AL QAEDA ASSHOLES APPARENTLY DISGUISED IT TO BLEND IN WITH THE GUTS OF A REGULAR OLD LOW-PRESSURE SODIUM LAMP.
CHRIST, YOU'RE SURE IT'S AL QAEDA?
NO, BUT THAT'S WHY I CAME TO *YOU* WITH IT, AND NOT THE FBI. I KNOW YOU AND I HAVE HAD DIFFERENCES ABOUT YOUR *PAST*, BUT IF THERE'S EVER BEEN A TIME FOR YOUR... YOUR *POWERS*, IT'S NOW.
IT LOOKS LIKE THIS THING WAS ACTIVATED BY SOME KIND OF REMOTE CONTROL. IT'S A *MACHINE*, RIGHT? IF YOU COULD *TALK* TO IT...
AMY, THAT'S NOT HOW IT WORKS. I CAN COMMUNICATE WITH MACHINES ON A VERY BASIC LEVEL, BUT I CAN'T *INTERROGATE* THEM.

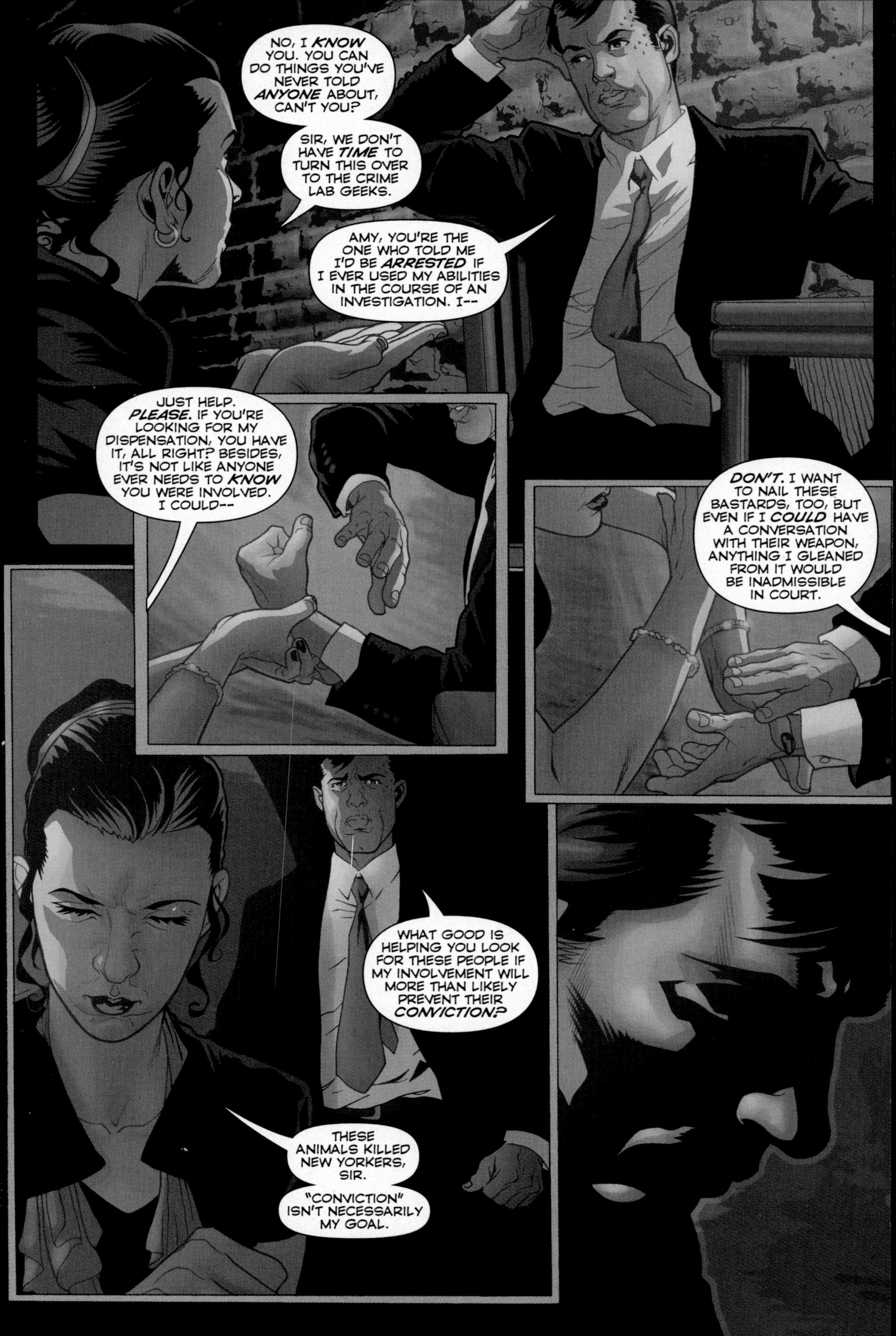
NO, I KNOW YOU. YOU CAN DO THINGS YOU'VE NEVER TOLD ANYONE ABOUT, CAN'T YOU?
SIR, WE DON'T HAVE TIME TO TURN THIS OVER TO THE CRIME LAB GEEKS.
AMY, YOU'RE THE ONE WHO TOLD ME I'D BE ARRESTED IF I EVER USED MY ABILITIES IN THE COURSE OF AN INVESTIGATION. I--
JUST HELP. PLEASE. IF YOU'RE LOOKING FOR MY DISPENSATION, YOU HAVE IT, ALL RIGHT? BESIDES, IT'S NOT LIKE ANYONE EVER NEEDS TO KNOW YOU WERE INVOLVED. I COULD--
DON'T. I WANT TO NAIL THESE BASTARDS, TOO, BUT EVEN IF I COULD HAVE A CONVERSATION WITH THEIR WEAPON, ANYTHING I GLEANED FROM IT WOULD BE INADMISSIBLE IN COURT.
WHAT GOOD IS HELPING YOU LOOK FOR THESE PEOPLE IF MY INVOLVEMENT WILL MORE THAN LIKELY PREVENT THEIR CONVICTION?
THESE ANIMALS KILLED NEW YORKERS, SIR.
"CONVICTION" ISN'T NECESSARILY MY GOAL.

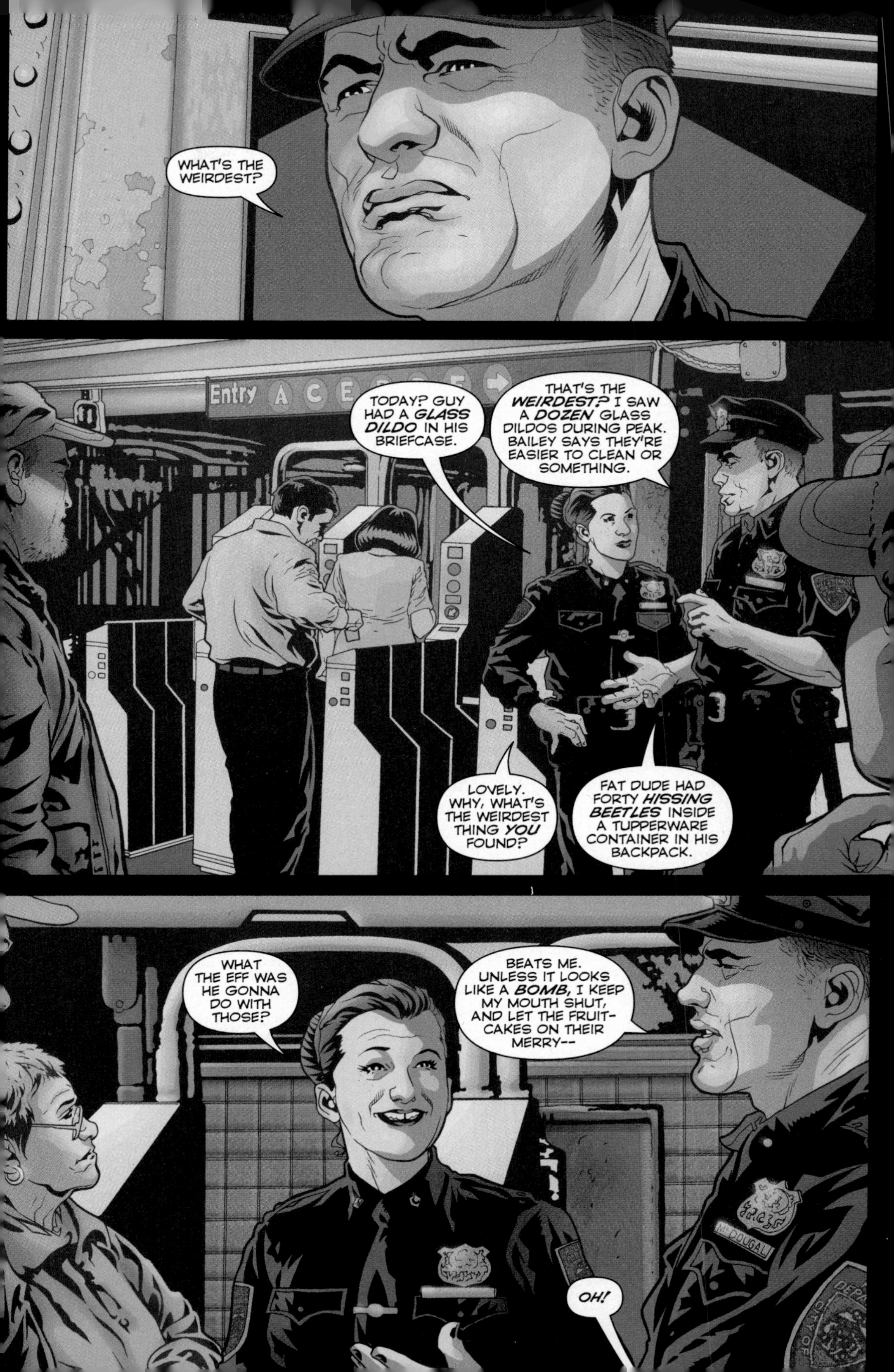
WHAT'S THE WEIRDEST?
Entry A C E
TODAY? GUY HAD A GLASS DILDO IN HIS BRIEFCASE.
THAT'S THE WEIRDEST? I SAW A DOZEN GLASS DILDOS DURING PEAK. BAILEY SAYS THEY'RE EASIER TO CLEAN OR SOMETHING.
LOVELY. WHY, WHAT'S THE WEIRDEST THING YOU FOUND?
FAT DUDE HAD FORTY HISSING BEETLES INSIDE A TUPPERWARE CONTAINER IN HIS BACKPACK.
WHAT THE EFF WAS HE GONNA DO WITH THOSE?
BEATS ME. UNLESS IT LOOKS LIKE A BOMB, I KEEP MY MOUTH SHUT, AND LET THE FRUIT-CAKES ON THEIR MERRY--
McDOUGAL
OH!

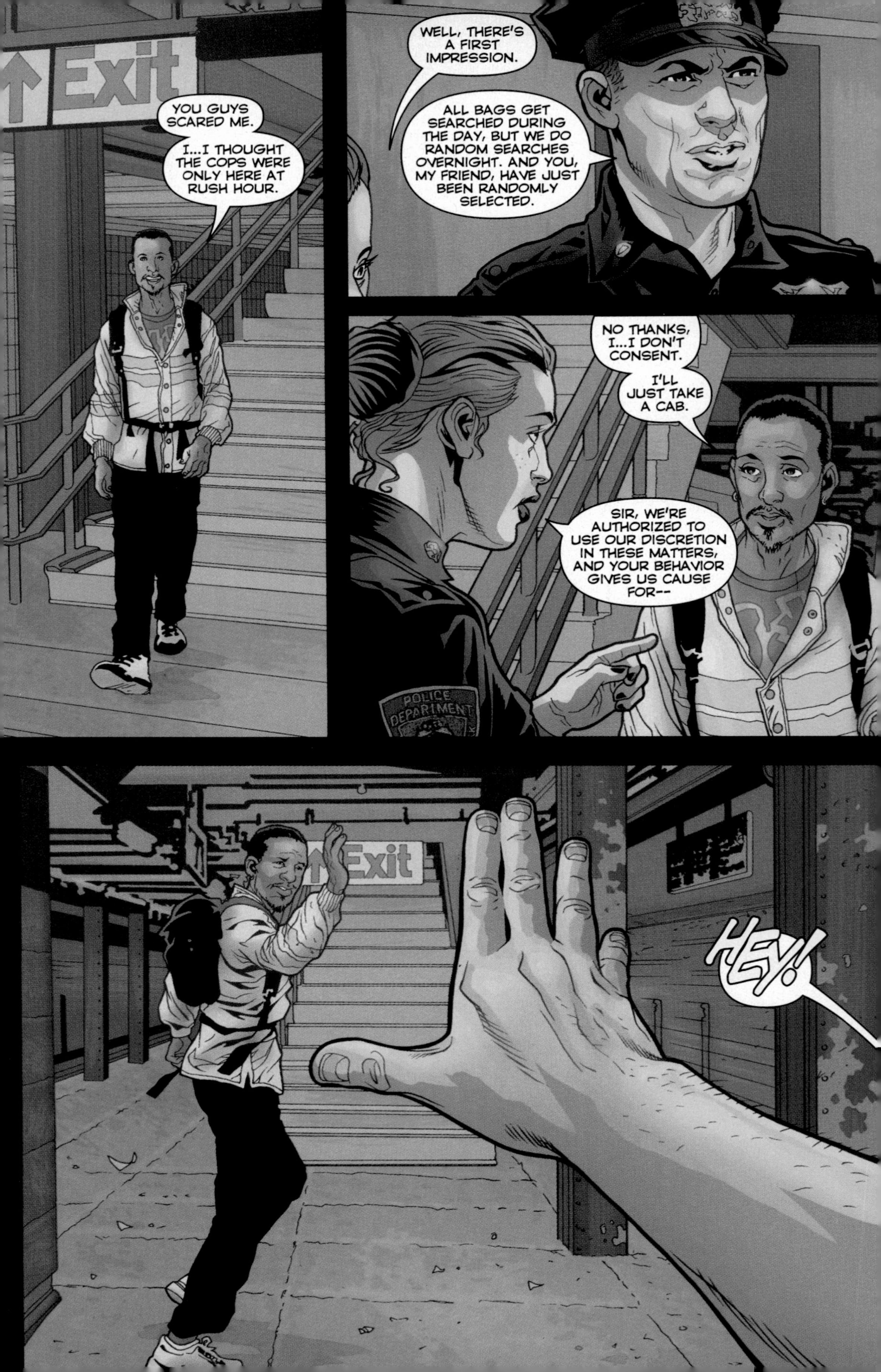
Exit
YOU GUYS SCARED ME.
I...I THOUGHT THE COPS WERE ONLY HERE AT RUSH HOUR.
WELL, THERE'S A FIRST IMPRESSION.
ALL BAGS GET SEARCHED DURING THE DAY, BUT WE DO RANDOM SEARCHES OVERNIGHT. AND YOU, MY FRIEND, HAVE JUST BEEN RANDOMLY SELECTED.
NO THANKS, I...I DON'T CONSENT.
I'LL JUST TAKE A CAB.
SIR, WE'RE AUTHORIZED TO USE OUR DISCRETION IN THESE MATTERS, AND YOUR BEHAVIOR GIVES US CAUSE FOR--
POLICE DEPARTMENT
Exit
HEY!

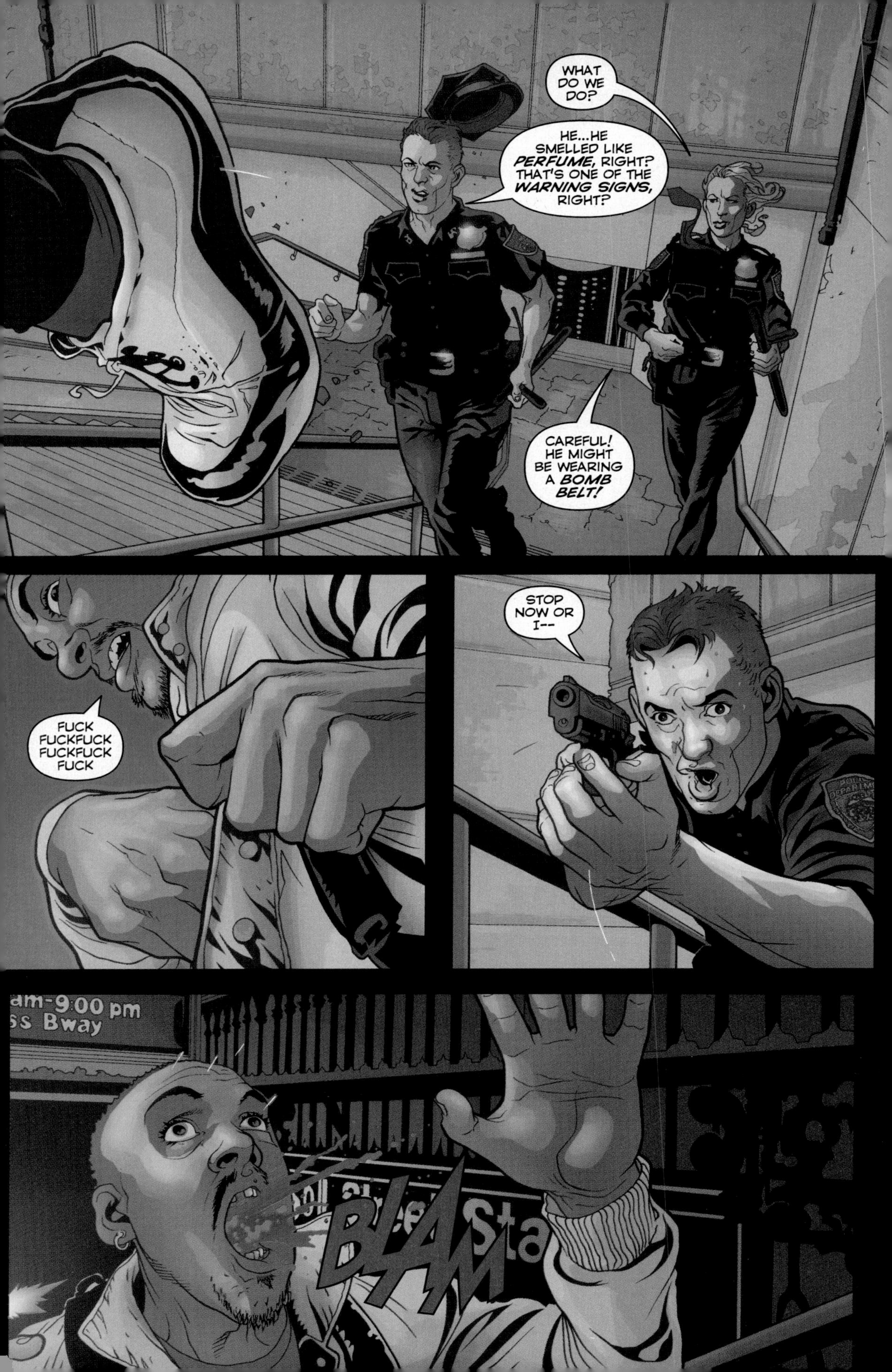
WHAT DO WE DO?
HE...HE SMELLED LIKE PERFUME, RIGHT? THAT'S ONE OF THE WARNING SIGNS, RIGHT?
CAREFUL! HE MIGHT BE WEARING A BOMB BELT!
FUCK FUCKFUCK FUCKFUCK FUCK
STOP NOW OR I--
am-9:00 pm
ss Bway
BLAM

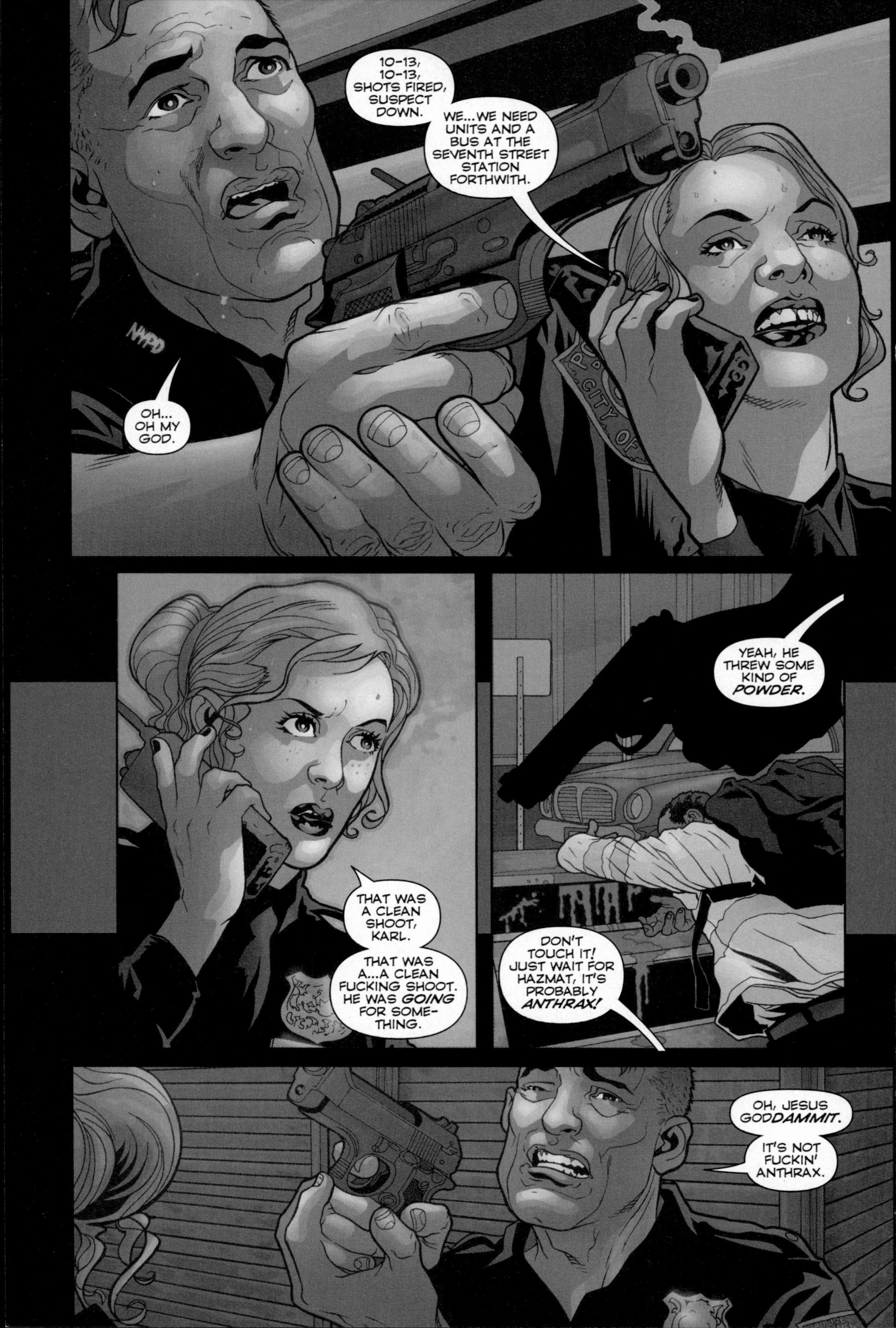
10-13, 10-13, SHOTS FIRED, SUSPECT DOWN.
WE...WE NEED UNITS AND A BUS AT THE SEVENTH STREET STATION FORTHWITH.
OH... OH MY GOD.
NYPD
THAT WAS A CLEAN SHOOT, KARL.
THAT WAS A...A CLEAN FUCKING SHOOT. HE WAS GOING FOR SOME-THING.
YEAH, HE THREW SOME KIND OF POWDER.
DON'T TOUCH IT! JUST WAIT FOR HAZMAT, IT'S PROBABLY ANTHRAX!
OH, JESUS GODDAMMIT.
IT'S NOT FUCKIN' ANTHRAX.

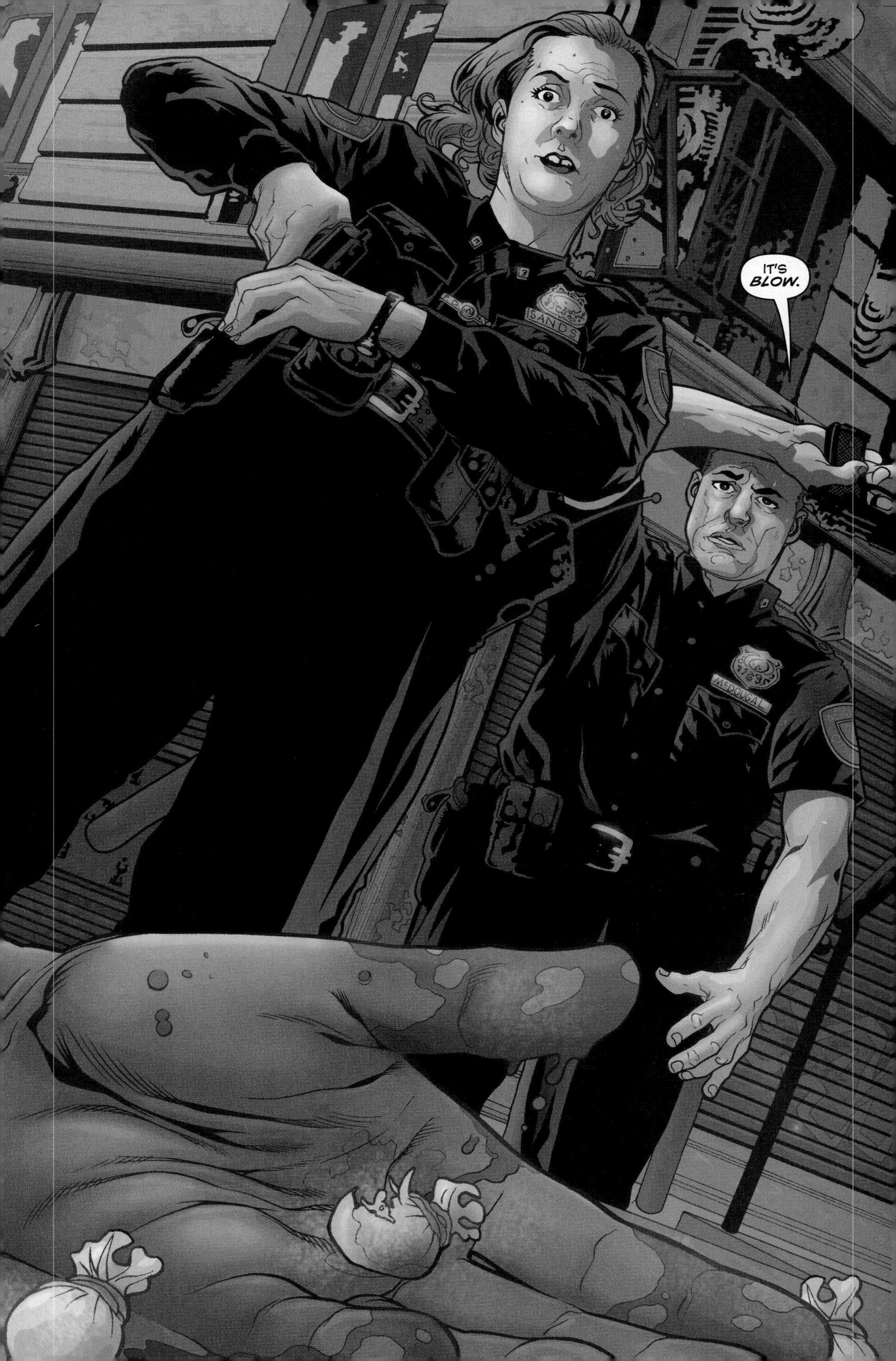
IT'S BLOW.

CHAPTER 4 March to War

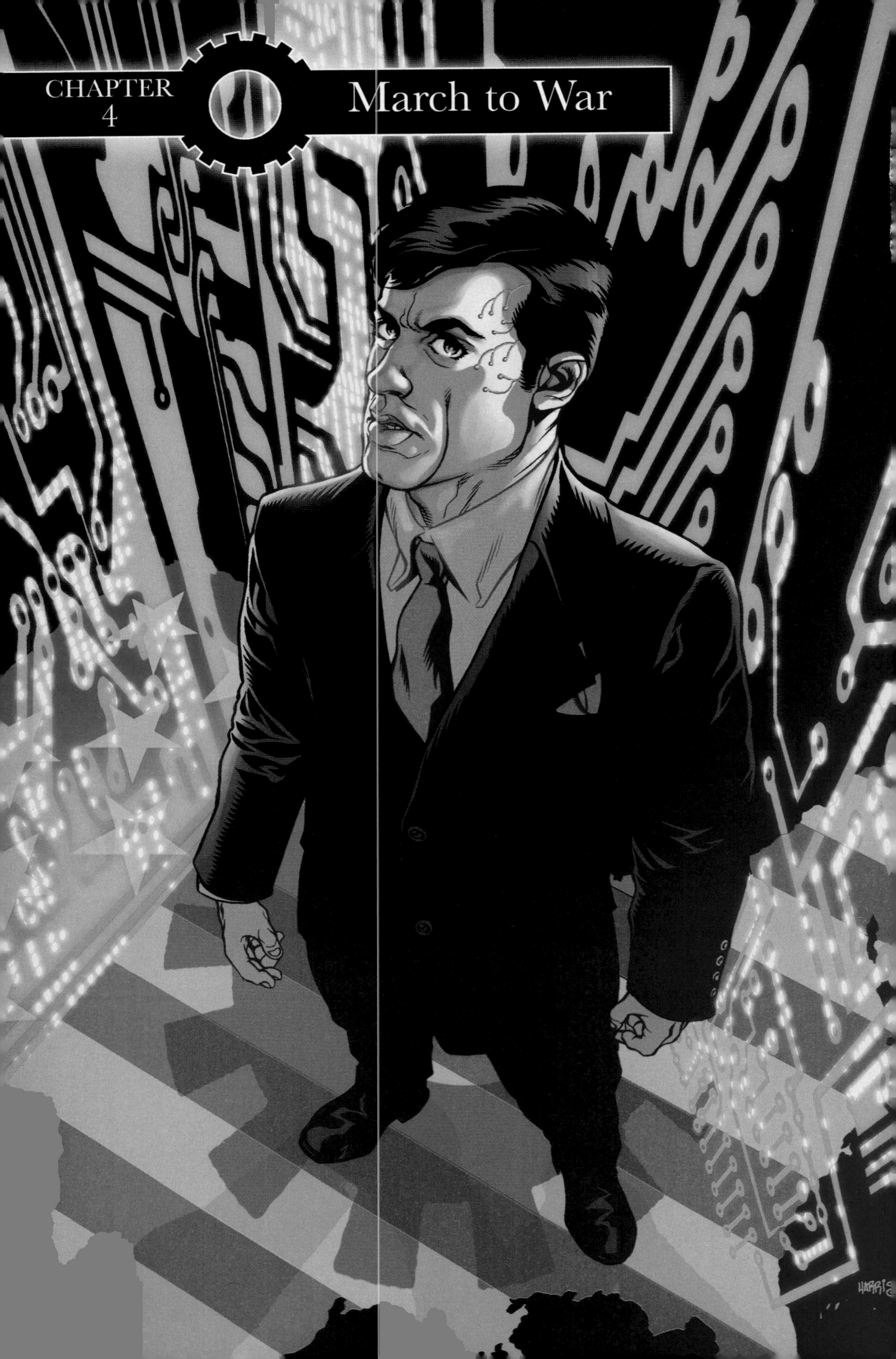

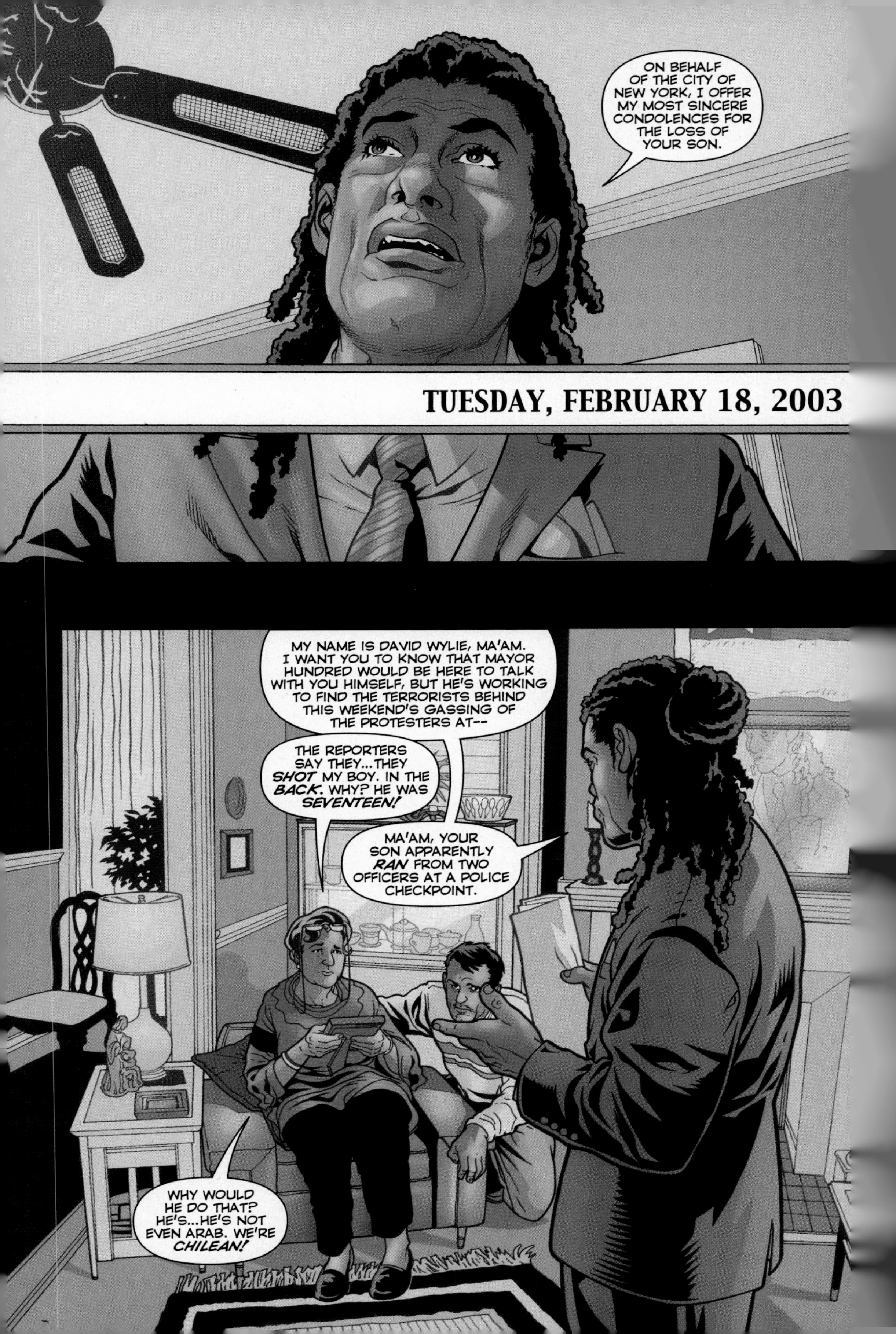
ON BEHALF OF THE CITY OF NEW YORK, I OFFER MY MOST SINCERE CONDOLENCES FOR THE LOSS OF YOUR SON.
TUESDAY, FEBRUARY 18, 2003
MY NAME IS DAVID WYLIE, MA'AM. I WANT YOU TO KNOW THAT MAYOR HUNDRED WOULD BE HERE TO TALK WITH YOU HIMSELF, BUT HE'S WORKING TO FIND THE TERRORISTS BEHIND THIS WEEKEND'S GASSING OF THE PROTESTERS AT--
THE REPORTERS SAY THEY...THEY *SHOT* MY BOY. IN THE *BACK*. WHY? HE WAS *SEVENTEEN!*
MA'AM, YOUR SON APPARENTLY *RAN* FROM TWO OFFICERS AT A POLICE CHECKPOINT.
WHY WOULD HE DO THAT? HE'S...HE'S NOT EVEN ARAB. WE'RE *CHILEAN!*

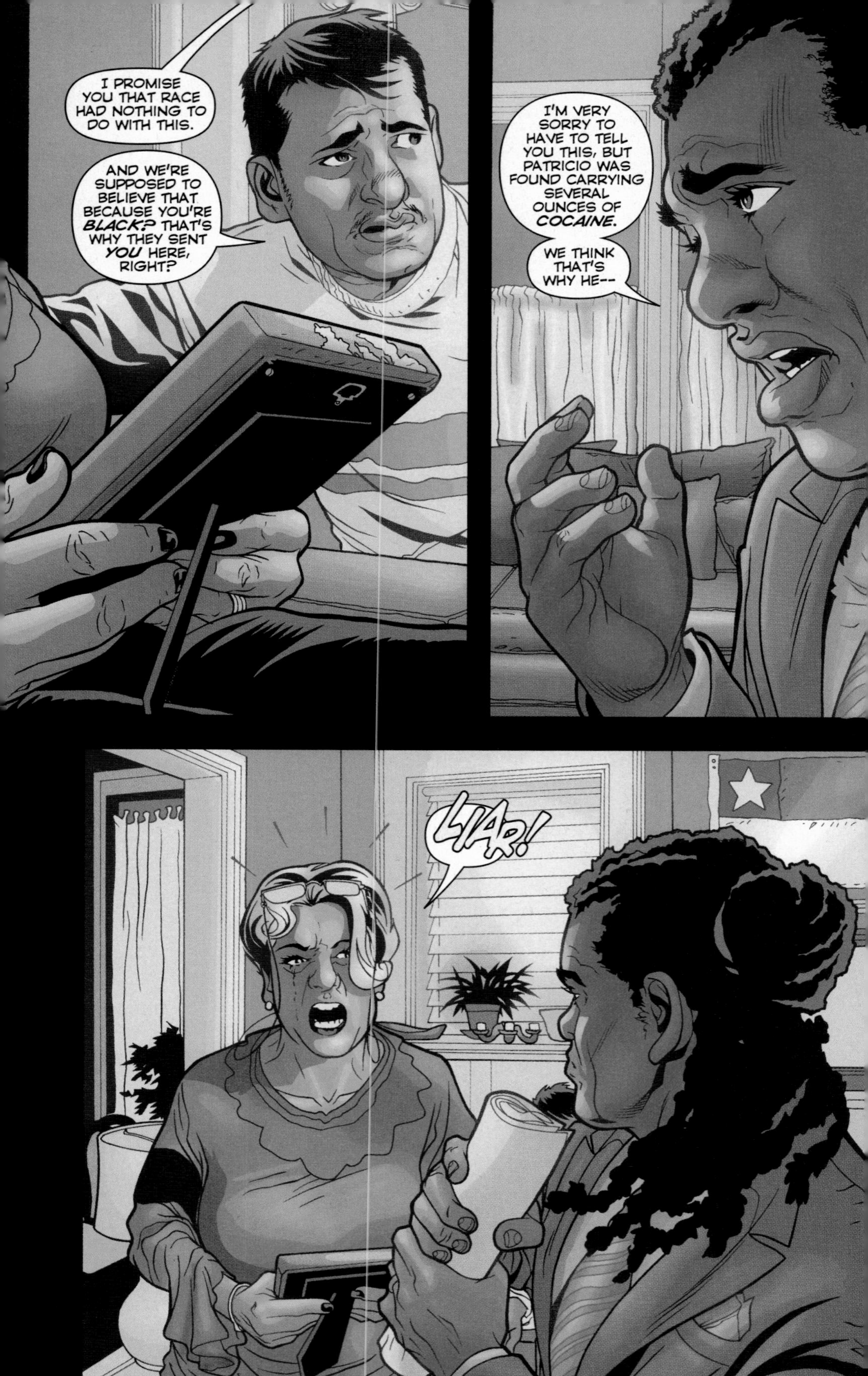
I PROMISE YOU THAT RACE HAD NOTHING TO DO WITH THIS.
AND WE'RE SUPPOSED TO BELIEVE THAT BECAUSE YOU'RE *BLACK?* THAT'S WHY THEY SENT *YOU* HERE, RIGHT?
I'M VERY SORRY TO HAVE TO TELL YOU THIS, BUT PATRICIO WAS FOUND CARRYING SEVERAL OUNCES OF *COCAINE*.
WE THINK THAT'S WHY HE--
LIAR!

MOM, ENOUGH.

¡VAYA AL INFIERNO!

WE DON'T *WANT* AN INVESTIGATION, MR. DEPUTY MAYOR. MY FAMILY HAS NO INTENTION OF TAKING ACTION AGAINST THE CITY.

I GRADUATED WEST POINT. I...I UNDERSTAND THAT HONEST MISTAKES HAPPEN IN THE FOG OF WAR.

I KNOW PAST ADMINISTRATIONS HAVE AUTOMATICALLY SIDED WITH THE NYPD IN INCIDENTS LIKE THIS, BUT I SWEAR TO YOU THAT THERE WILL BE A FULL AND VIGOROUS INVESTIGATION.

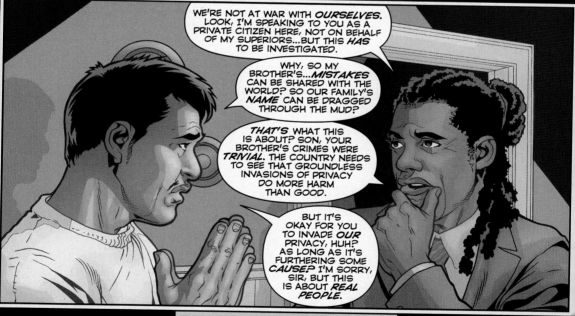

WE'RE NOT AT WAR WITH *OURSELVES.* LOOK, I'M SPEAKING TO YOU AS A PRIVATE CITIZEN HERE, NOT ON BEHALF OF MY SUPERIORS...BUT THIS *HAS* TO BE INVESTIGATED.

WHY, SO MY BROTHER'S...*MISTAKES* CAN BE SHARED WITH THE WORLD? SO OUR FAMILY'S *NAME* CAN BE DRAGGED THROUGH THE MUD?

THAT'S WHAT THIS IS ABOUT? SON, YOUR BROTHER'S CRIMES WERE *TRIVIAL.* THE COUNTRY NEEDS TO SEE THAT GROUNDLESS INVASIONS OF PRIVACY DO MORE HARM THAN GOOD.

BUT IT'S OKAY FOR YOU TO INVADE *OUR* PRIVACY, HUH? AS LONG AS IT'S FURTHERING SOME *CAUSE?* I'M SORRY, SIR, BUT THIS IS ABOUT *REAL PEOPLE.*

WHY CAN'T THE FOLKS IN CHARGE EVER UNDERSTAND THAT?

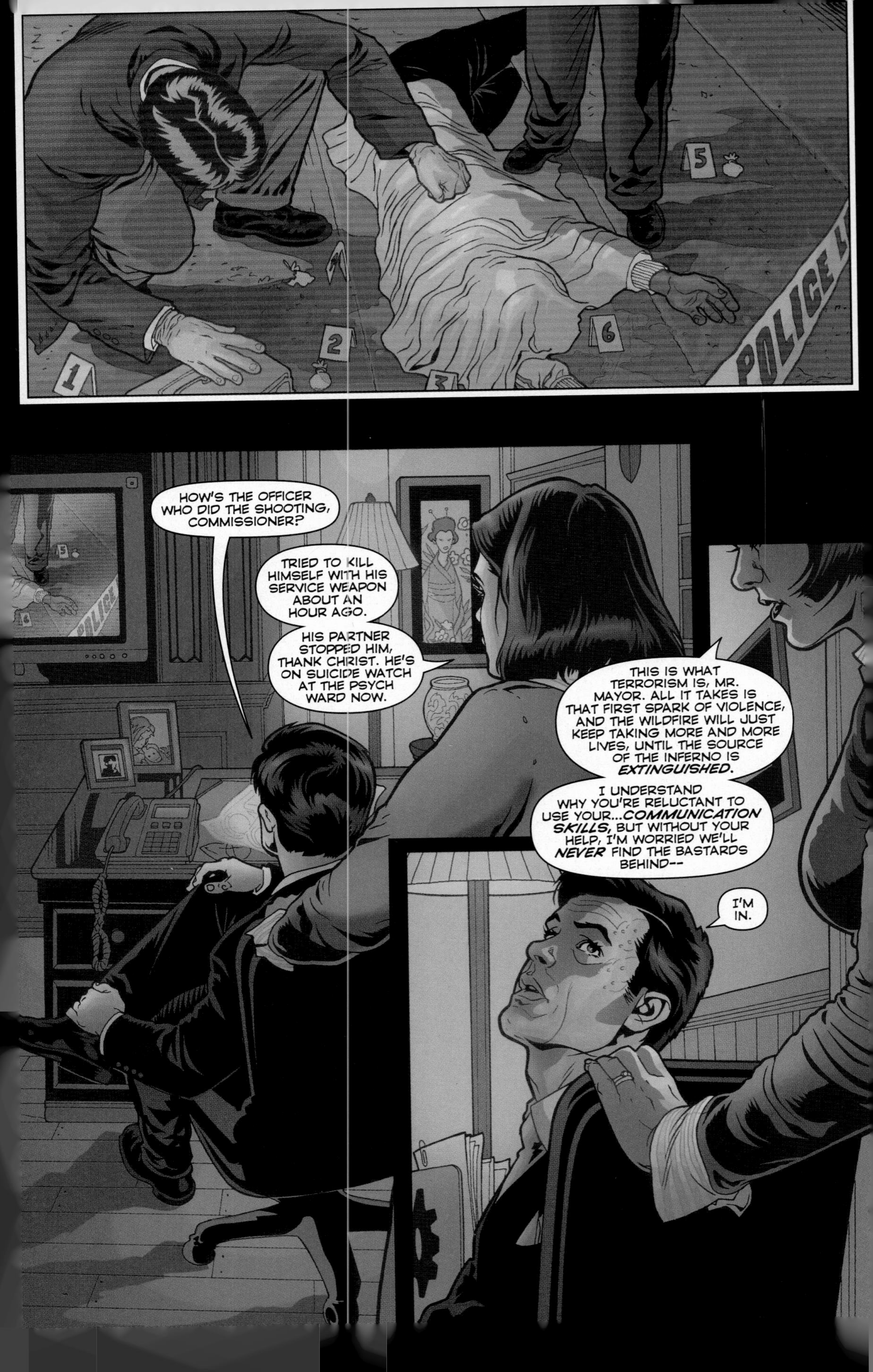

POLICE
HOW'S THE OFFICER WHO DID THE SHOOTING, COMMISSIONER?
TRIED TO KILL HIMSELF WITH HIS SERVICE WEAPON ABOUT AN HOUR AGO.
HIS PARTNER STOPPED HIM, THANK CHRIST. HE'S ON SUICIDE WATCH AT THE PSYCH WARD NOW.
THIS IS WHAT TERRORISM IS, MR. MAYOR. ALL IT TAKES IS THAT FIRST SPARK OF VIOLENCE, AND THE WILDFIRE WILL JUST KEEP TAKING MORE AND MORE LIVES, UNTIL THE SOURCE OF THE INFERNO IS EXTINGUISHED.
I UNDERSTAND WHY YOU'RE RELUCTANT TO USE YOUR...COMMUNICATION SKILLS, BUT WITHOUT YOUR HELP, I'M WORRIED WE'LL NEVER FIND THE BASTARDS BEHIND--
I'M IN.

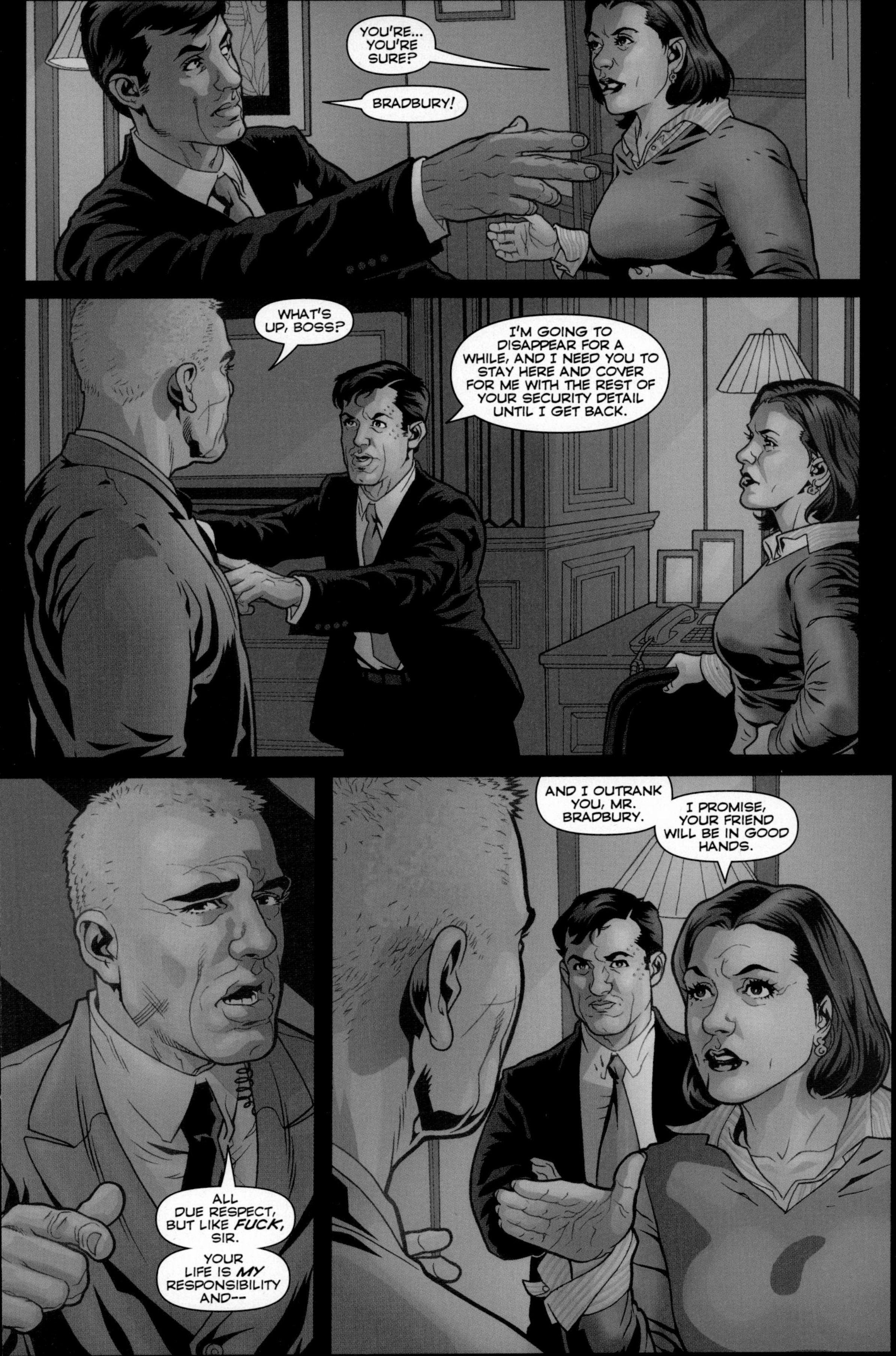
YOU'RE... YOU'RE SURE?
BRADBURY!
WHAT'S UP, BOSS?
I'M GOING TO DISAPPEAR FOR A WHILE, AND I NEED YOU TO STAY HERE AND COVER FOR ME WITH THE REST OF YOUR SECURITY DETAIL UNTIL I GET BACK.
ALL DUE RESPECT, BUT LIKE *FUCK*, SIR.
YOUR LIFE IS *MY* RESPONSIBILITY AND--
AND I OUTRANK YOU, MR. BRADBURY.
I PROMISE, YOUR FRIEND WILL BE IN GOOD HANDS.

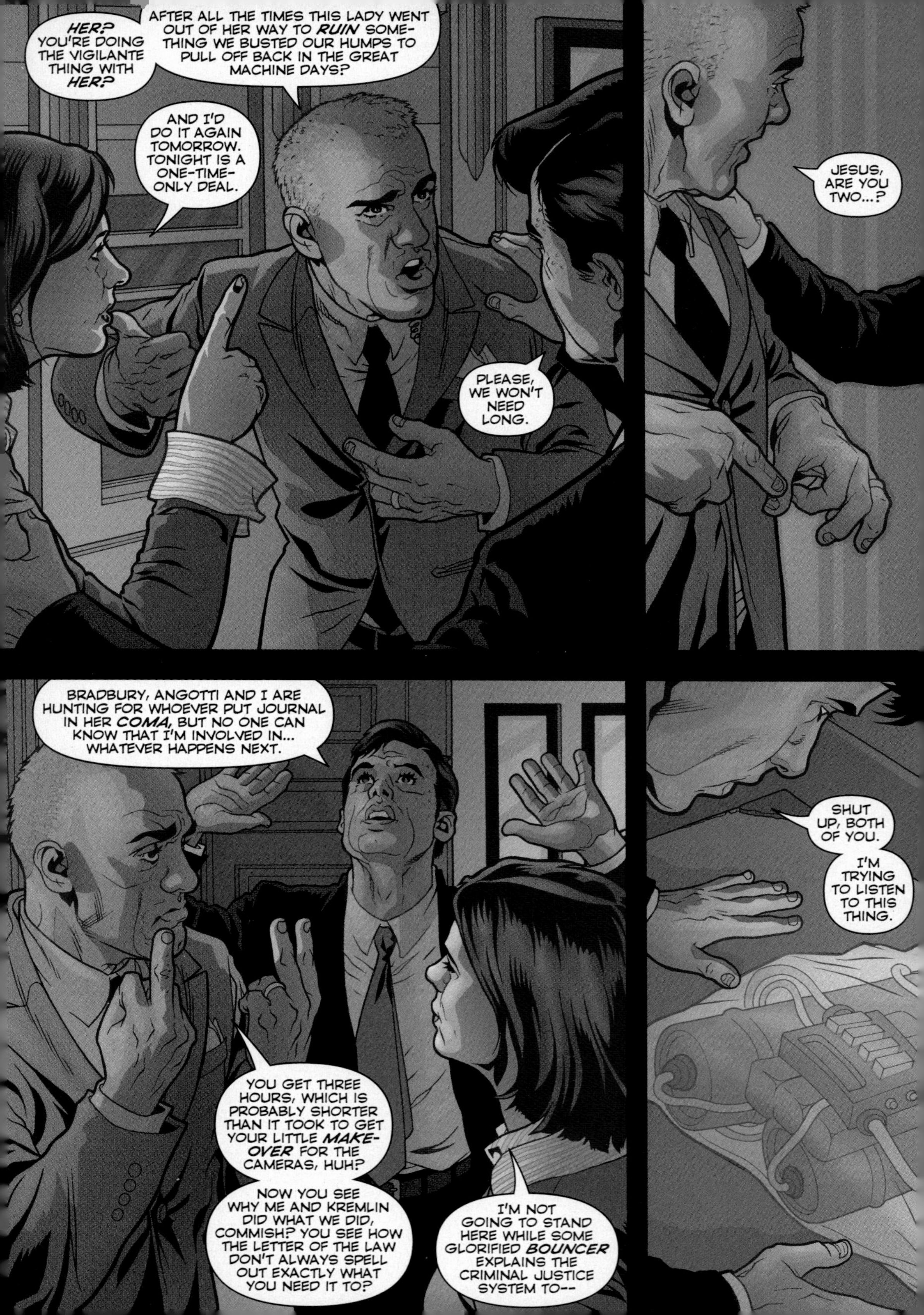
HER? YOU'RE DOING THE VIGILANTE THING WITH HER?
AFTER ALL THE TIMES THIS LADY WENT OUT OF HER WAY TO RUIN SOMETHING WE BUSTED OUR HUMPS TO PULL OFF BACK IN THE GREAT MACHINE DAYS?
AND I'D DO IT AGAIN TOMORROW. TONIGHT IS A ONE-TIME-ONLY DEAL.
PLEASE, WE WON'T NEED LONG.
JESUS, ARE YOU TWO...?
BRADBURY, ANGOTTI AND I ARE HUNTING FOR WHOEVER PUT JOURNAL IN HER COMA, BUT NO ONE CAN KNOW THAT I'M INVOLVED IN... WHATEVER HAPPENS NEXT.
YOU GET THREE HOURS, WHICH IS PROBABLY SHORTER THAN IT TOOK TO GET YOUR LITTLE MAKE-OVER FOR THE CAMERAS, HUH?
NOW YOU SEE WHY ME AND KREMLIN DID WHAT WE DID, COMMISH? YOU SEE HOW THE LETTER OF THE LAW DON'T ALWAYS SPELL OUT EXACTLY WHAT YOU NEED IT TO?
I'M NOT GOING TO STAND HERE WHILE SOME GLORIFIED BOUNCER EXPLAINS THE CRIMINAL JUSTICE SYSTEM TO--
SHUT UP, BOTH OF YOU.
I'M TRYING TO LISTEN TO THIS THING.

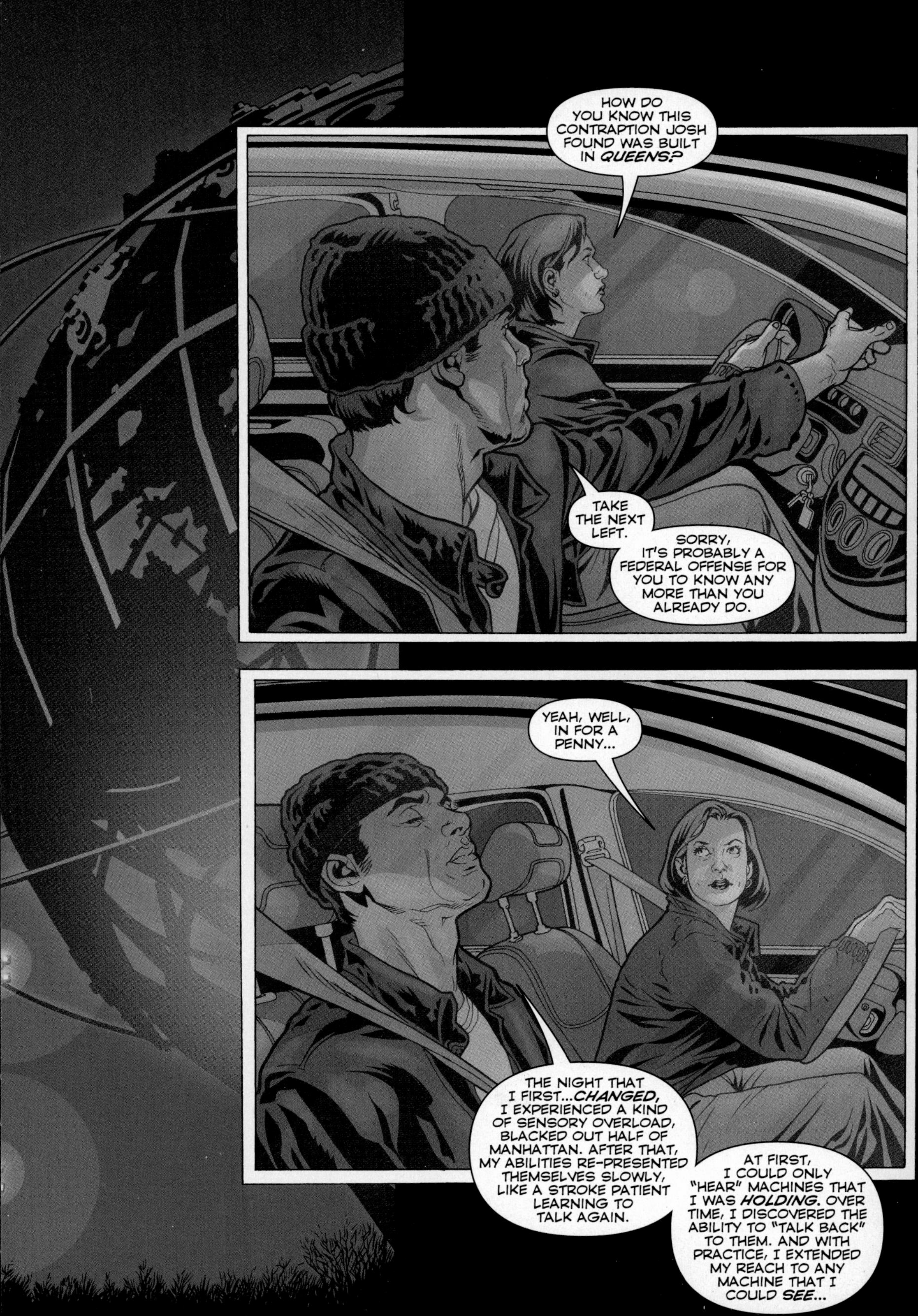
HOW DO YOU KNOW THIS CONTRAPTION JOSH FOUND WAS BUILT IN *QUEENS?*
TAKE THE NEXT LEFT.
SORRY, IT'S PROBABLY A FEDERAL OFFENSE FOR YOU TO KNOW ANY MORE THAN YOU ALREADY DO.
YEAH, WELL, IN FOR A PENNY...
THE NIGHT THAT I FIRST...*CHANGED,* I EXPERIENCED A KIND OF SENSORY OVERLOAD, BLACKED OUT HALF OF MANHATTAN. AFTER THAT, MY ABILITIES RE-PRESENTED THEMSELVES SLOWLY, LIKE A STROKE PATIENT LEARNING TO TALK AGAIN.
AT FIRST, I COULD ONLY "HEAR" MACHINES THAT I WAS *HOLDING.* OVER TIME, I DISCOVERED THE ABILITY TO "TALK BACK" TO THEM. AND WITH PRACTICE, I EXTENDED MY REACH TO ANY MACHINE THAT I COULD *SEE...*

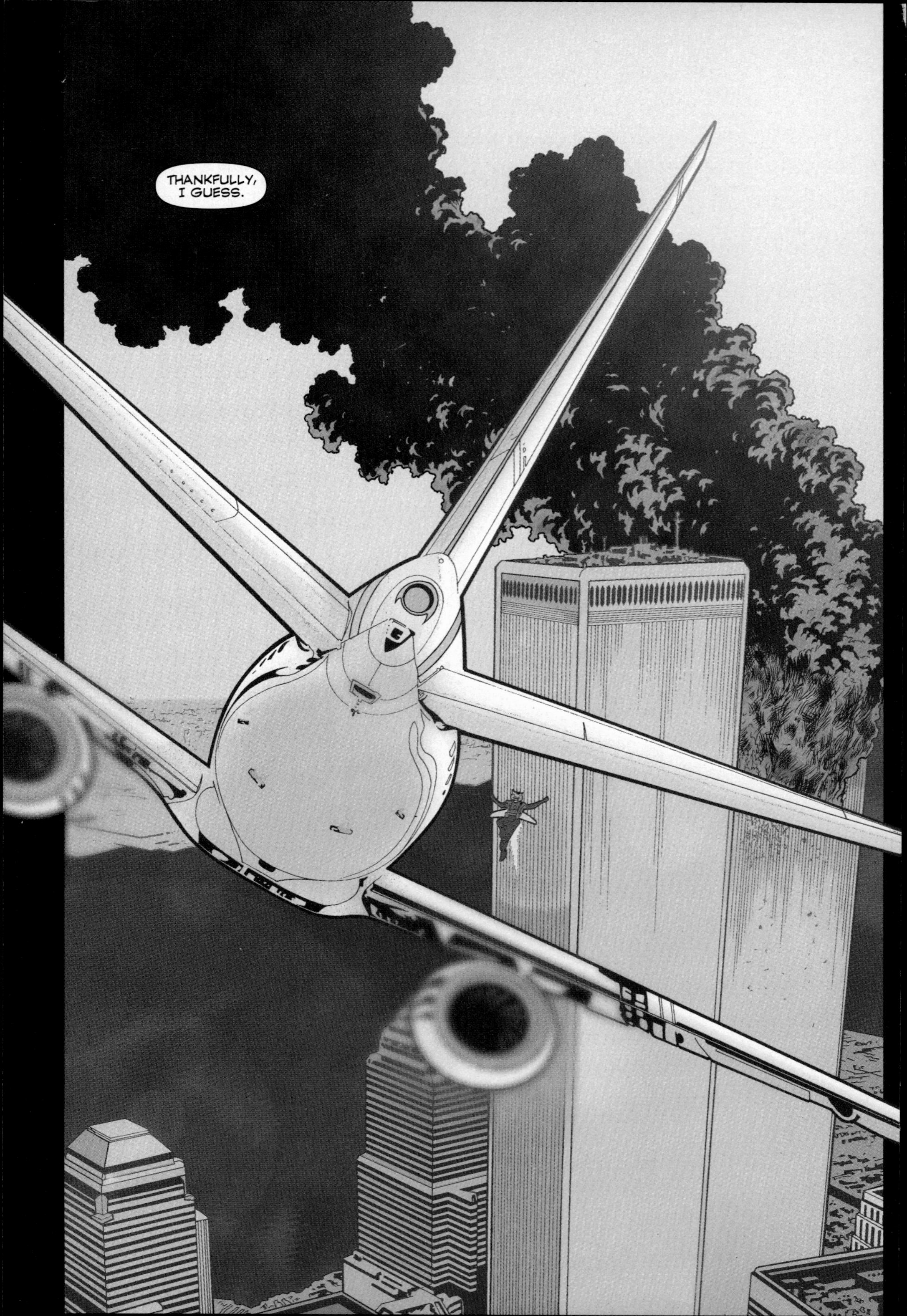
THANKFULLY, I GUESS.

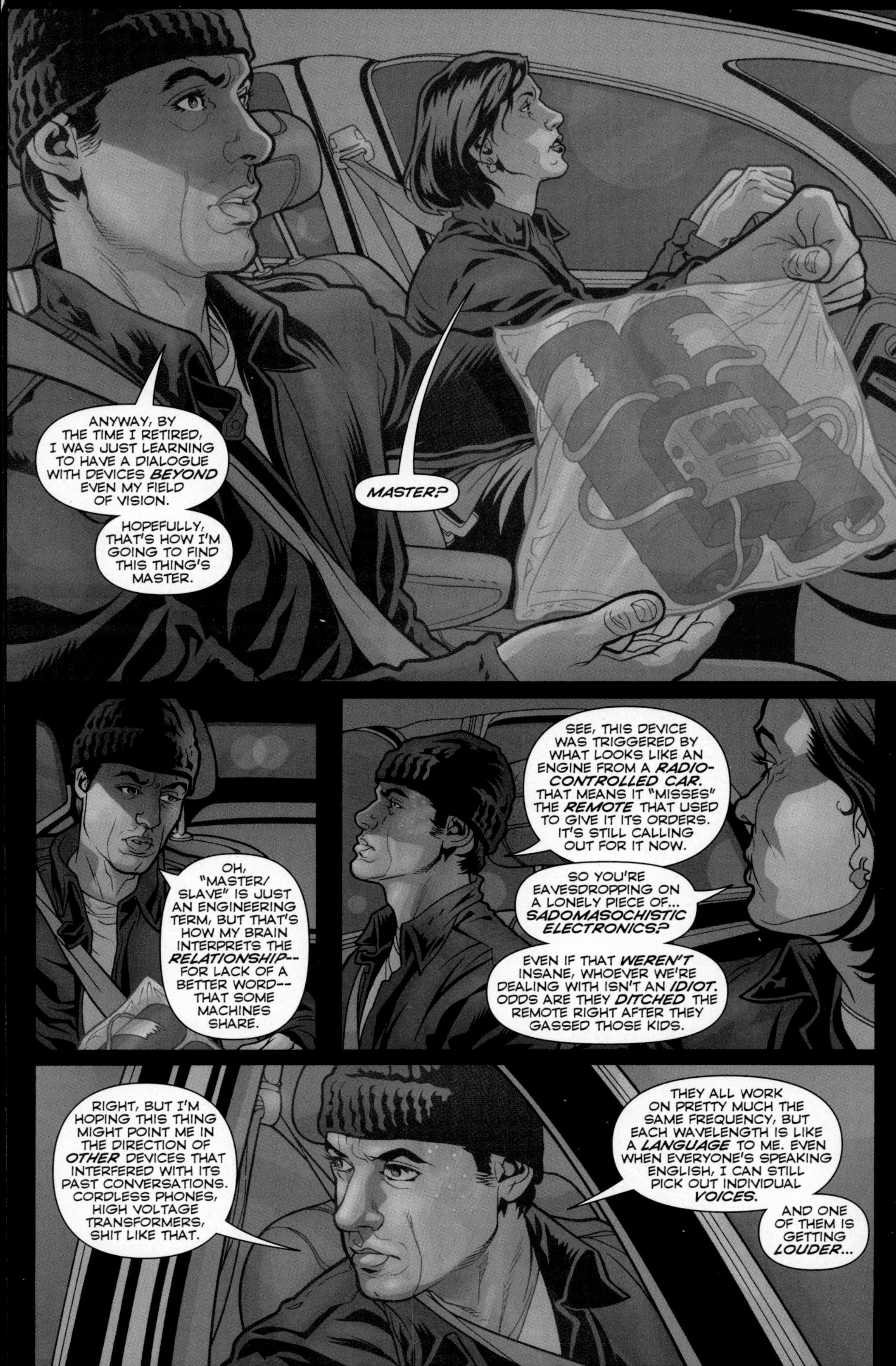
ANYWAY, BY THE TIME I RETIRED, I WAS JUST LEARNING TO HAVE A DIALOGUE WITH DEVICES *BEYOND* EVEN MY FIELD OF VISION.
HOPEFULLY, THAT'S HOW I'M GOING TO FIND THIS THING'S MASTER.
MASTER?
OH, "MASTER/ SLAVE" IS JUST AN ENGINEERING TERM, BUT THAT'S HOW MY BRAIN INTERPRETS THE *RELATIONSHIP*-- FOR LACK OF A BETTER WORD-- THAT SOME MACHINES SHARE.
SEE, THIS DEVICE WAS TRIGGERED BY WHAT LOOKS LIKE AN ENGINE FROM A *RADIO-CONTROLLED CAR*. THAT MEANS IT "MISSES" THE *REMOTE* THAT USED TO GIVE IT ITS ORDERS. IT'S STILL CALLING OUT FOR IT NOW.
SO YOU'RE EAVESDROPPING ON A LONELY PIECE OF... *SADOMASOCHISTIC ELECTRONICS?*
EVEN IF THAT *WEREN'T* INSANE, WHOEVER WE'RE DEALING WITH ISN'T AN *IDIOT*. ODDS ARE THEY *DITCHED* THE REMOTE RIGHT AFTER THEY GASSED THOSE KIDS.
RIGHT, BUT I'M HOPING THIS THING MIGHT POINT ME IN THE DIRECTION OF *OTHER* DEVICES THAT INTERFERED WITH ITS PAST CONVERSATIONS. CORDLESS PHONES, HIGH VOLTAGE TRANSFORMERS, SHIT LIKE THAT.
THEY ALL WORK ON PRETTY MUCH THE SAME FREQUENCY, BUT EACH WAVELENGTH IS LIKE A *LANGUAGE* TO ME. EVEN WHEN EVERYONE'S SPEAKING ENGLISH, I CAN STILL PICK OUT INDIVIDUAL *VOICES*.
AND ONE OF THEM IS GETTING *LOUDER...*

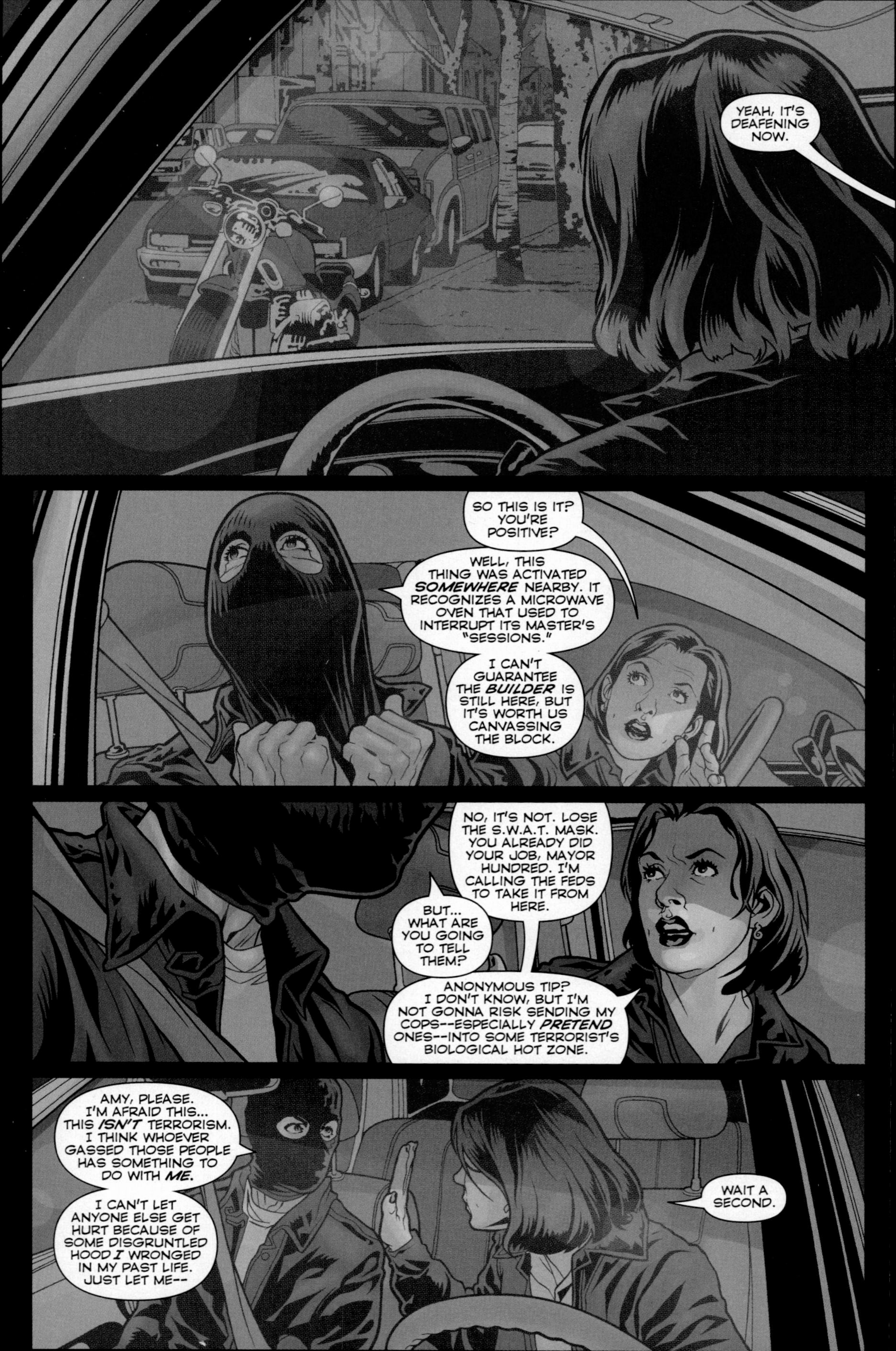
YEAH, IT'S DEAFENING NOW.
SO THIS IS IT? YOU'RE POSITIVE?
WELL, THIS THING WAS ACTIVATED SOMEWHERE NEARBY. IT RECOGNIZES A MICROWAVE OVEN THAT USED TO INTERRUPT ITS MASTER'S "SESSIONS."
I CAN'T GUARANTEE THE BUILDER IS STILL HERE, BUT IT'S WORTH US CANVASSING THE BLOCK.
NO, IT'S NOT. LOSE THE S.W.A.T. MASK. YOU ALREADY DID YOUR JOB, MAYOR HUNDRED. I'M CALLING THE FEDS TO TAKE IT FROM HERE.
BUT... WHAT ARE YOU GOING TO TELL THEM?
ANONYMOUS TIP? I DON'T KNOW, BUT I'M NOT GONNA RISK SENDING MY COPS--ESPECIALLY PRETEND ONES--INTO SOME TERRORIST'S BIOLOGICAL HOT ZONE.
AMY, PLEASE. I'M AFRAID THIS... THIS ISN'T TERRORISM. I THINK WHOEVER GASSED THOSE PEOPLE HAS SOMETHING TO DO WITH ME.
I CAN'T LET ANYONE ELSE GET HURT BECAUSE OF SOME DISGRUNTLED HOOD I WRONGED IN MY PAST LIFE. JUST LET ME--
WAIT A SECOND.

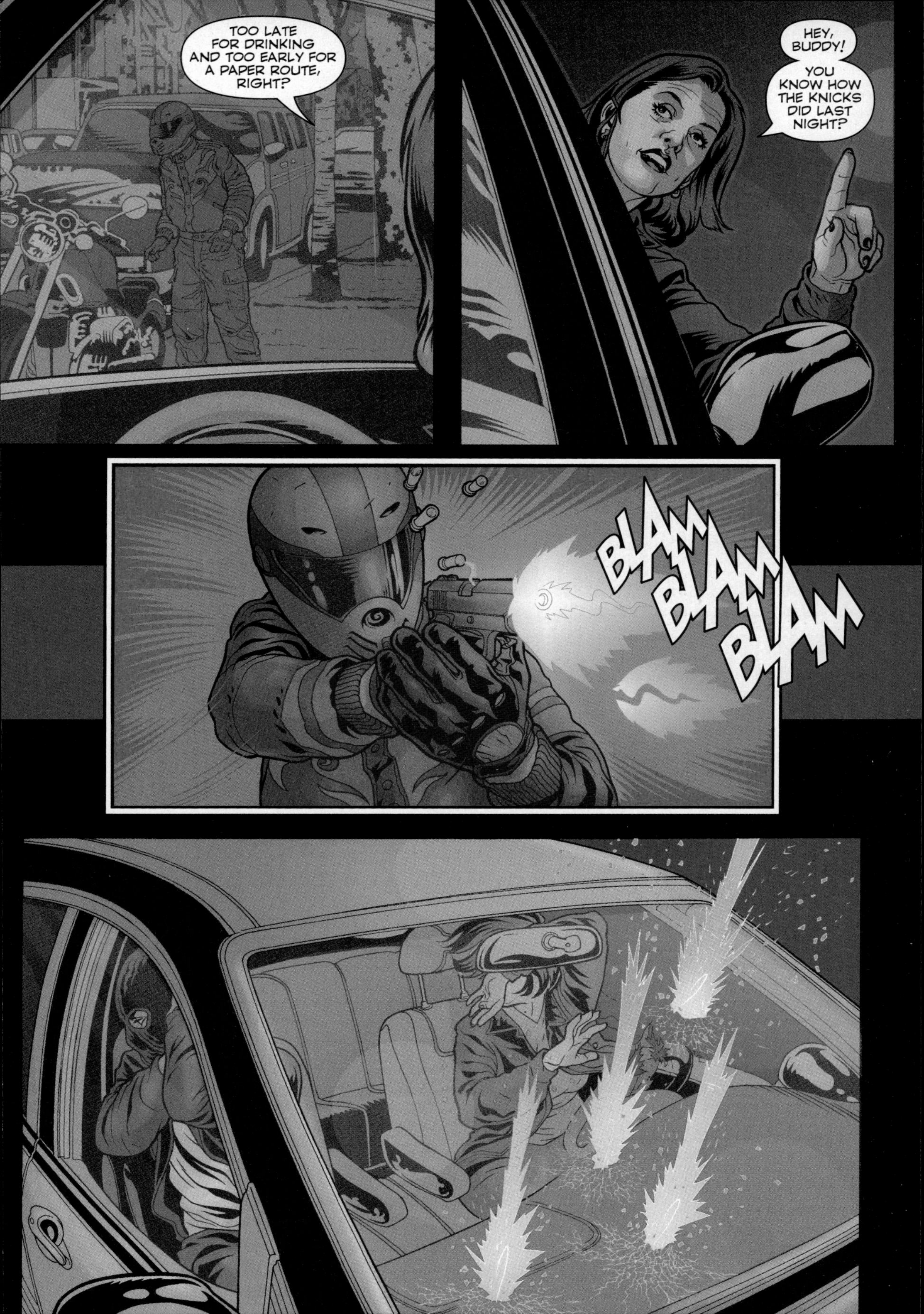
TOO LATE FOR DRINKING AND TOO EARLY FOR A PAPER ROUTE, RIGHT?
HEY, BUDDY!
YOU KNOW HOW THE KNICKS DID LAST NIGHT?
BLAM BLAM BLAM

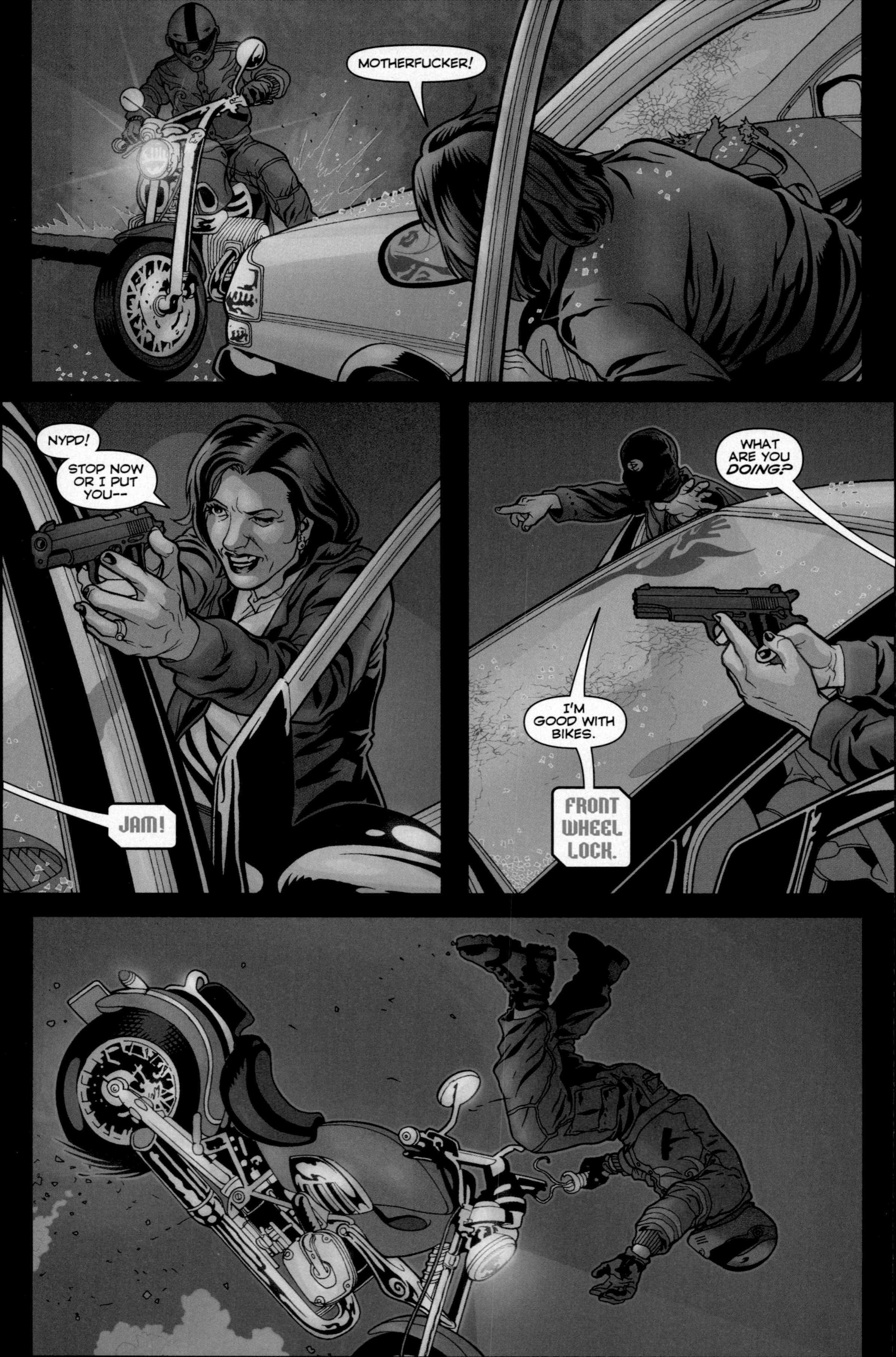
MOTHERFUCKER!
NYPD!
STOP NOW OR I PUT YOU--
JAM!
WHAT ARE YOU DOING?
I'M GOOD WITH BIKES.
FRONT WHEEL LOCK.

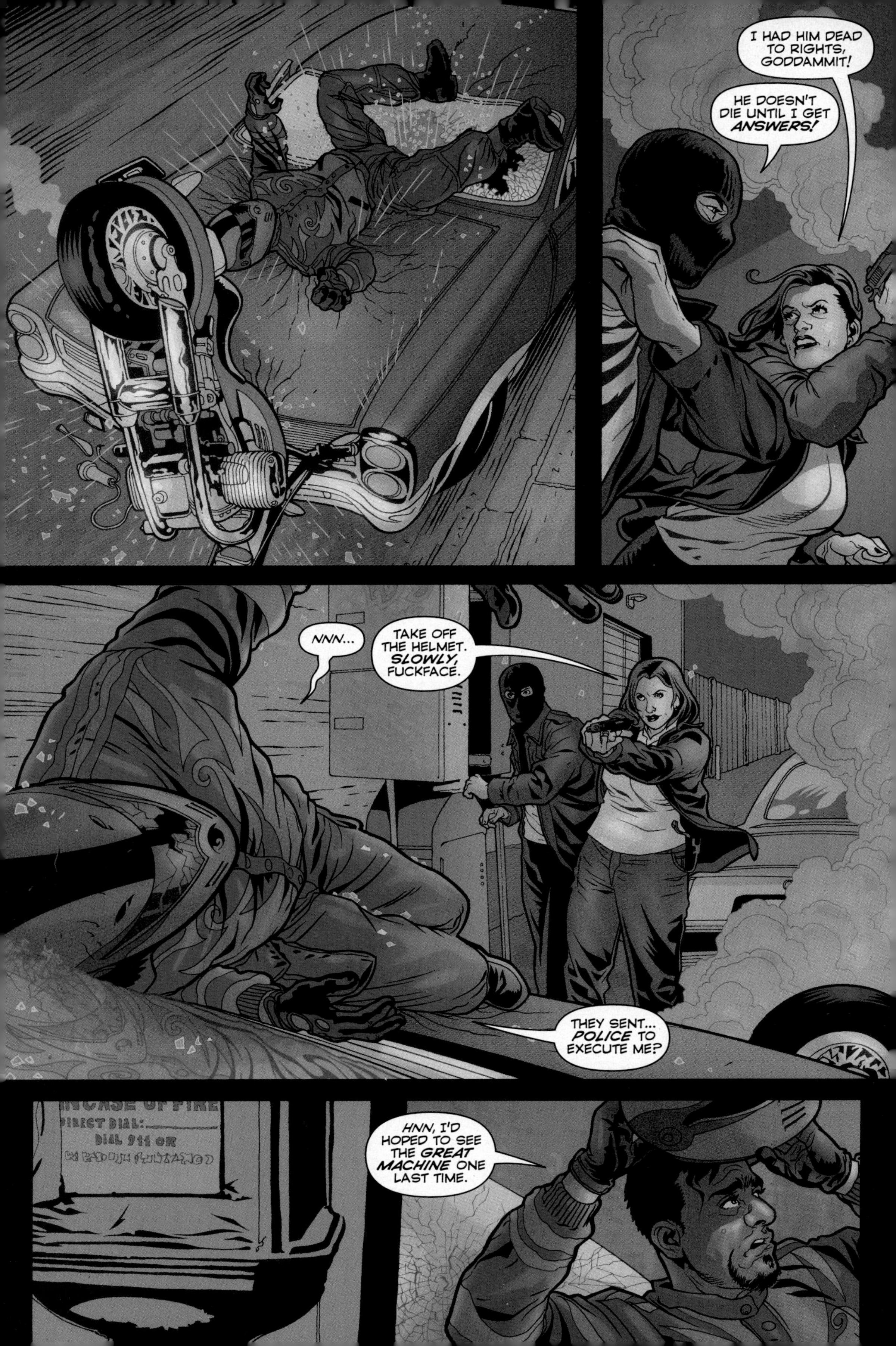
I HAD HIM DEAD TO RIGHTS, GODDAMMIT!
HE DOESN'T DIE UNTIL I GET *ANSWERS!*
NNN...
TAKE OFF THE HELMET. *SLOWLY,* FUCKFACE.
THEY SENT... *POLICE* TO EXECUTE ME?
DIRECT DIAL:
DIAL 911 OR
HNN, I'D HOPED TO SEE THE *GREAT MACHINE* ONE LAST TIME.

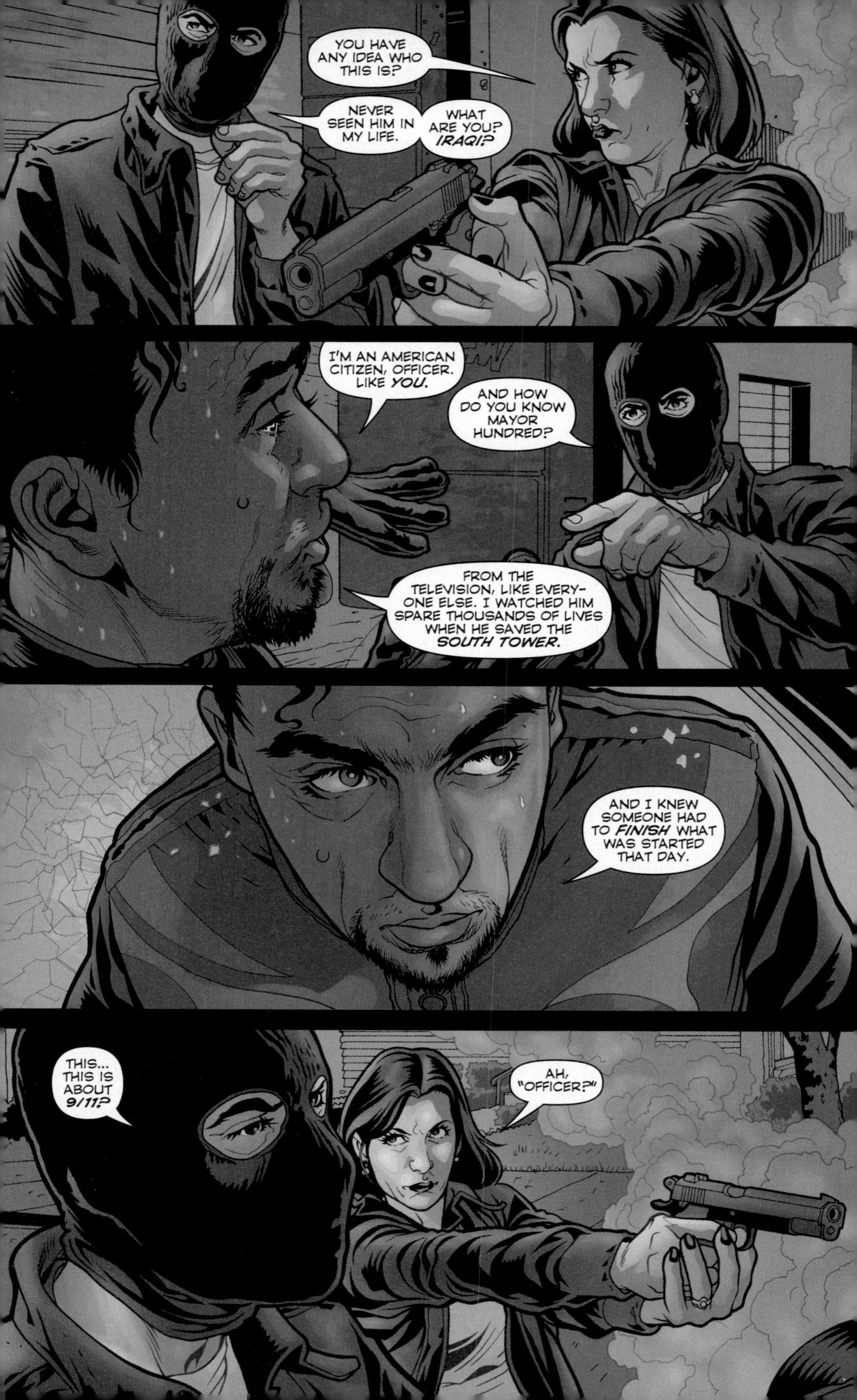
YOU HAVE ANY IDEA WHO THIS IS?
NEVER SEEN HIM IN MY LIFE.
WHAT ARE YOU? *IRAQI?*
I'M AN AMERICAN CITIZEN, OFFICER. LIKE *YOU.*
AND HOW DO YOU KNOW MAYOR HUNDRED?
FROM THE TELEVISION, LIKE EVERY-ONE ELSE. I WATCHED HIM SPARE THOUSANDS OF LIVES WHEN HE SAVED THE *SOUTH TOWER.*
AND I KNEW SOMEONE HAD TO *FINISH* WHAT WAS STARTED THAT DAY.
THIS... THIS IS ABOUT *9/11?*
AH, "OFFICER?"

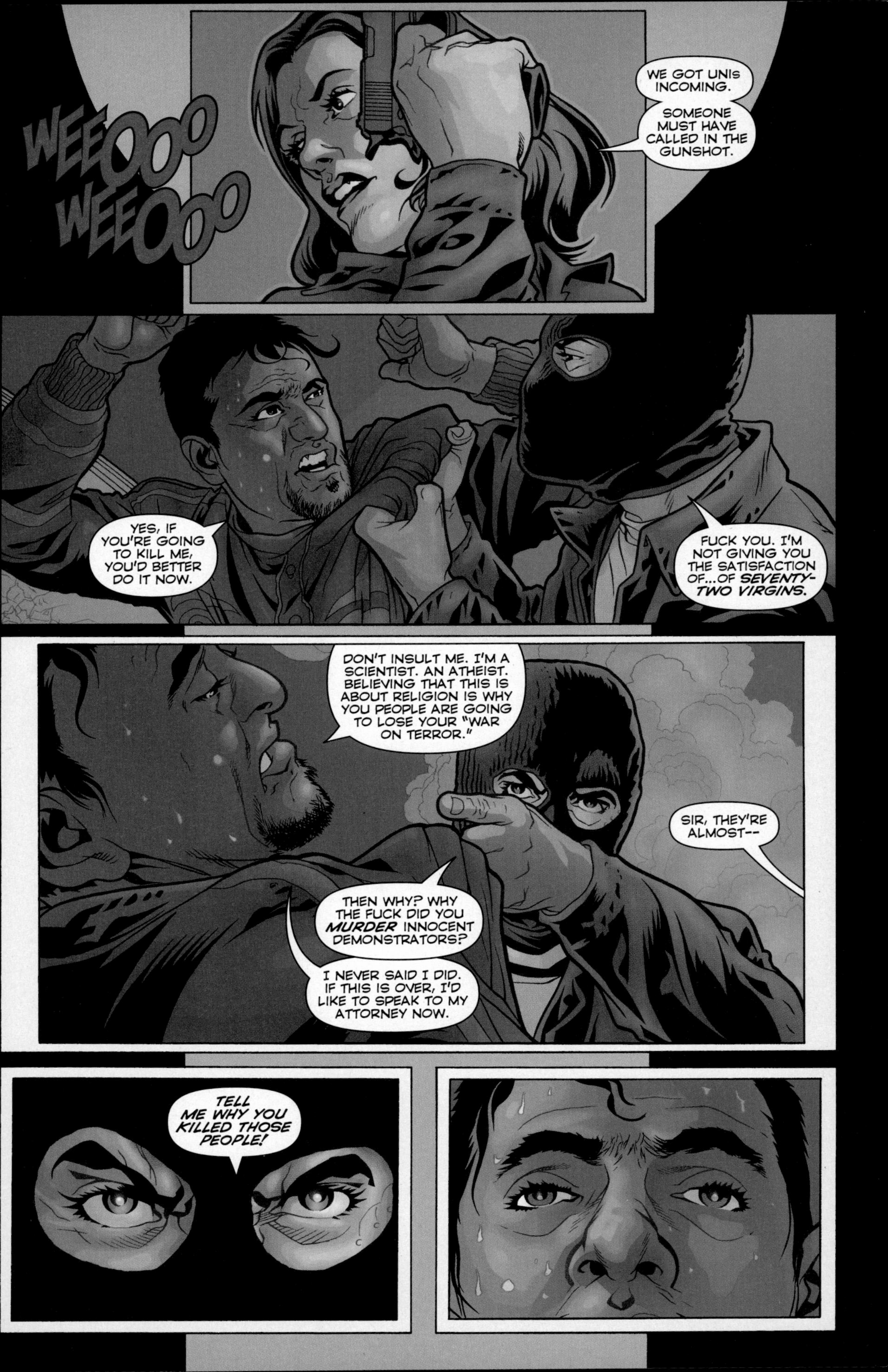
WEEOOO
WEEOOO
WE GOT UNIs INCOMING.
SOMEONE MUST HAVE CALLED IN THE GUNSHOT.
YES, IF YOU'RE GOING TO KILL ME, YOU'D BETTER DO IT NOW.
FUCK YOU. I'M NOT GIVING YOU THE SATISFACTION OF...OF SEVENTY-TWO VIRGINS.
DON'T INSULT ME. I'M A SCIENTIST. AN ATHEIST. BELIEVING THAT THIS IS ABOUT RELIGION IS WHY YOU PEOPLE ARE GOING TO LOSE YOUR "WAR ON TERROR."
SIR, THEY'RE ALMOST--
THEN WHY? WHY THE FUCK DID YOU MURDER INNOCENT DEMONSTRATORS?
I NEVER SAID I DID. IF THIS IS OVER, I'D LIKE TO SPEAK TO MY ATTORNEY NOW.
TELL ME WHY YOU KILLED THOSE PEOPLE!

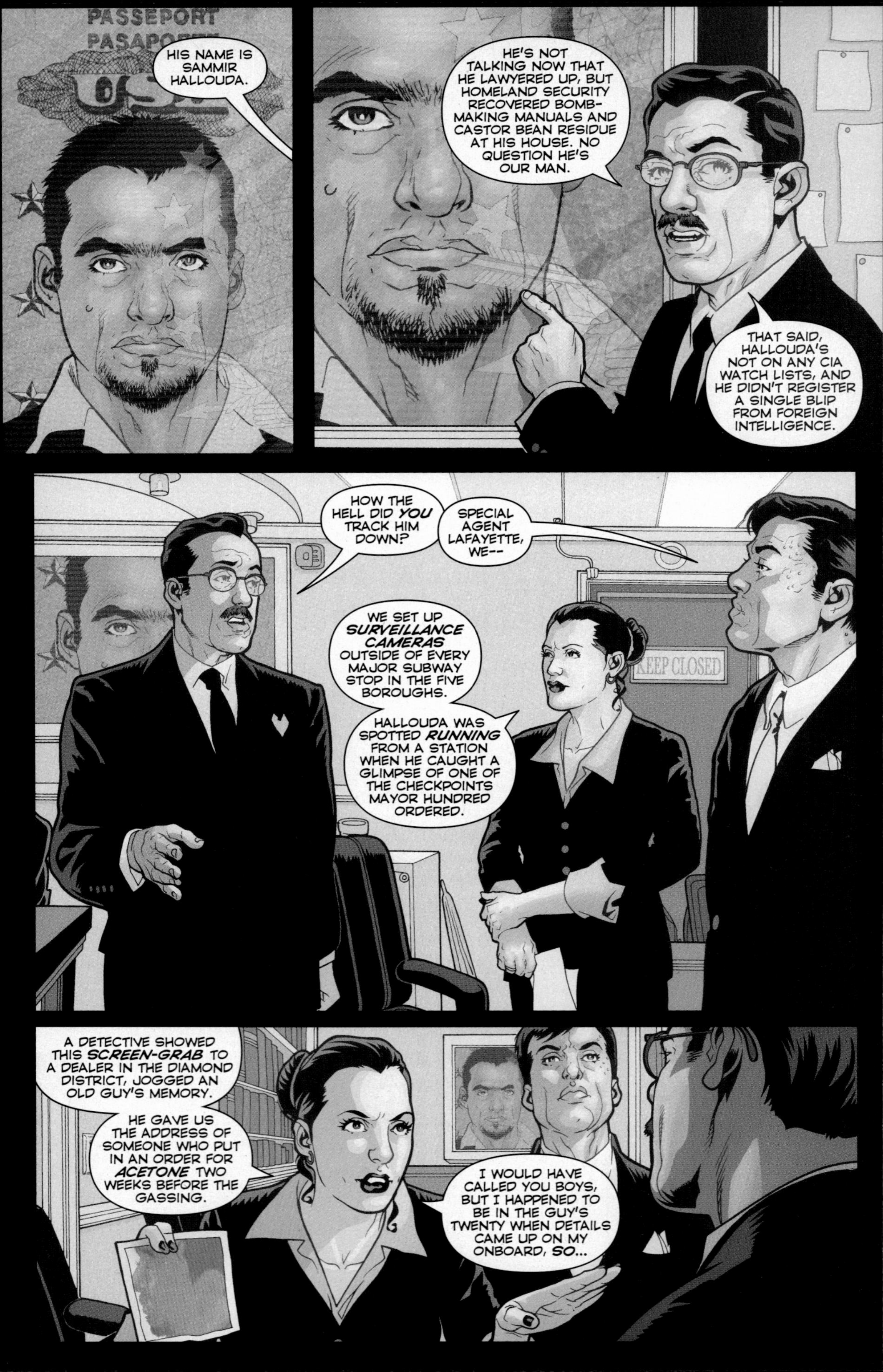
PASSEPORT
PASAPORTE
HIS NAME IS SAMMIR HALLOUDA.
HE'S NOT TALKING NOW THAT HE LAWYERED UP, BUT HOMELAND SECURITY RECOVERED BOMB-MAKING MANUALS AND CASTOR BEAN RESIDUE AT HIS HOUSE. NO QUESTION HE'S OUR MAN.
THAT SAID, HALLOUDA'S NOT ON ANY CIA WATCH LISTS, AND HE DIDN'T REGISTER A SINGLE BLIP FROM FOREIGN INTELLIGENCE.
HOW THE HELL DID YOU TRACK HIM DOWN?
SPECIAL AGENT LAFAYETTE, WE--
WE SET UP SURVEILLANCE CAMERAS OUTSIDE OF EVERY MAJOR SUBWAY STOP IN THE FIVE BOROUGHS.
HALLOUDA WAS SPOTTED RUNNING FROM A STATION WHEN HE CAUGHT A GLIMPSE OF ONE OF THE CHECKPOINTS MAYOR HUNDRED ORDERED.
KEEP CLOSED
A DETECTIVE SHOWED THIS SCREEN-GRAB TO A DEALER IN THE DIAMOND DISTRICT, JOGGED AN OLD GUY'S MEMORY.
HE GAVE US THE ADDRESS OF SOMEONE WHO PUT IN AN ORDER FOR ACETONE TWO WEEKS BEFORE THE GASSING.
I WOULD HAVE CALLED YOU BOYS, BUT I HAPPENED TO BE IN THE GUY'S TWENTY WHEN DETAILS CAME UP ON MY ONBOARD, SO...

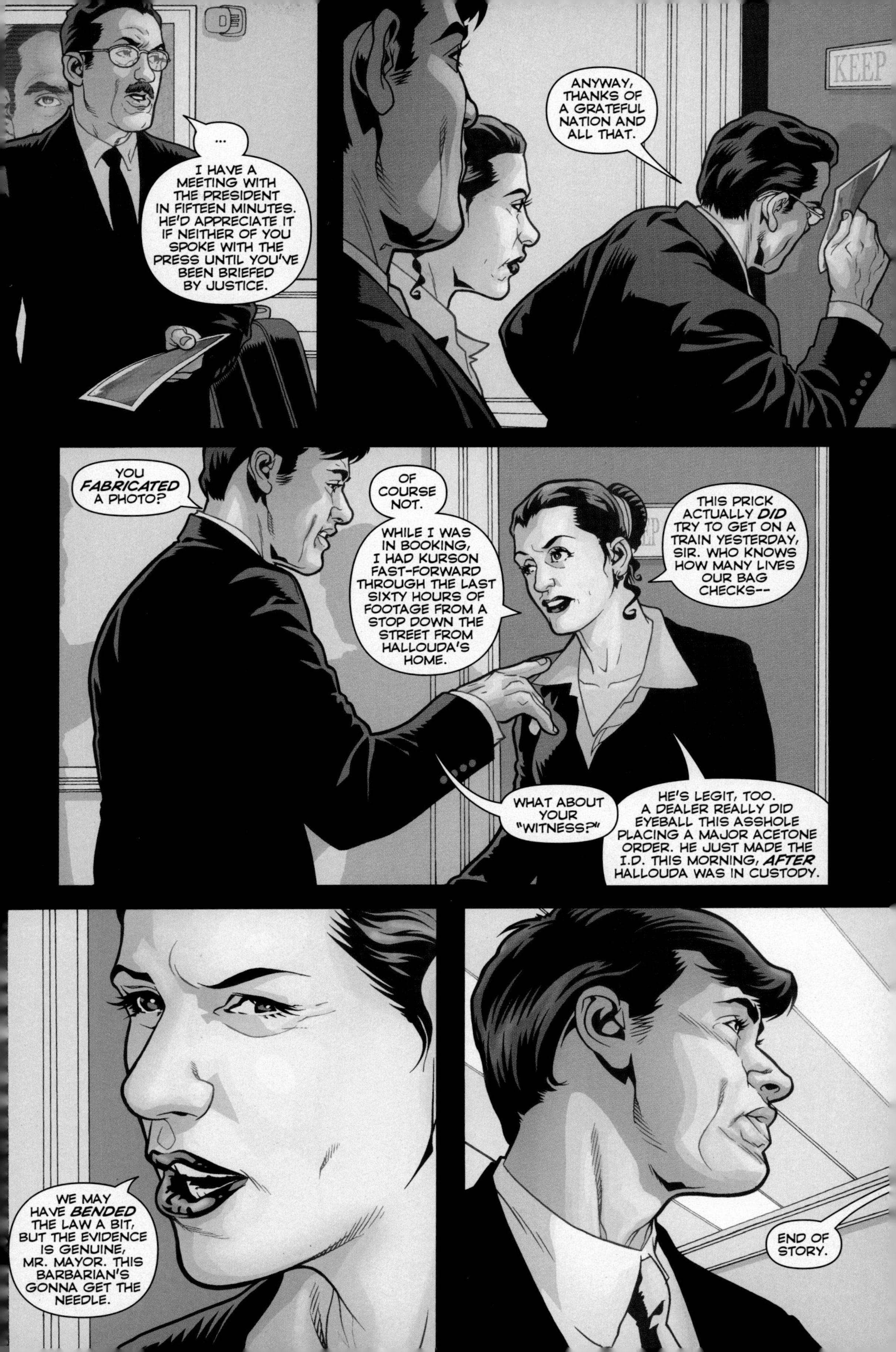
...
I HAVE A MEETING WITH THE PRESIDENT IN FIFTEEN MINUTES. HE'D APPRECIATE IT IF NEITHER OF YOU SPOKE WITH THE PRESS UNTIL YOU'VE BEEN BRIEFED BY JUSTICE.
KEEP
ANYWAY, THANKS OF A GRATEFUL NATION AND ALL THAT.
YOU *FABRICATED* A PHOTO?
OF COURSE NOT.
WHILE I WAS IN BOOKING, I HAD KURSON FAST-FORWARD THROUGH THE LAST SIXTY HOURS OF FOOTAGE FROM A STOP DOWN THE STREET FROM HALLOUDA'S HOME.
THIS PRICK ACTUALLY *DID* TRY TO GET ON A TRAIN YESTERDAY, SIR. WHO KNOWS HOW MANY LIVES OUR BAG CHECKS--
WHAT ABOUT YOUR "WITNESS?"
HE'S LEGIT, TOO. A DEALER REALLY DID EYEBALL THIS ASSHOLE PLACING A MAJOR ACETONE ORDER. HE JUST MADE THE I.D. THIS MORNING, *AFTER* HALLOUDA WAS IN CUSTODY.
WE MAY HAVE *BENDED* THE LAW A BIT, BUT THE EVIDENCE IS GENUINE, MR. MAYOR. THIS BARBARIAN'S GONNA GET THE NEEDLE.
END OF STORY.

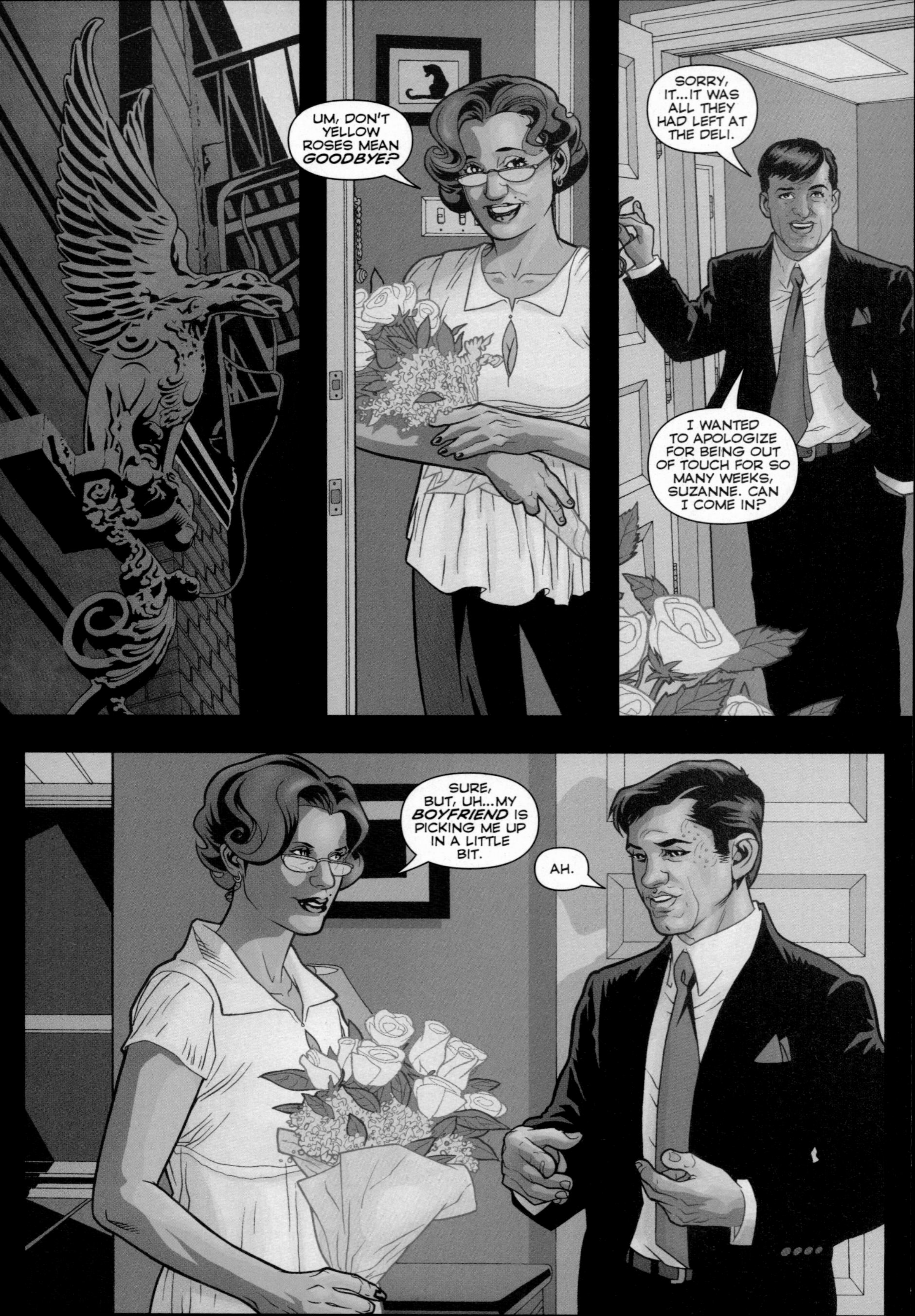
UM, DON'T YELLOW ROSES MEAN *GOODBYE?*
SORRY, IT...IT WAS ALL THEY HAD LEFT AT THE DELI.
I WANTED TO APOLOGIZE FOR BEING OUT OF TOUCH FOR SO MANY WEEKS, SUZANNE. CAN I COME IN?
SURE, BUT, UH...MY *BOYFRIEND* IS PICKING ME UP IN A LITTLE BIT.
AH.

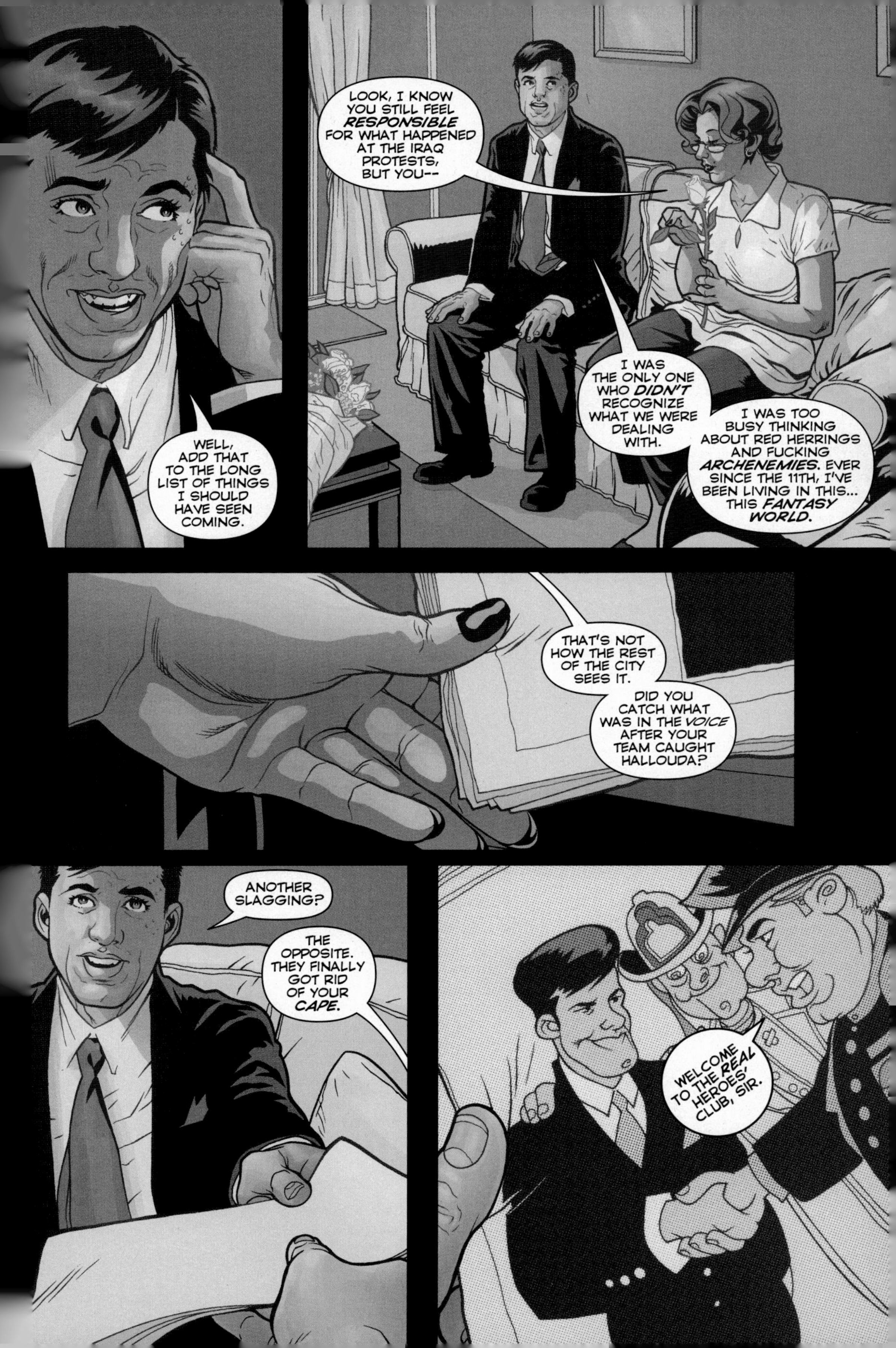
WELL, ADD THAT TO THE LONG LIST OF THINGS I SHOULD HAVE SEEN COMING.
LOOK, I KNOW YOU STILL FEEL *RESPONSIBLE* FOR WHAT HAPPENED AT THE IRAQ PROTESTS, BUT YOU--
I WAS THE ONLY ONE WHO *DIDN'T* RECOGNIZE WHAT WE WERE DEALING WITH.
I WAS TOO BUSY THINKING ABOUT RED HERRINGS AND FUCKING *ARCHENEMIES*. EVER SINCE THE 11TH, I'VE BEEN LIVING IN THIS... THIS *FANTASY WORLD*.
THAT'S NOT HOW THE REST OF THE CITY SEES IT.
DID YOU CATCH WHAT WAS IN THE *VOICE* AFTER YOUR TEAM CAUGHT HALLOUDA?
ANOTHER SLAGGING?
THE OPPOSITE. THEY FINALLY GOT RID OF YOUR *CAPE*.
WELCOME TO THE *REAL* HEROES' CLUB, SIR.

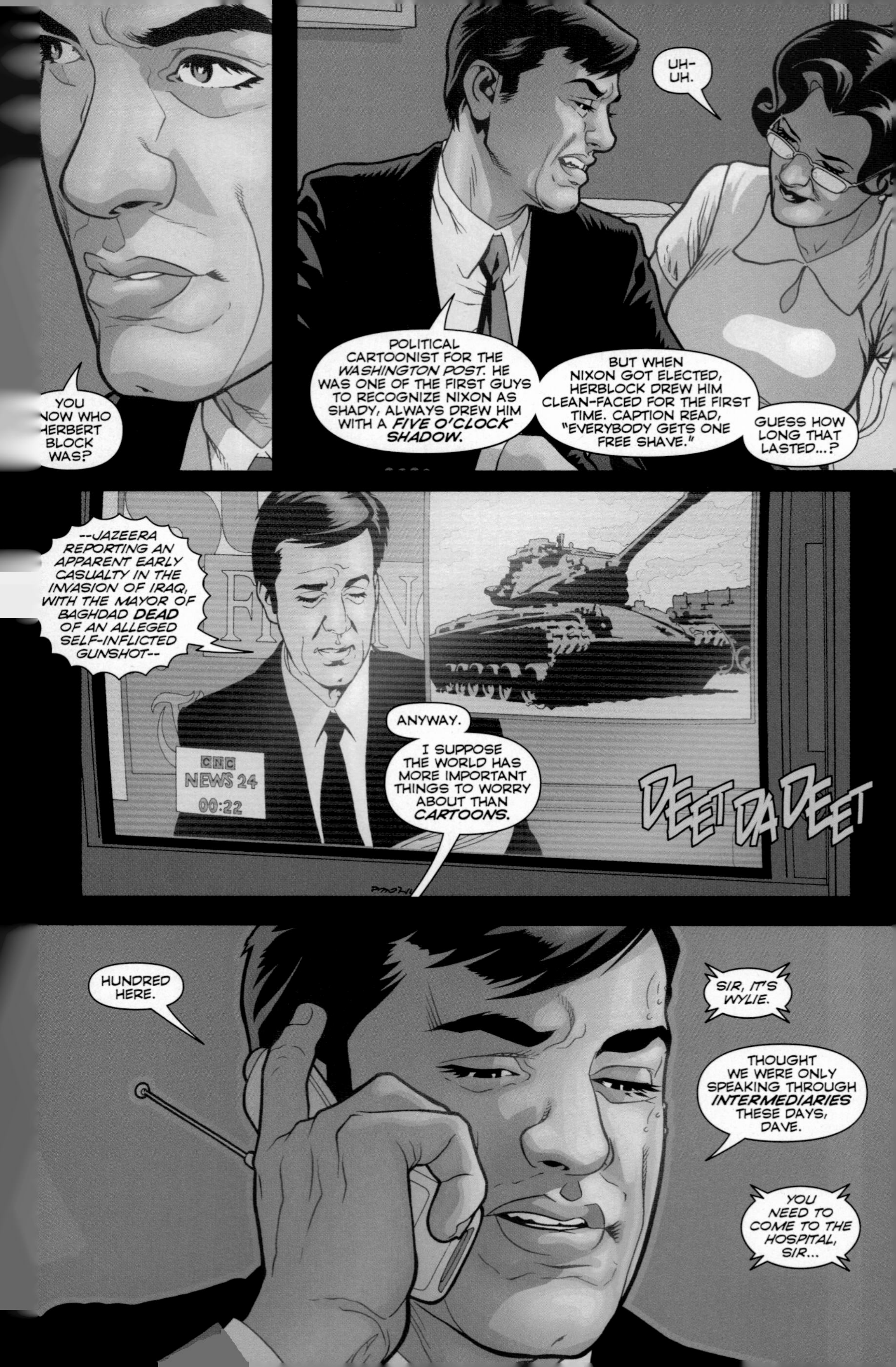
YOU [K]NOW WHO HERBERT BLOCK WAS?
UH-UH.
POLITICAL CARTOONIST FOR THE WASHINGTON POST. HE WAS ONE OF THE FIRST GUYS TO RECOGNIZE NIXON AS SHADY, ALWAYS DREW HIM WITH A FIVE O'CLOCK SHADOW.
BUT WHEN NIXON GOT ELECTED, HERBLOCK DREW HIM CLEAN-FACED FOR THE FIRST TIME. CAPTION READ, "EVERYBODY GETS ONE FREE SHAVE."
GUESS HOW LONG THAT LASTED...?
--JAZEERA REPORTING AN APPARENT EARLY CASUALTY IN THE INVASION OF IRAQ, WITH THE MAYOR OF BAGHDAD DEAD OF AN ALLEGED SELF-INFLICTED GUNSHOT--
CNC NEWS 24 00:22
ANYWAY.
I SUPPOSE THE WORLD HAS MORE IMPORTANT THINGS TO WORRY ABOUT THAN CARTOONS.
DEET DA DEET
HUNDRED HERE.
SIR, IT'S WYLIE.
THOUGHT WE WERE ONLY SPEAKING THROUGH INTERMEDIARIES THESE DAYS, DAVE.
YOU NEED TO COME TO THE HOSPITAL, SIR...

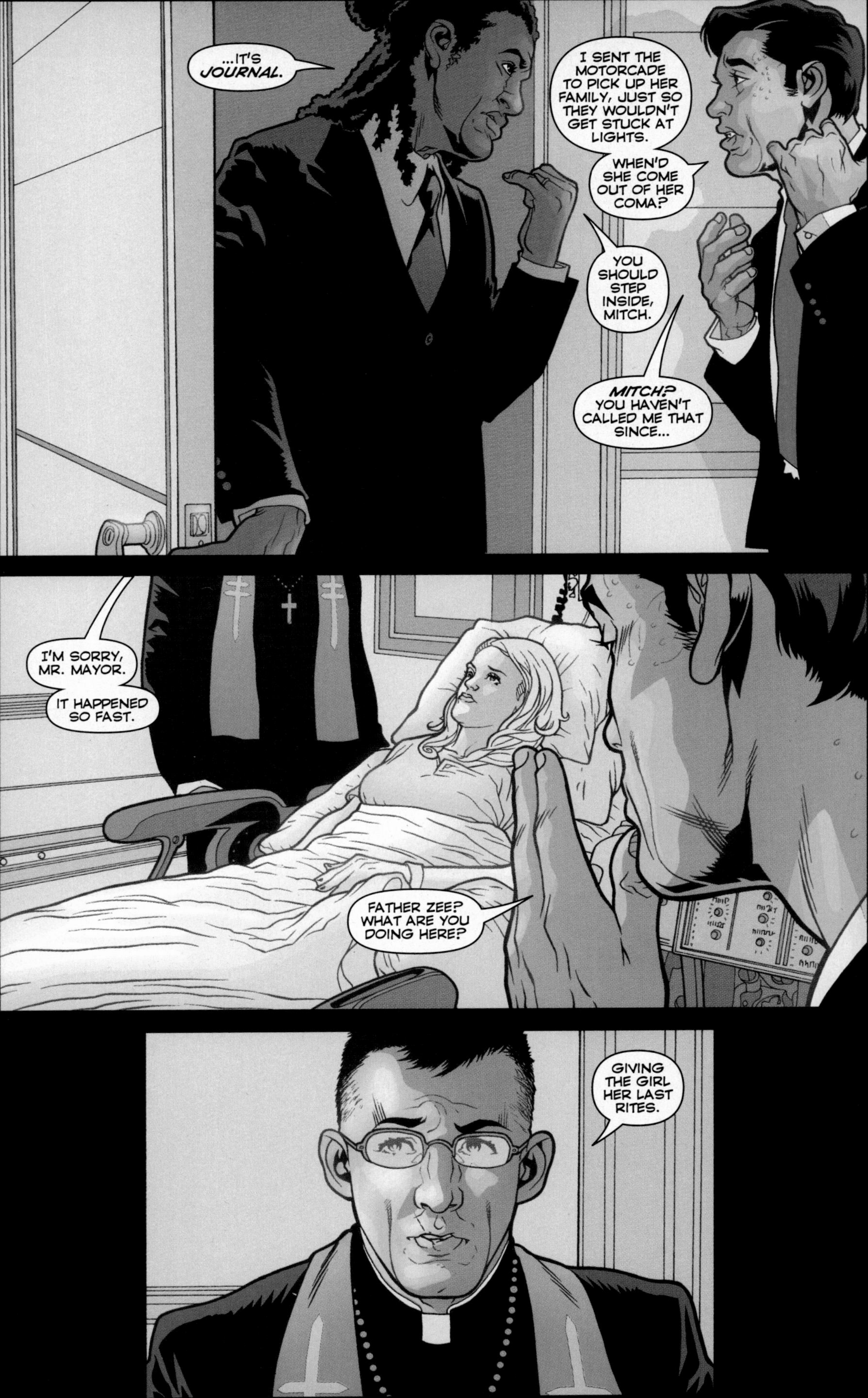
...IT'S *JOURNAL*.
I SENT THE MOTORCADE TO PICK UP HER FAMILY, JUST SO THEY WOULDN'T GET STUCK AT LIGHTS.
WHEN'D SHE COME OUT OF HER COMA?
YOU SHOULD STEP INSIDE, MITCH.
MITCH? YOU HAVEN'T CALLED ME THAT SINCE...
I'M SORRY, MR. MAYOR.
IT HAPPENED SO FAST.
FATHER ZEE? WHAT ARE YOU DOING HERE?
GIVING THE GIRL HER LAST RITES.

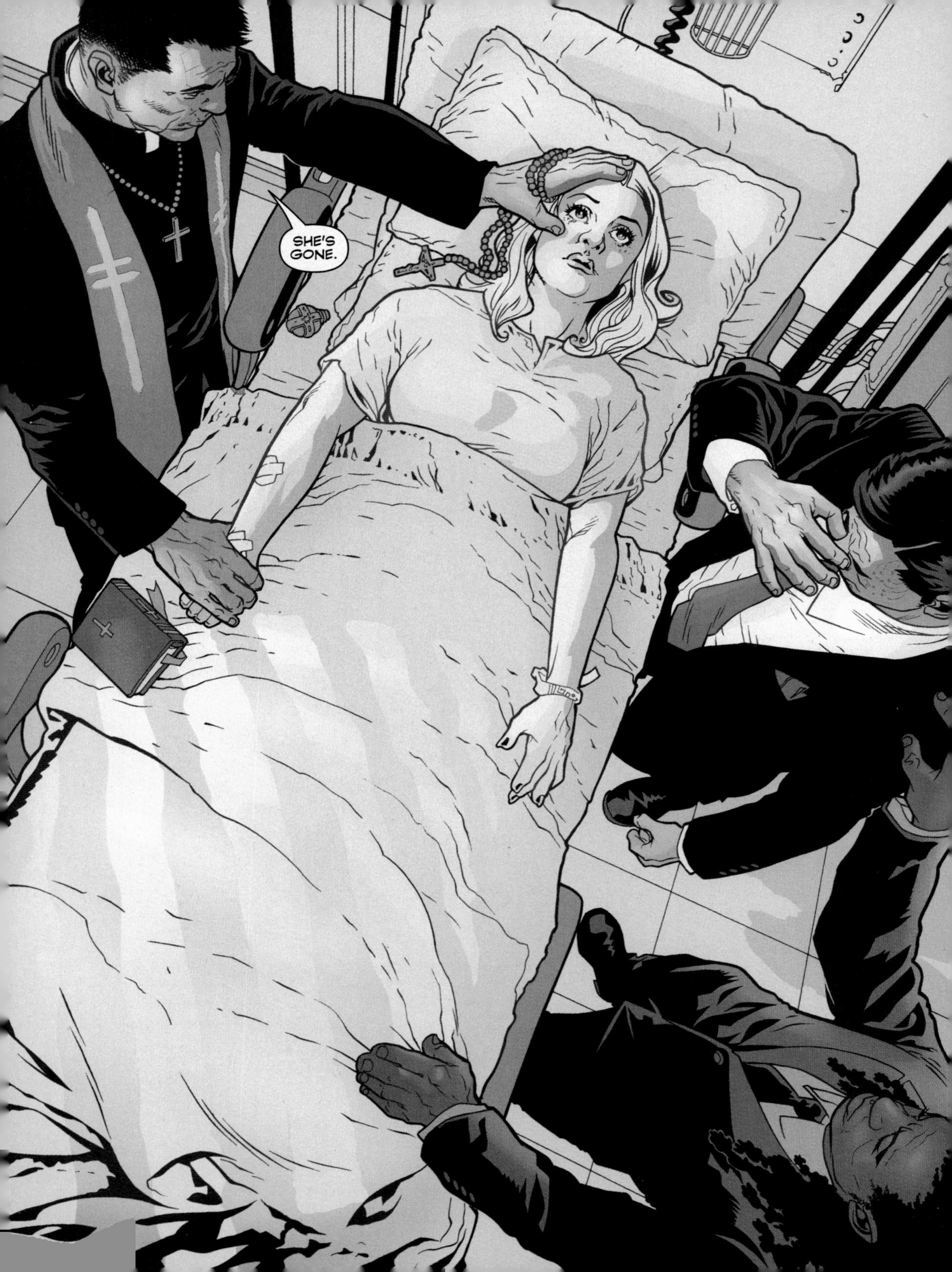
SHE'S GONE.

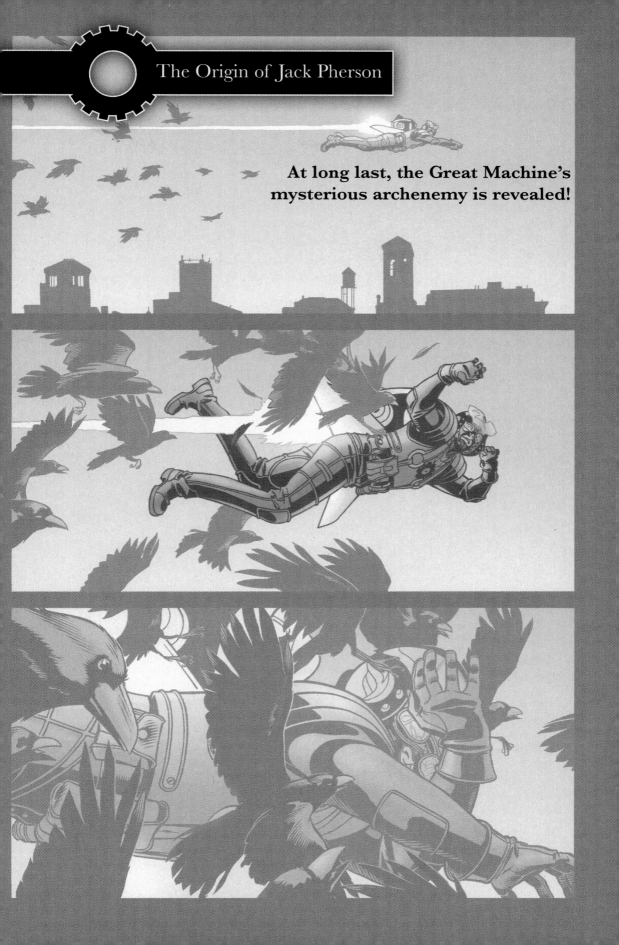

The Origin of Jack Pherson

At long last, the Great Machine's mysterious archenemy is revealed!

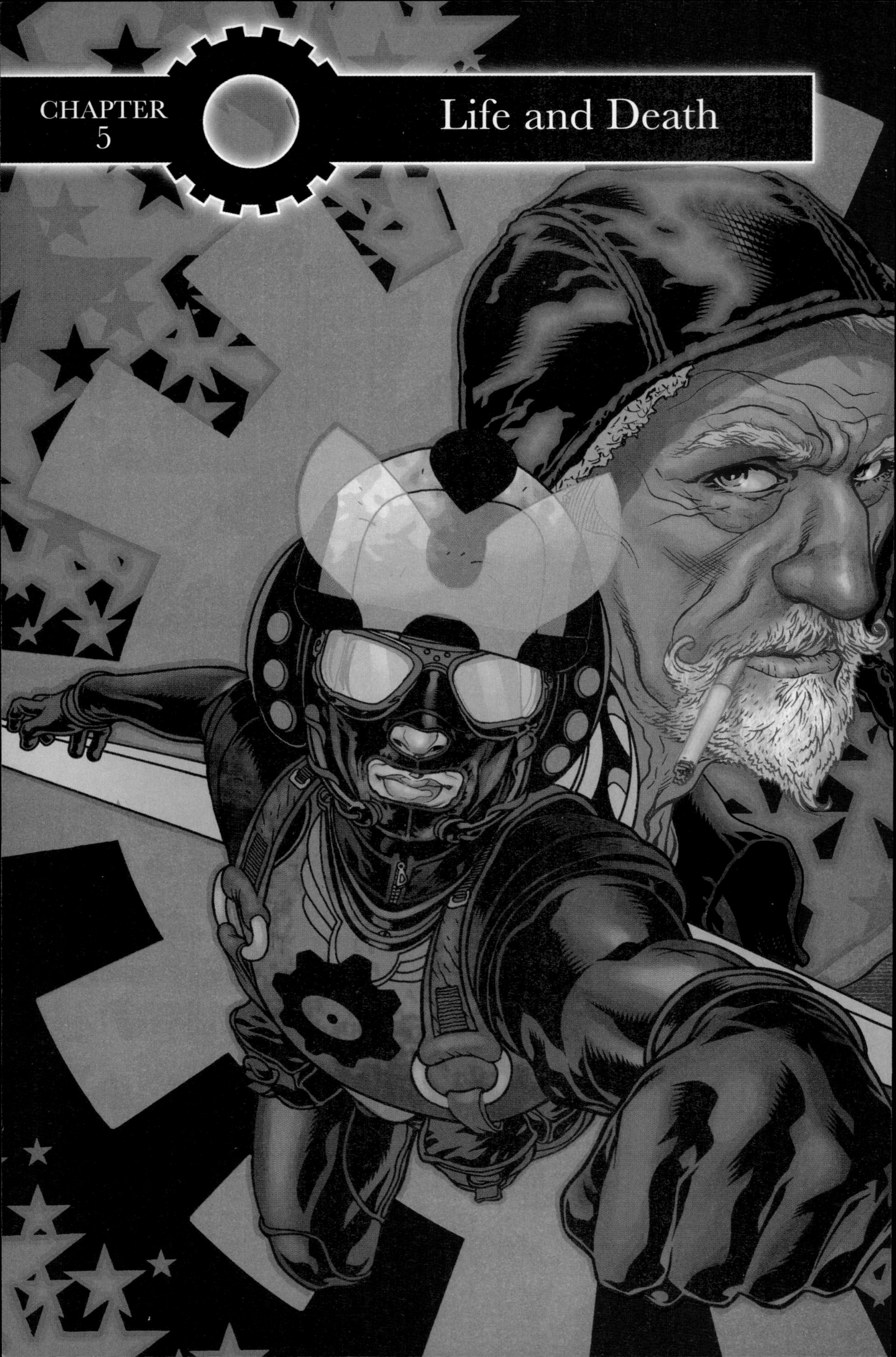
CHAPTER
5
Life and Death

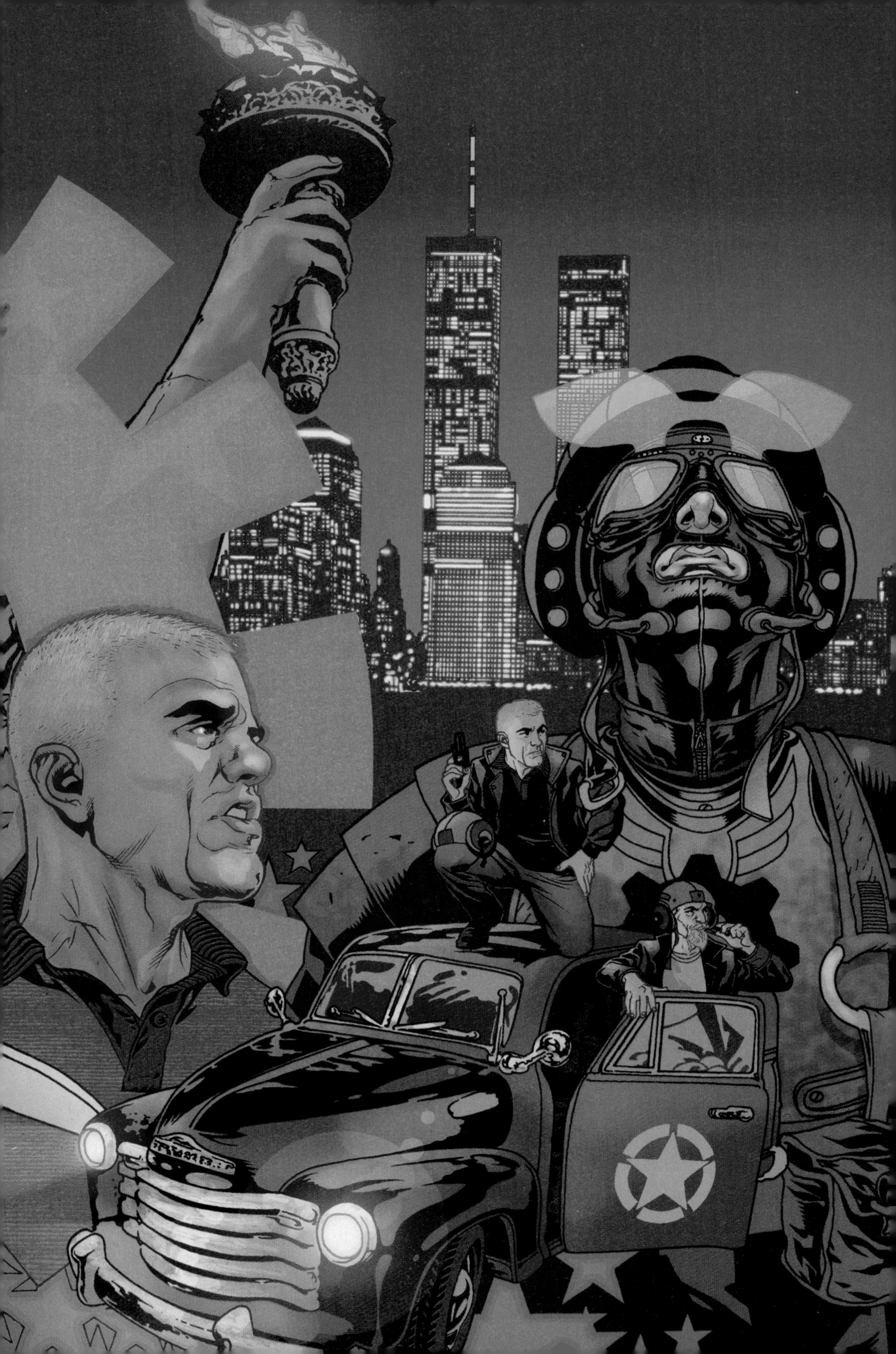

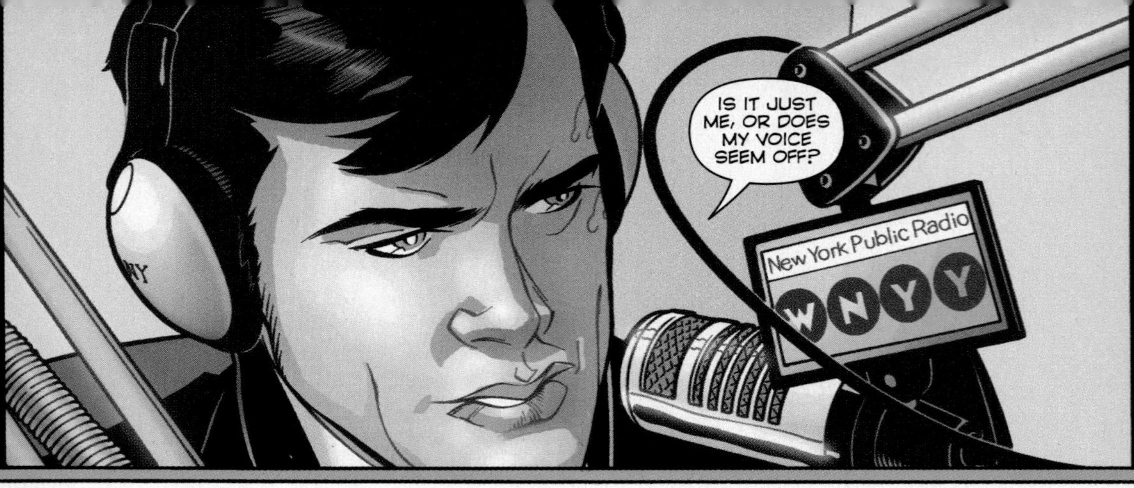
IS IT JUST ME, OR DOES MY VOICE SEEM OFF?
New York Public Radio
WNYY

TUESDAY, MARCH 4, 2003

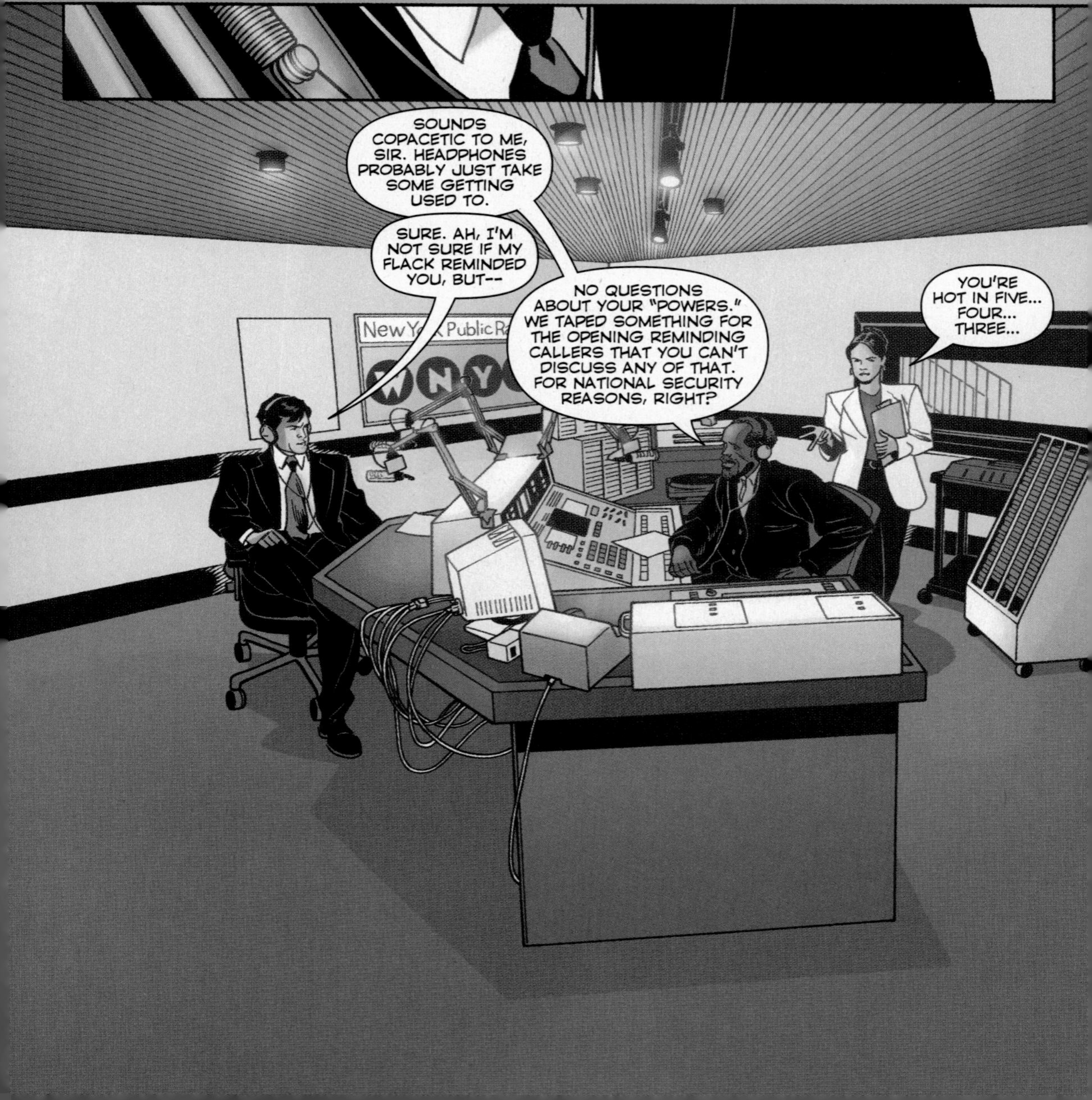
SOUNDS COPACETIC TO ME, SIR. HEADPHONES PROBABLY JUST TAKE SOME GETTING USED TO.
SURE. AH, I'M NOT SURE IF MY FLACK REMINDED YOU, BUT--
NO QUESTIONS ABOUT YOUR "POWERS." WE TAPED SOMETHING FOR THE OPENING REMINDING CALLERS THAT YOU CAN'T DISCUSS ANY OF THAT. FOR NATIONAL SECURITY REASONS, RIGHT?
YOU'RE HOT IN FIVE... FOUR... THREE...

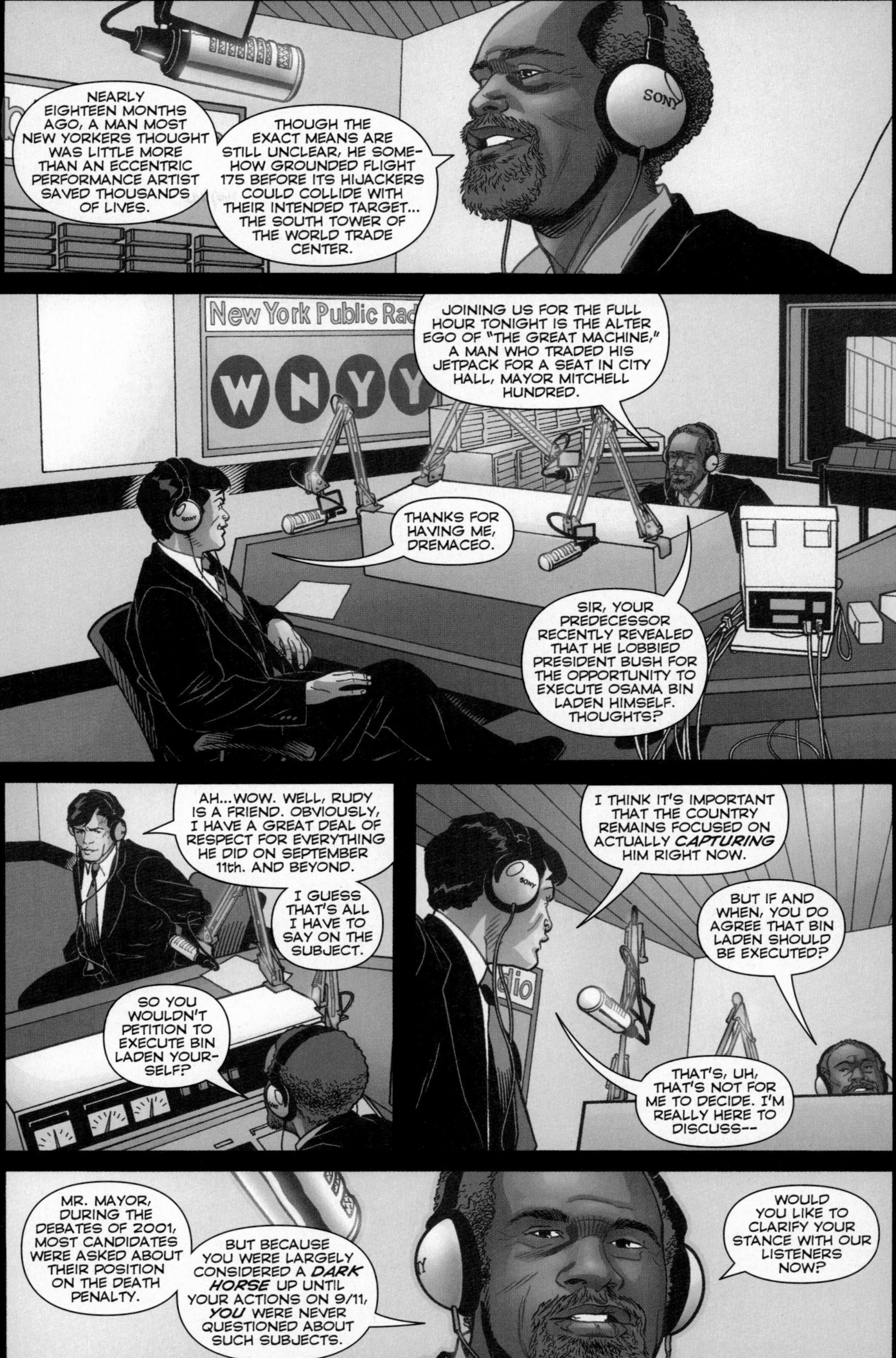

NEARLY EIGHTEEN MONTHS AGO, A MAN MOST NEW YORKERS THOUGHT WAS LITTLE MORE THAN AN ECCENTRIC PERFORMANCE ARTIST SAVED THOUSANDS OF LIVES.
THOUGH THE EXACT MEANS ARE STILL UNCLEAR, HE SOMEHOW GROUNDED FLIGHT 175 BEFORE ITS HIJACKERS COULD COLLIDE WITH THEIR INTENDED TARGET... THE SOUTH TOWER OF THE WORLD TRADE CENTER.
SONY
New York Public Rad
WNYY
JOINING US FOR THE FULL HOUR TONIGHT IS THE ALTER EGO OF "THE GREAT MACHINE," A MAN WHO TRADED HIS JETPACK FOR A SEAT IN CITY HALL, MAYOR MITCHELL HUNDRED.
THANKS FOR HAVING ME, DREMACEO.
SIR, YOUR PREDECESSOR RECENTLY REVEALED THAT HE LOBBIED PRESIDENT BUSH FOR THE OPPORTUNITY TO EXECUTE OSAMA BIN LADEN HIMSELF. THOUGHTS?
AH...WOW. WELL, RUDY IS A FRIEND. OBVIOUSLY, I HAVE A GREAT DEAL OF RESPECT FOR EVERYTHING HE DID ON SEPTEMBER 11th. AND BEYOND.
I GUESS THAT'S ALL I HAVE TO SAY ON THE SUBJECT.
SO YOU WOULDN'T PETITION TO EXECUTE BIN LADEN YOURSELF?
I THINK IT'S IMPORTANT THAT THE COUNTRY REMAINS FOCUSED ON ACTUALLY *CAPTURING* HIM RIGHT NOW.
BUT IF AND WHEN, YOU DO AGREE THAT BIN LADEN SHOULD BE EXECUTED?
THAT'S, UH, THAT'S NOT FOR ME TO DECIDE. I'M REALLY HERE TO DISCUSS--
MR. MAYOR, DURING THE DEBATES OF 2001, MOST CANDIDATES WERE ASKED ABOUT THEIR POSITION ON THE DEATH PENALTY.
BUT BECAUSE YOU WERE LARGELY CONSIDERED A *DARK HORSE* UP UNTIL YOUR ACTIONS ON 9/11, *YOU* WERE NEVER QUESTIONED ABOUT SUCH SUBJECTS.
WOULD YOU LIKE TO CLARIFY YOUR STANCE WITH OUR LISTENERS NOW?

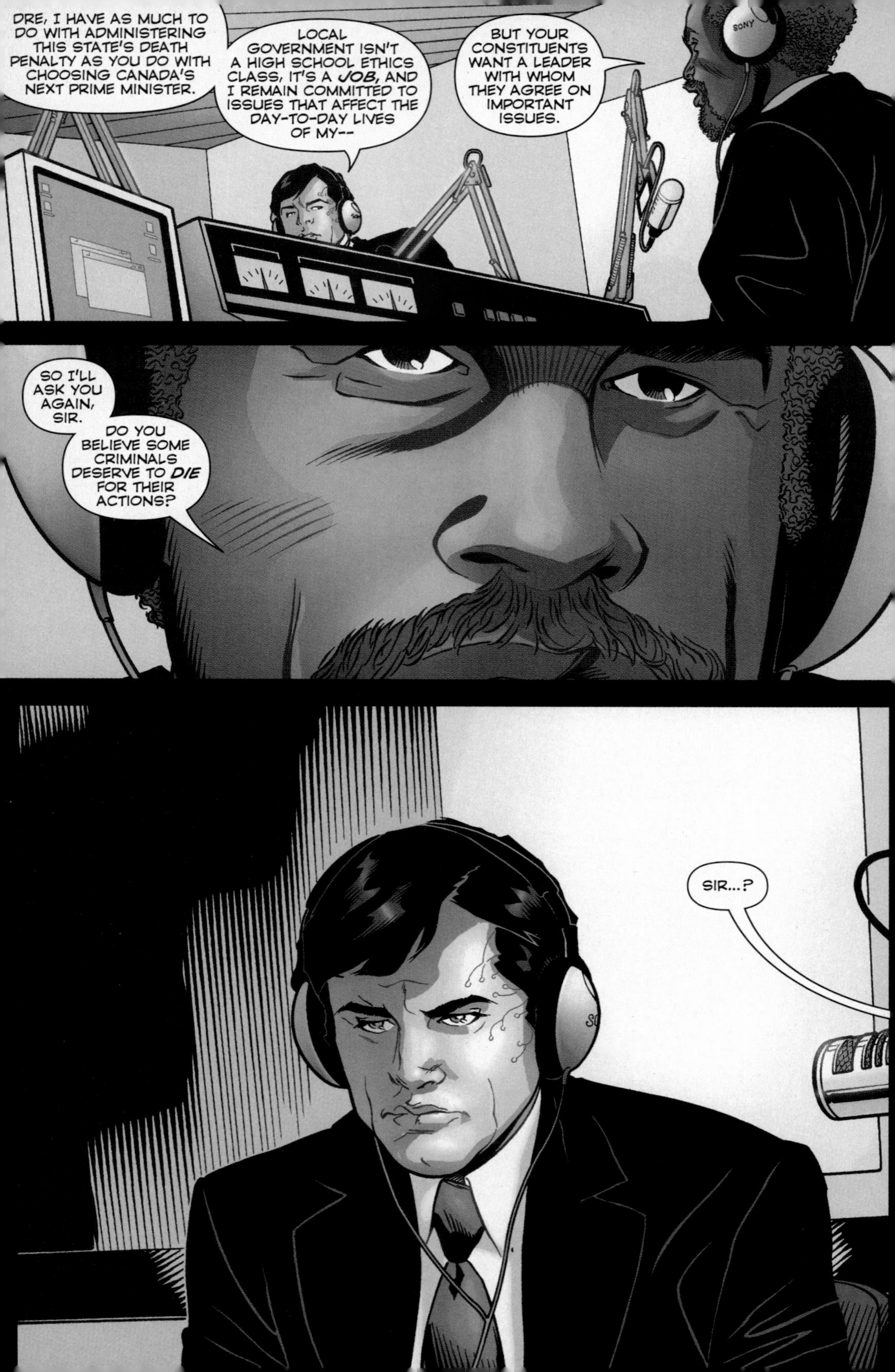
DRE, I HAVE AS MUCH TO DO WITH ADMINISTERING THIS STATE'S DEATH PENALTY AS YOU DO WITH CHOOSING CANADA'S NEXT PRIME MINISTER.
LOCAL GOVERNMENT ISN'T A HIGH SCHOOL ETHICS CLASS, IT'S A JOB, AND I REMAIN COMMITTED TO ISSUES THAT AFFECT THE DAY-TO-DAY LIVES OF MY--
BUT YOUR CONSTITUENTS WANT A LEADER WITH WHOM THEY AGREE ON IMPORTANT ISSUES.
SONY
SO I'LL ASK YOU AGAIN, SIR.
DO YOU BELIEVE SOME CRIMINALS DESERVE TO DIE FOR THEIR ACTIONS?
SIR...?

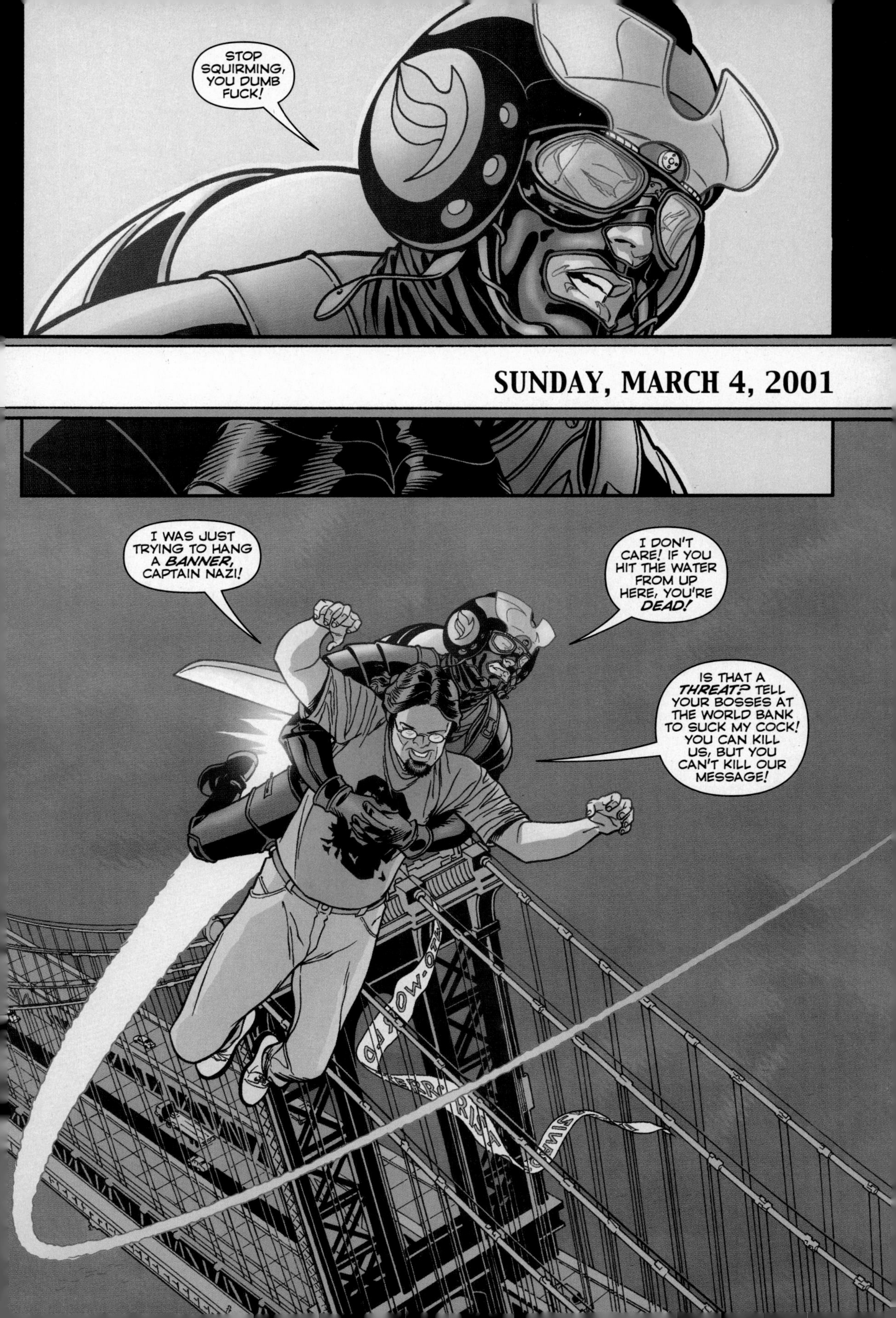
STOP SQUIRMING, YOU DUMB FUCK!
SUNDAY, MARCH 4, 2001
I WAS JUST TRYING TO HANG A BANNER, CAPTAIN NAZI!
I DON'T CARE! IF YOU HIT THE WATER FROM UP HERE, YOU'RE DEAD!
IS THAT A THREAT? TELL YOUR BOSSES AT THE WORLD BANK TO SUCK MY COCK! YOU CAN KILL US, BUT YOU CAN'T KILL OUR MESSAGE!

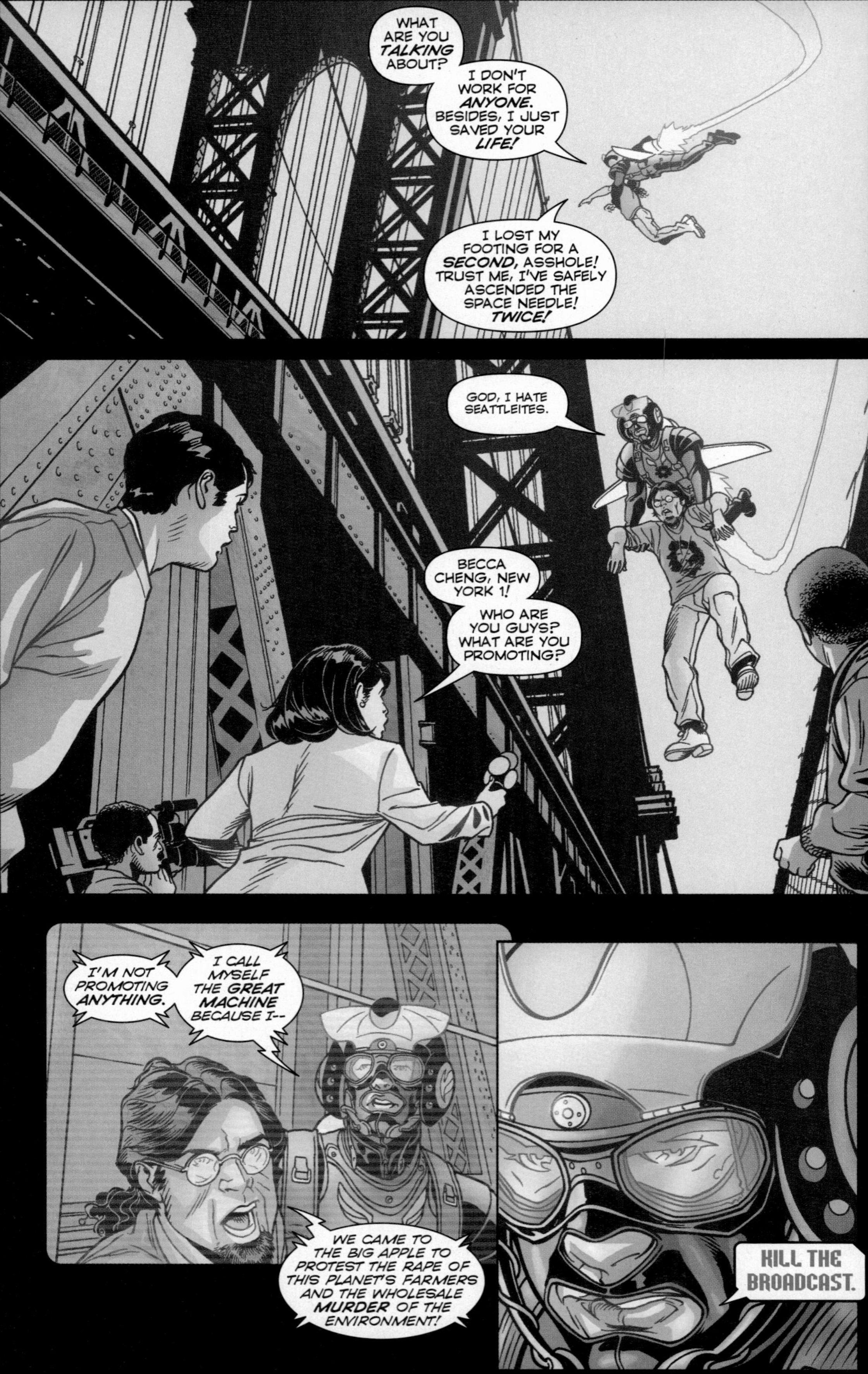

WHAT ARE YOU TALKING ABOUT?
I DON'T WORK FOR ANYONE. BESIDES, I JUST SAVED YOUR LIFE!
I LOST MY FOOTING FOR A SECOND, ASSHOLE! TRUST ME, I'VE SAFELY ASCENDED THE SPACE NEEDLE! TWICE!
GOD, I HATE SEATTLEITES.
BECCA CHENG, NEW YORK 1!
WHO ARE YOU GUYS? WHAT ARE YOU PROMOTING?
I'M NOT PROMOTING ANYTHING.
I CALL MYSELF THE GREAT MACHINE BECAUSE I--
WE CAME TO THE BIG APPLE TO PROTEST THE RAPE OF THIS PLANET'S FARMERS AND THE WHOLESALE MURDER OF THE ENVIRONMENT!
KILL THE BROADCAST.

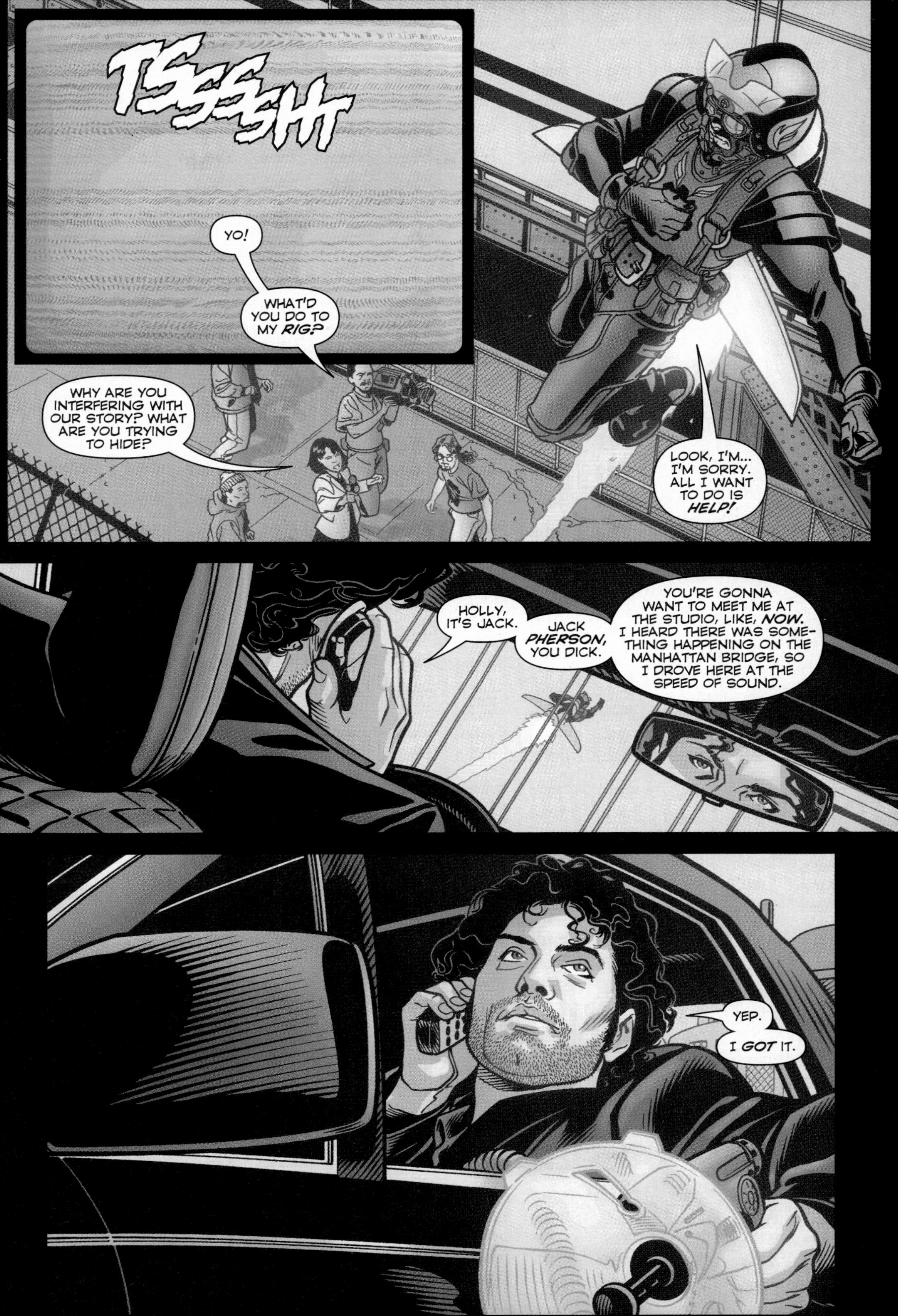

TSSSSHT
YO!
WHAT'D YOU DO TO MY *RIG?*
WHY ARE YOU INTERFERING WITH OUR STORY? WHAT ARE YOU TRYING TO HIDE?
LOOK, I'M... I'M SORRY. ALL I WANT TO DO IS *HELP!*
HOLLY, IT'S JACK.
JACK *PHERSON,* YOU DICK.
YOU'RE GONNA WANT TO MEET ME AT THE STUDIO, LIKE, *NOW.* I HEARD THERE WAS SOMETHING HAPPENING ON THE MANHATTAN BRIDGE, SO I DROVE HERE AT THE SPEED OF SOUND.
YEP.
I *GOT* IT.

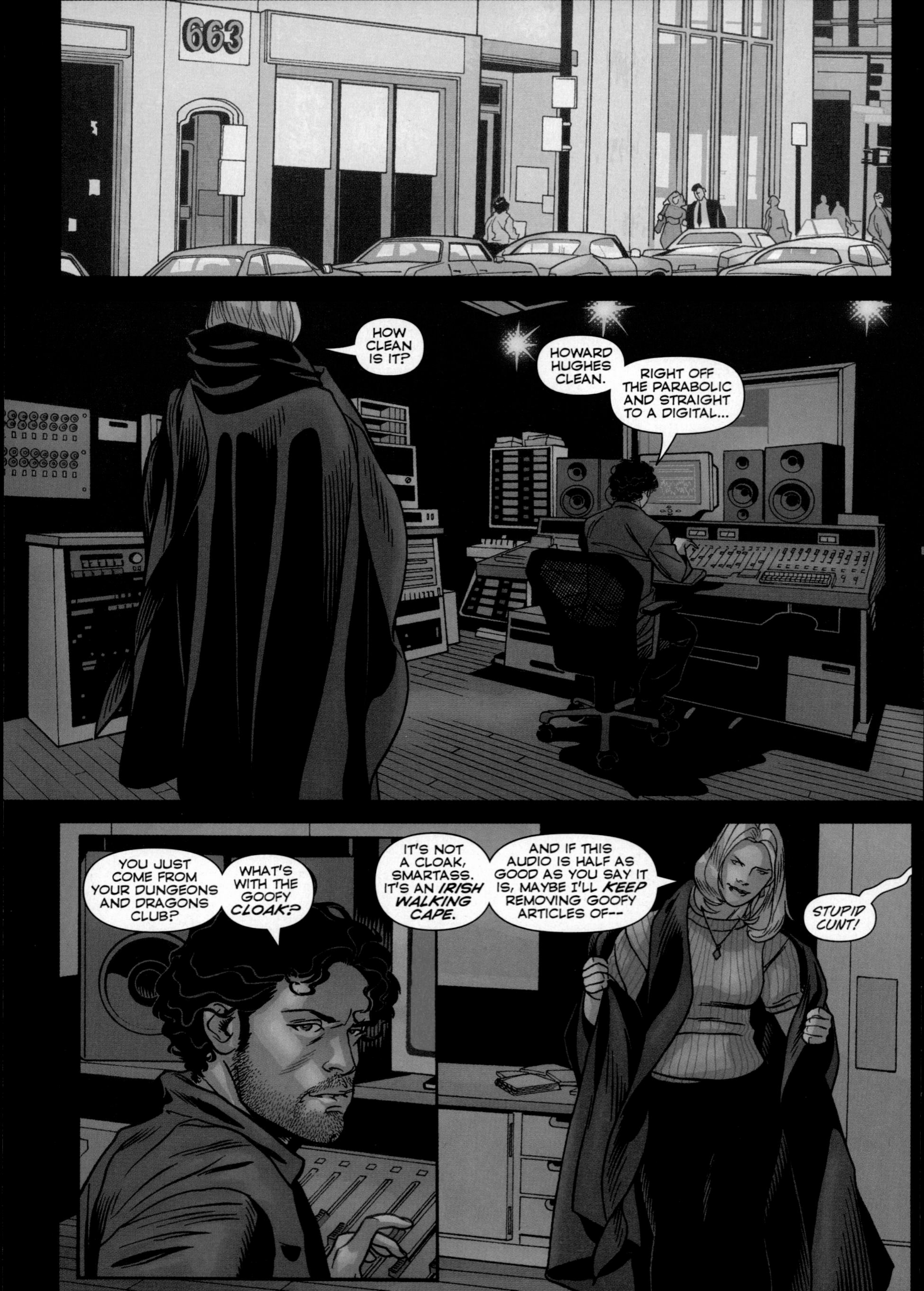
663
HOW CLEAN IS IT?
HOWARD HUGHES CLEAN.
RIGHT OFF THE PARABOLIC AND STRAIGHT TO A DIGITAL...
YOU JUST COME FROM YOUR DUNGEONS AND DRAGONS CLUB?
WHAT'S WITH THE GOOFY *CLOAK?*
IT'S NOT A CLOAK, SMARTASS. IT'S AN *IRISH WALKING CAPE.*
AND IF THIS AUDIO IS HALF AS GOOD AS YOU SAY IT IS, MAYBE I'LL *KEEP* REMOVING GOOFY ARTICLES OF--
STUPID CUNT!

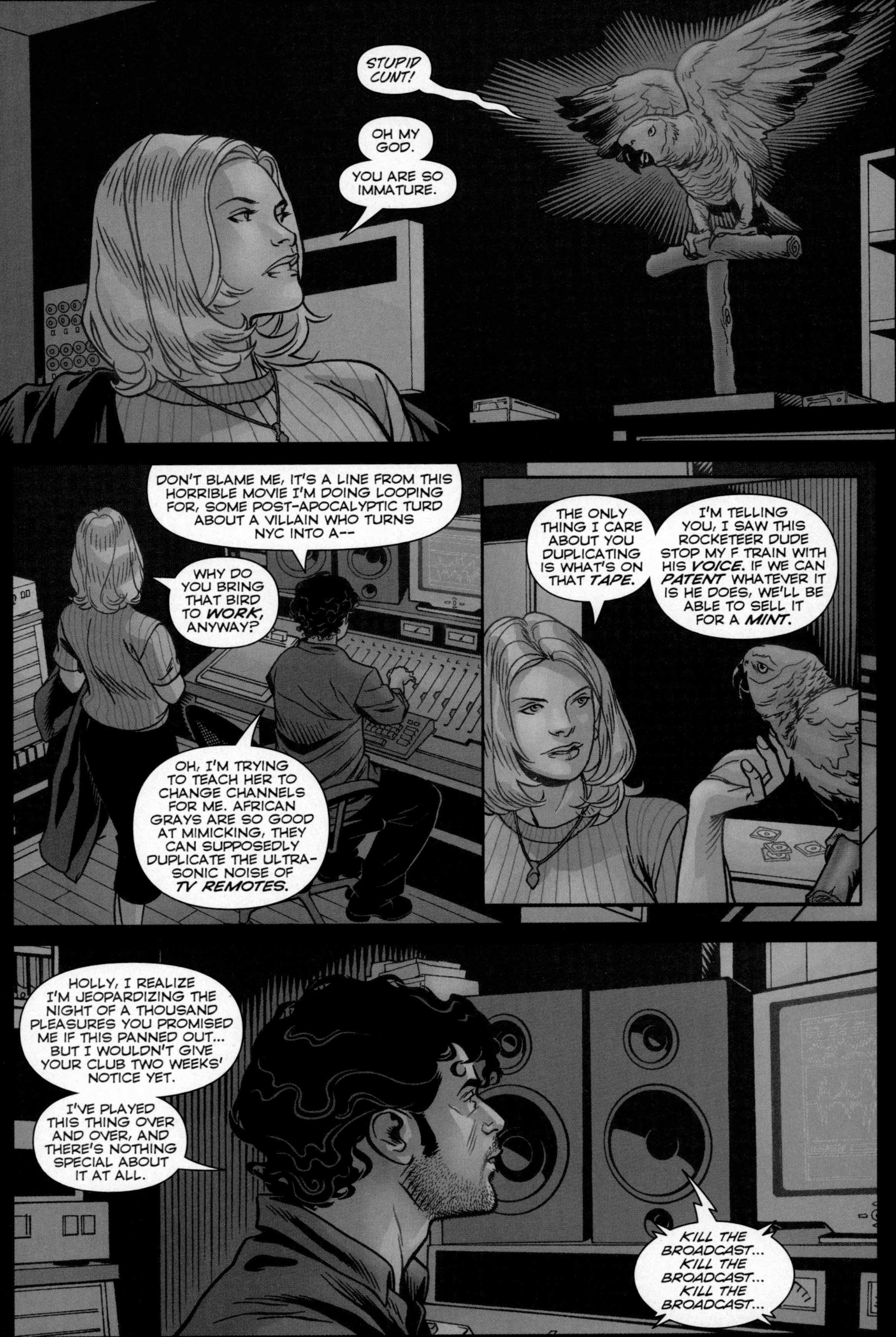
STUPID CUNT!
OH MY GOD.
YOU ARE SO IMMATURE.
DON'T BLAME ME, IT'S A LINE FROM THIS HORRIBLE MOVIE I'M DOING LOOPING FOR, SOME POST-APOCALYPTIC TURD ABOUT A VILLAIN WHO TURNS NYC INTO A--
WHY DO YOU BRING THAT BIRD TO WORK, ANYWAY?
OH, I'M TRYING TO TEACH HER TO CHANGE CHANNELS FOR ME. AFRICAN GRAYS ARE SO GOOD AT MIMICKING, THEY CAN SUPPOSEDLY DUPLICATE THE ULTRA-SONIC NOISE OF TV REMOTES.
THE ONLY THING I CARE ABOUT YOU DUPLICATING IS WHAT'S ON THAT TAPE.
I'M TELLING YOU, I SAW THIS ROCKETEER DUDE STOP MY F TRAIN WITH HIS VOICE. IF WE CAN PATENT WHATEVER IT IS HE DOES, WE'LL BE ABLE TO SELL IT FOR A MINT.
HOLLY, I REALIZE I'M JEOPARDIZING THE NIGHT OF A THOUSAND PLEASURES YOU PROMISED ME IF THIS PANNED OUT... BUT I WOULDN'T GIVE YOUR CLUB TWO WEEKS' NOTICE YET.
I'VE PLAYED THIS THING OVER AND OVER, AND THERE'S NOTHING SPECIAL ABOUT IT AT ALL.
KILL THE BROADCAST... KILL THE BROADCAST... KILL THE BROADCAST...

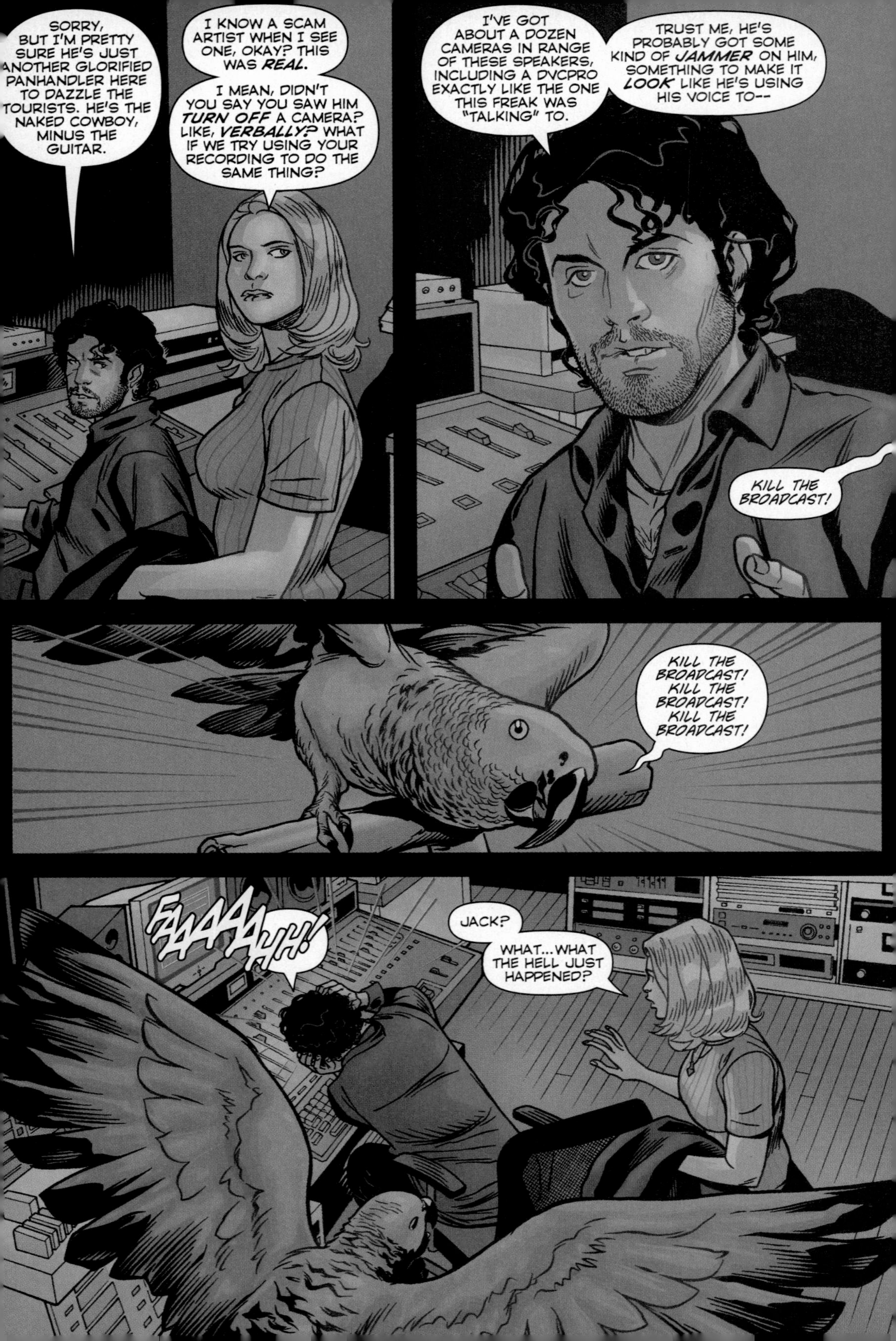
SORRY, BUT I'M PRETTY SURE HE'S JUST ANOTHER GLORIFIED PANHANDLER HERE TO DAZZLE THE TOURISTS. HE'S THE NAKED COWBOY, MINUS THE GUITAR.
I KNOW A SCAM ARTIST WHEN I SEE ONE, OKAY? THIS WAS REAL.
I MEAN, DIDN'T YOU SAY YOU SAW HIM TURN OFF A CAMERA? LIKE, VERBALLY? WHAT IF WE TRY USING YOUR RECORDING TO DO THE SAME THING?
I'VE GOT ABOUT A DOZEN CAMERAS IN RANGE OF THESE SPEAKERS, INCLUDING A DVCPRO EXACTLY LIKE THE ONE THIS FREAK WAS "TALKING" TO.
TRUST ME, HE'S PROBABLY GOT SOME KIND OF JAMMER ON HIM, SOMETHING TO MAKE IT LOOK LIKE HE'S USING HIS VOICE TO--
KILL THE BROADCAST!
KILL THE BROADCAST! KILL THE BROADCAST! KILL THE BROADCAST!
FAAAAAAHH!
JACK?
WHAT...WHAT THE HELL JUST HAPPENED?

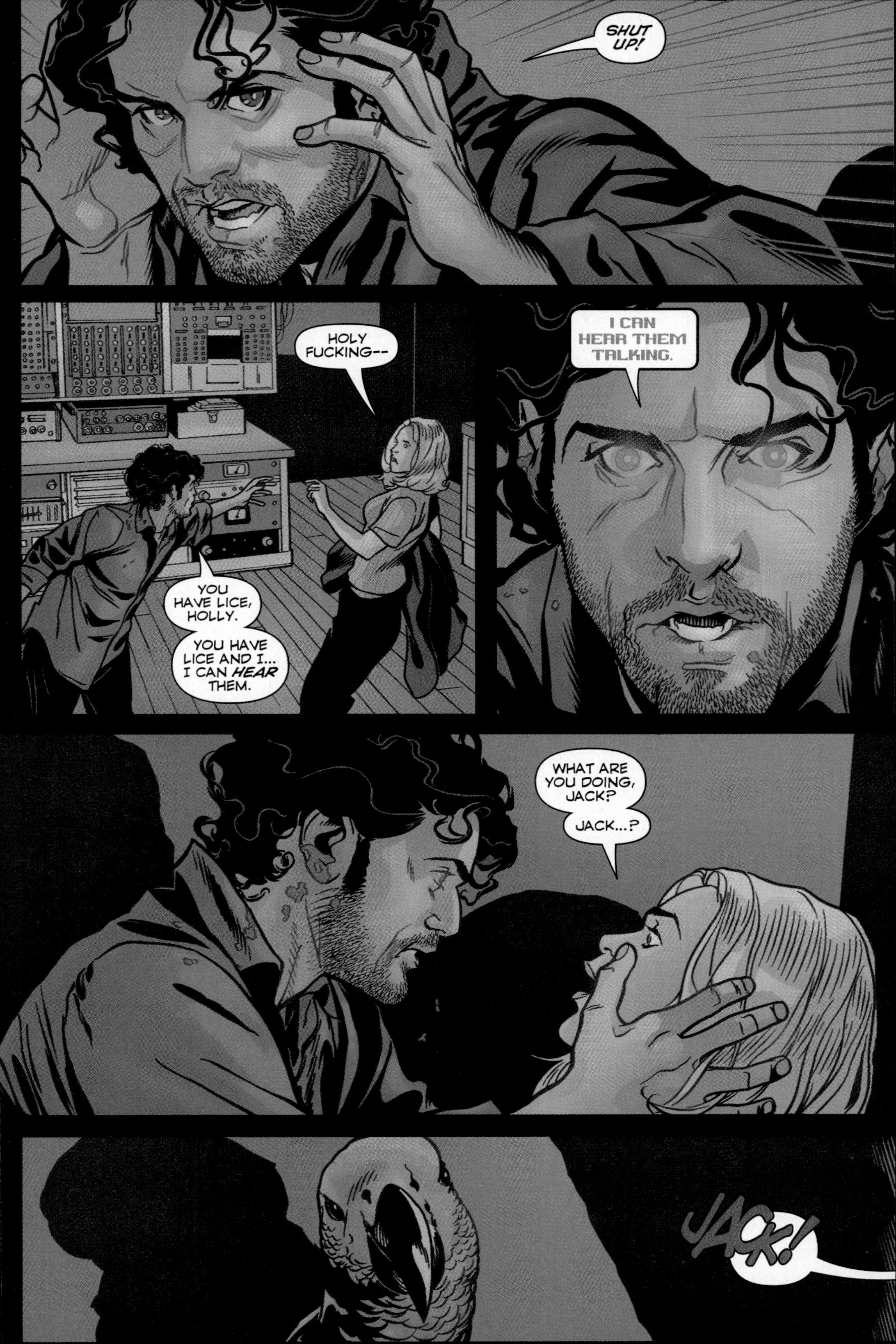
SHUT UP!
HOLY FUCKING--
YOU HAVE LICE, HOLLY.
YOU HAVE LICE AND I... I CAN *HEAR* THEM.
I CAN HEAR THEM TALKING.
WHAT ARE YOU DOING, JACK?
JACK...?
JACK!

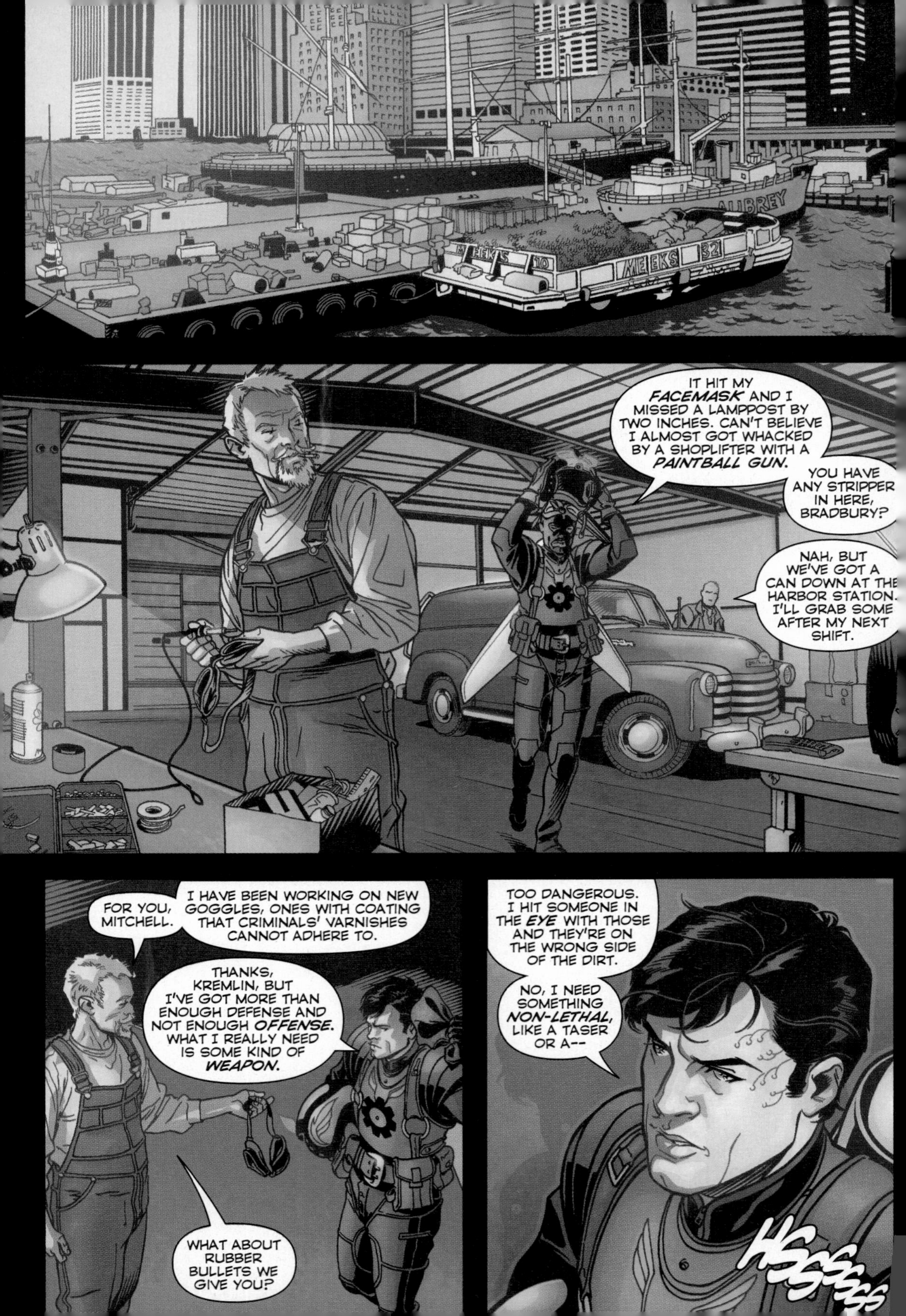
IT HIT MY FACEMASK AND I MISSED A LAMPPOST BY TWO INCHES. CAN'T BELIEVE I ALMOST GOT WHACKED BY A SHOPLIFTER WITH A PAINTBALL GUN.
YOU HAVE ANY STRIPPER IN HERE, BRADBURY?
NAH, BUT WE'VE GOT A CAN DOWN AT THE HARBOR STATION. I'LL GRAB SOME AFTER MY NEXT SHIFT.
FOR YOU, MITCHELL.
I HAVE BEEN WORKING ON NEW GOGGLES, ONES WITH COATING THAT CRIMINALS' VARNISHES CANNOT ADHERE TO.
THANKS, KREMLIN, BUT I'VE GOT MORE THAN ENOUGH DEFENSE AND NOT ENOUGH OFFENSE. WHAT I REALLY NEED IS SOME KIND OF WEAPON.
WHAT ABOUT RUBBER BULLETS WE GIVE YOU?
TOO DANGEROUS. I HIT SOMEONE IN THE EYE WITH THOSE AND THEY'RE ON THE WRONG SIDE OF THE DIRT.
NO, I NEED SOMETHING NON-LETHAL, LIKE A TASER OR A--

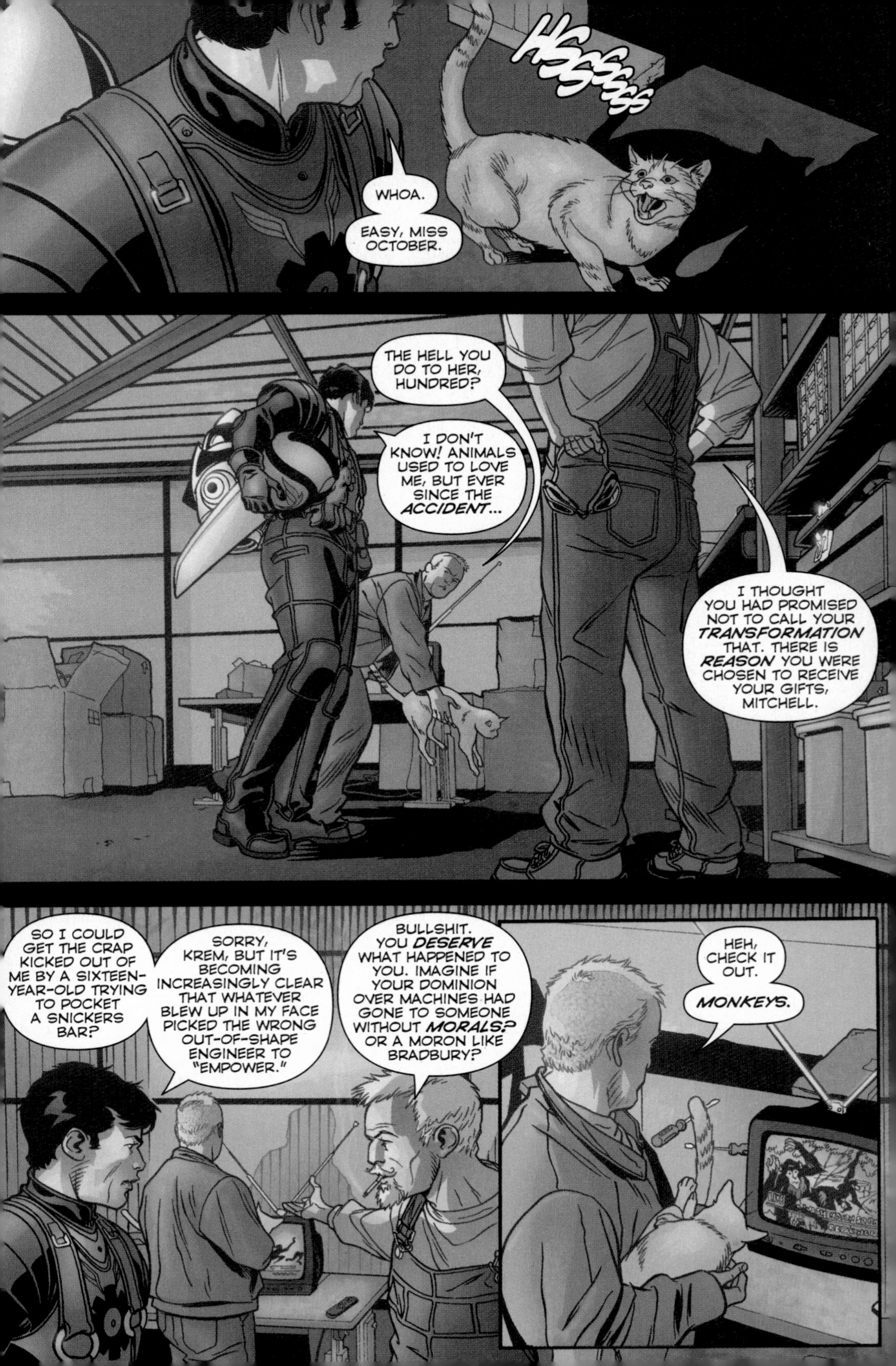
HSSSSSS
WHOA.
EASY, MISS OCTOBER.
THE HELL YOU DO TO HER, HUNDRED?
I DON'T KNOW! ANIMALS USED TO LOVE ME, BUT EVER SINCE THE *ACCIDENT*...
I THOUGHT YOU HAD PROMISED NOT TO CALL YOUR *TRANSFORMATION* THAT. THERE IS *REASON* YOU WERE CHOSEN TO RECEIVE YOUR GIFTS, MITCHELL.
SO I COULD GET THE CRAP KICKED OUT OF ME BY A SIXTEEN-YEAR-OLD TRYING TO POCKET A SNICKERS BAR?
SORRY, KREM, BUT IT'S BECOMING INCREASINGLY CLEAR THAT WHATEVER BLEW UP IN MY FACE PICKED THE WRONG OUT-OF-SHAPE ENGINEER TO "EMPOWER."
BULLSHIT. YOU *DESERVE* WHAT HAPPENED TO YOU. IMAGINE IF YOUR DOMINION OVER MACHINES HAD GONE TO SOMEONE WITHOUT *MORALS?* OR A MORON LIKE BRADBURY?
HEH, CHECK IT OUT.
MONKEYS.

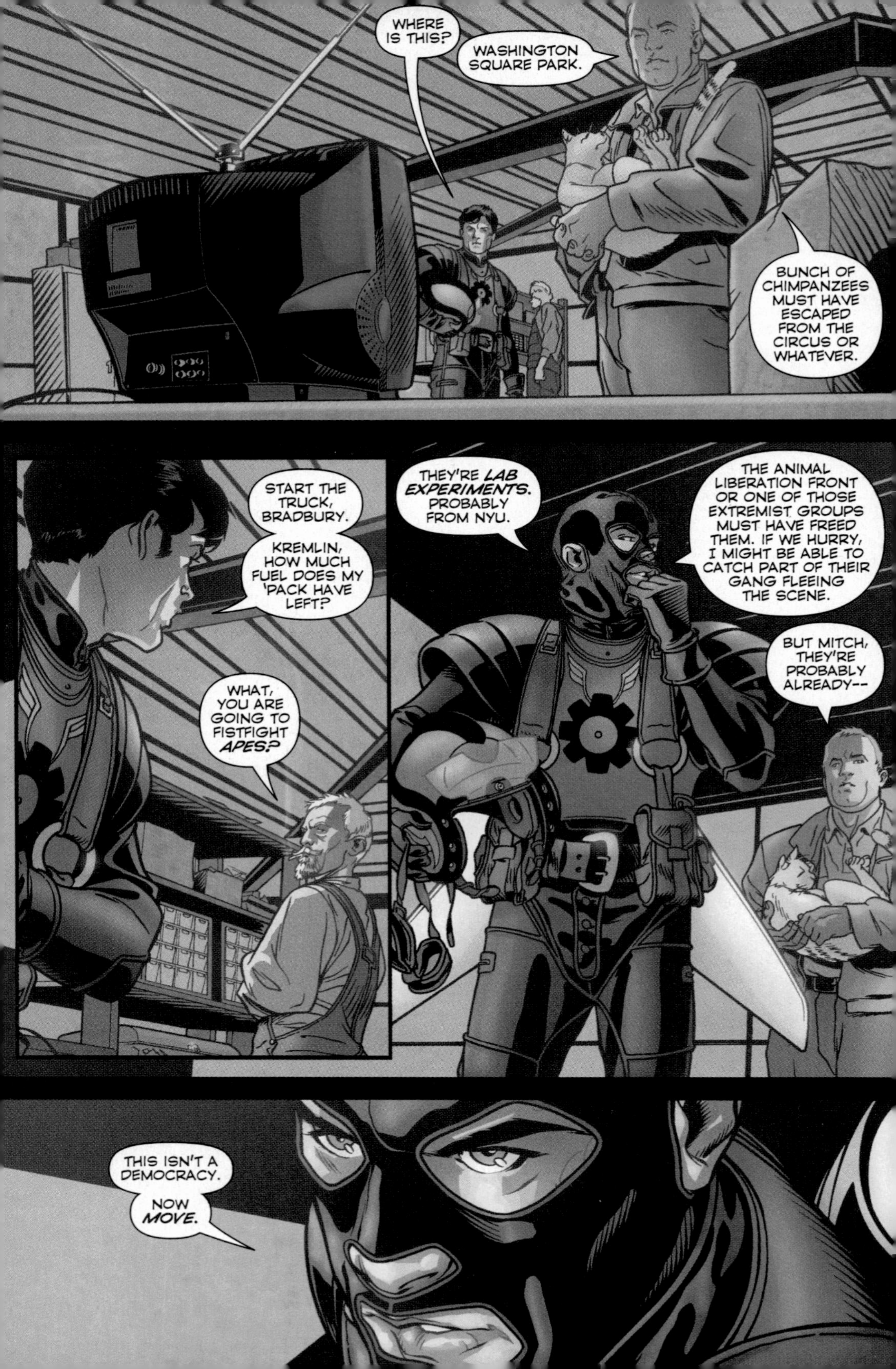
WHERE IS THIS?
WASHINGTON SQUARE PARK.
BUNCH OF CHIMPANZEES MUST HAVE ESCAPED FROM THE CIRCUS OR WHATEVER.
START THE TRUCK, BRADBURY.
KREMLIN, HOW MUCH FUEL DOES MY 'PACK HAVE LEFT?
WHAT, YOU ARE GOING TO FISTFIGHT *APES?*
THEY'RE *LAB EXPERIMENTS.* PROBABLY FROM NYU.
THE ANIMAL LIBERATION FRONT OR ONE OF THOSE EXTREMIST GROUPS MUST HAVE FREED THEM. IF WE HURRY, I MIGHT BE ABLE TO CATCH PART OF THEIR GANG FLEEING THE SCENE.
BUT MITCH, THEY'RE PROBABLY ALREADY--
THIS ISN'T A DEMOCRACY.
NOW *MOVE.*

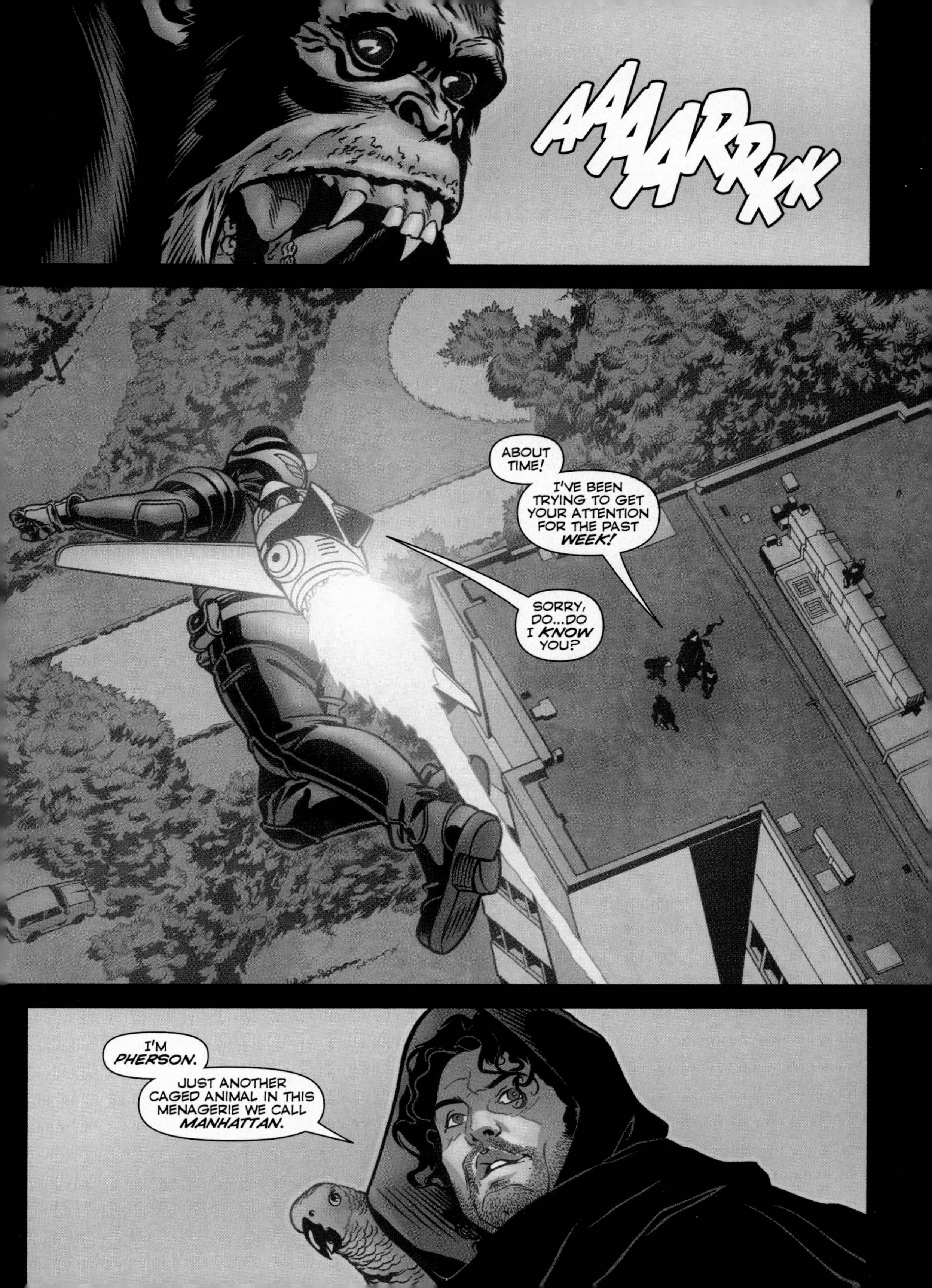
AAAARRRKK
ABOUT TIME!
I'VE BEEN TRYING TO GET YOUR ATTENTION FOR THE PAST WEEK!
SORRY, DO...DO I KNOW YOU?
I'M PHERSON.
JUST ANOTHER CAGED ANIMAL IN THIS MENAGERIE WE CALL MANHATTAN.

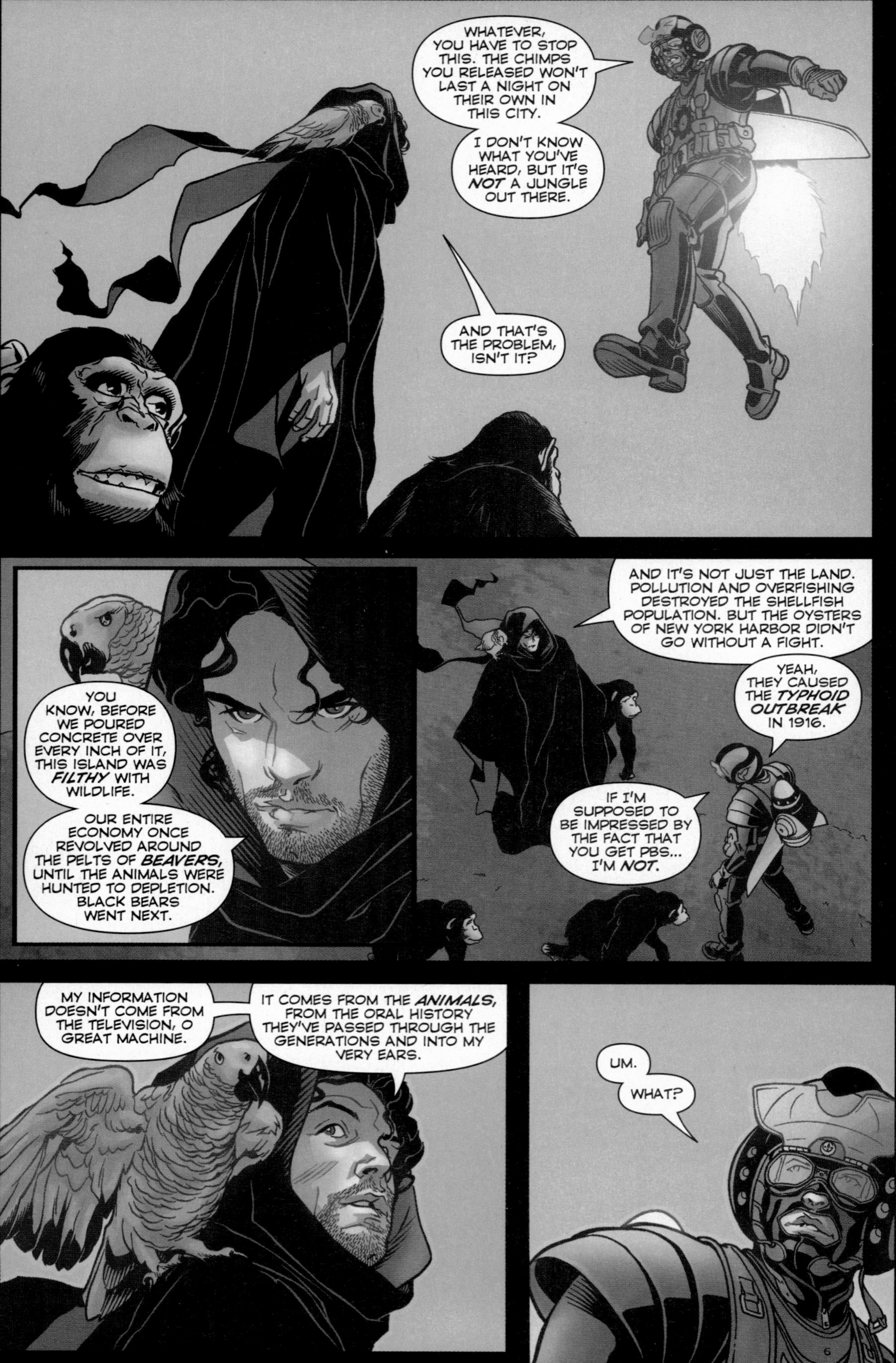
WHATEVER, YOU HAVE TO STOP THIS. THE CHIMPS YOU RELEASED WON'T LAST A NIGHT ON THEIR OWN IN THIS CITY.
I DON'T KNOW WHAT YOU'VE HEARD, BUT IT'S *NOT* A JUNGLE OUT THERE.
AND THAT'S THE PROBLEM, ISN'T IT?
YOU KNOW, BEFORE WE POURED CONCRETE OVER EVERY INCH OF IT, THIS ISLAND WAS *FILTHY* WITH WILDLIFE.
OUR ENTIRE ECONOMY ONCE REVOLVED AROUND THE PELTS OF *BEAVERS,* UNTIL THE ANIMALS WERE HUNTED TO DEPLETION. BLACK BEARS WENT NEXT.
AND IT'S NOT JUST THE LAND. POLLUTION AND OVERFISHING DESTROYED THE SHELLFISH POPULATION. BUT THE OYSTERS OF NEW YORK HARBOR DIDN'T GO WITHOUT A FIGHT.
YEAH, THEY CAUSED THE *TYPHOID OUTBREAK* IN 1916.
IF I'M SUPPOSED TO BE IMPRESSED BY THE FACT THAT YOU GET PBS... I'M *NOT*.
MY INFORMATION DOESN'T COME FROM THE TELEVISION, O GREAT MACHINE.
IT COMES FROM THE *ANIMALS,* FROM THE ORAL HISTORY THEY'VE PASSED THROUGH THE GENERATIONS AND INTO MY VERY EARS.
UM.
WHAT?

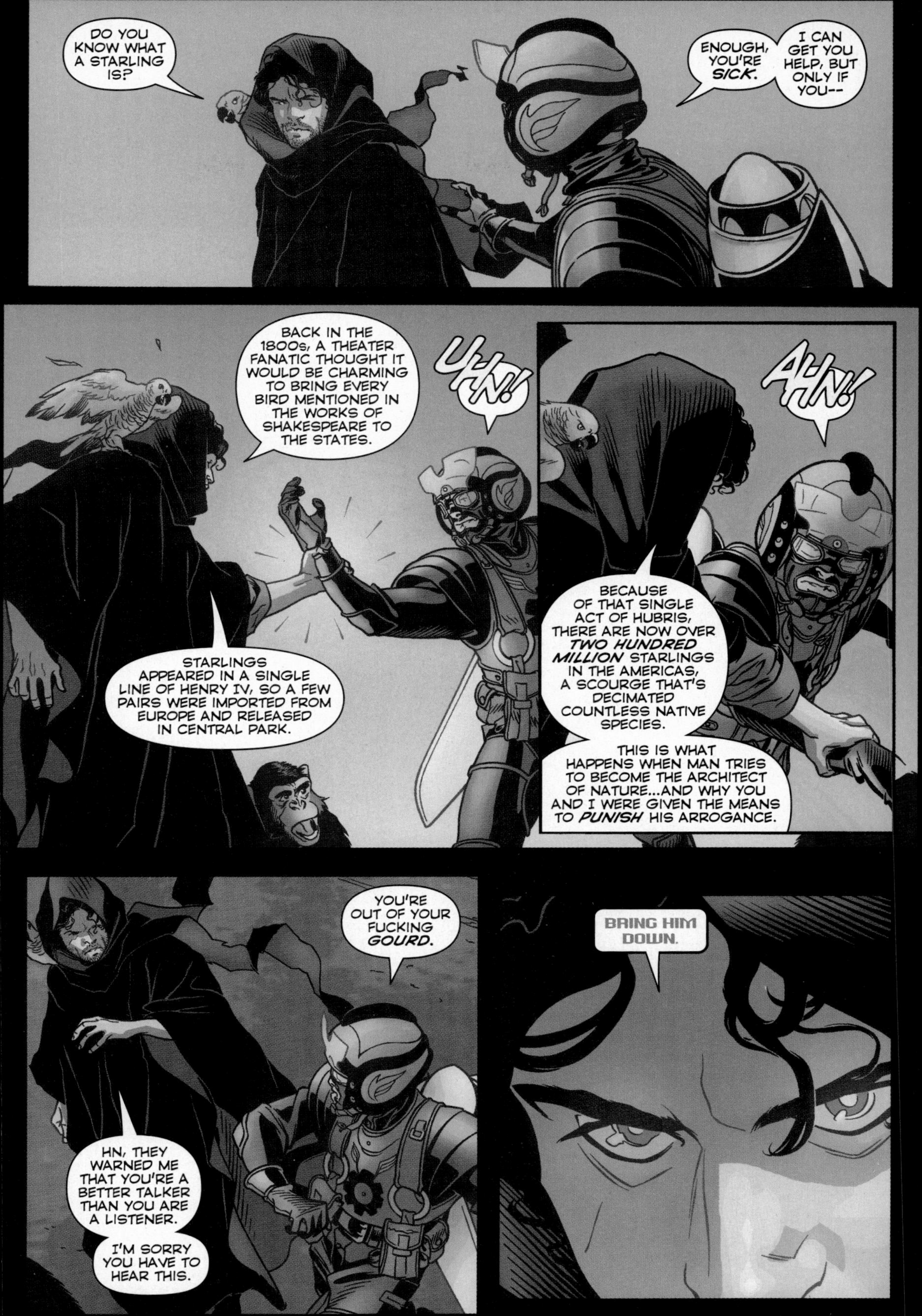
DO YOU KNOW WHAT A STARLING IS?
ENOUGH, YOU'RE *SICK*.
I CAN GET YOU HELP, BUT ONLY IF YOU--
BACK IN THE 1800s, A THEATER FANATIC THOUGHT IT WOULD BE CHARMING TO BRING EVERY BIRD MENTIONED IN THE WORKS OF SHAKESPEARE TO THE STATES.
UHN!
STARLINGS APPEARED IN A SINGLE LINE OF HENRY IV, SO A FEW PAIRS WERE IMPORTED FROM EUROPE AND RELEASED IN CENTRAL PARK.
AHN!
BECAUSE OF THAT SINGLE ACT OF HUBRIS, THERE ARE NOW OVER *TWO HUNDRED MILLION* STARLINGS IN THE AMERICAS, A SCOURGE THAT'S DECIMATED COUNTLESS NATIVE SPECIES.
THIS IS WHAT HAPPENS WHEN MAN TRIES TO BECOME THE ARCHITECT OF NATURE...AND WHY YOU AND I WERE GIVEN THE MEANS TO *PUNISH* HIS ARROGANCE.
YOU'RE OUT OF YOUR FUCKING *GOURD*.
HN, THEY WARNED ME THAT YOU'RE A BETTER TALKER THAN YOU ARE A LISTENER.
I'M SORRY YOU HAVE TO HEAR THIS.
BRING HIM DOWN.

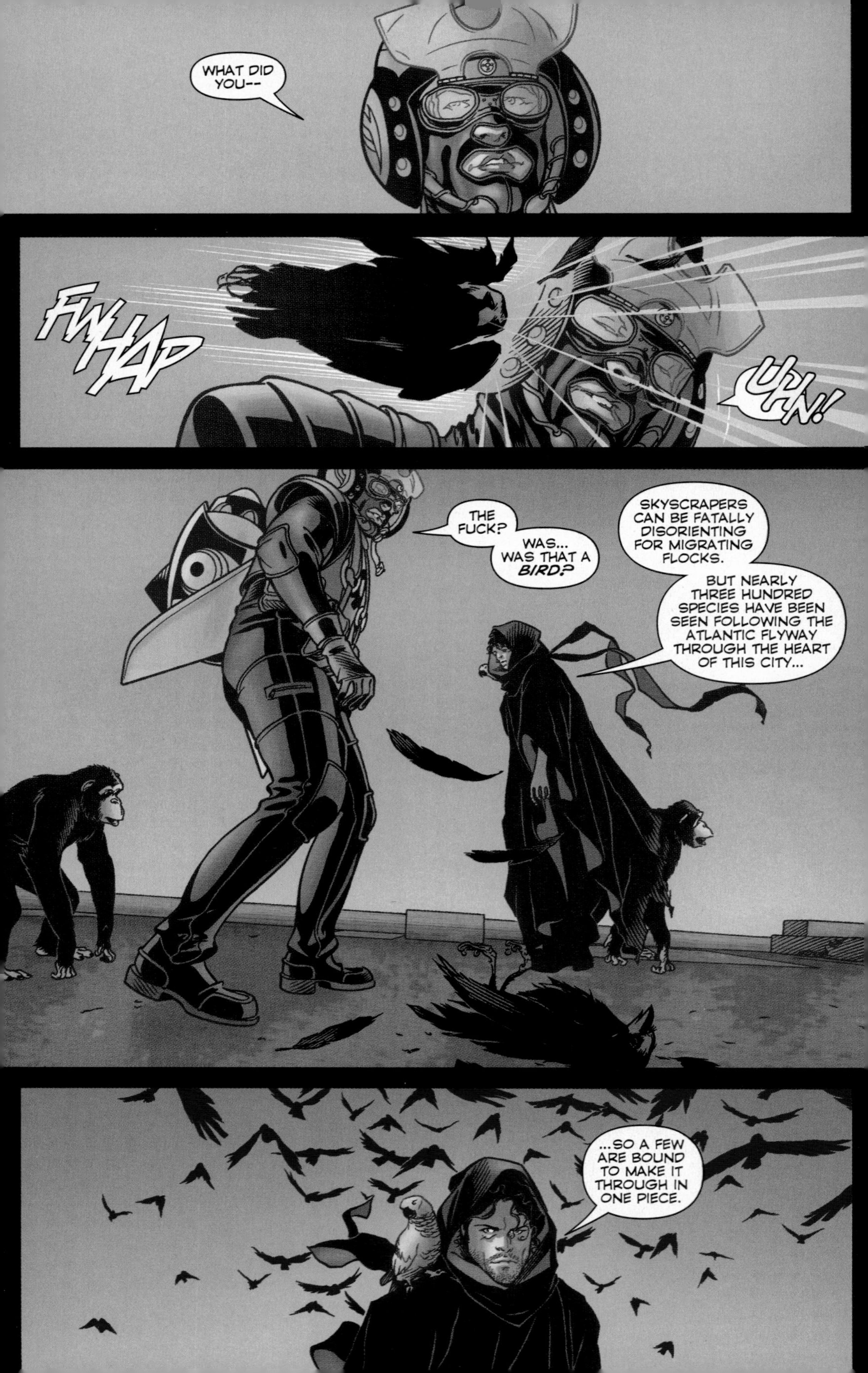

WHAT DID YOU--
FWHAP
UHN!
THE FUCK?
WAS... WAS THAT A *BIRD?*
SKYSCRAPERS CAN BE FATALLY DISORIENTING FOR MIGRATING FLOCKS.
BUT NEARLY THREE HUNDRED SPECIES HAVE BEEN SEEN FOLLOWING THE ATLANTIC FLYWAY THROUGH THE HEART OF THIS CITY...
...SO A FEW ARE BOUND TO MAKE IT THROUGH IN ONE PIECE.

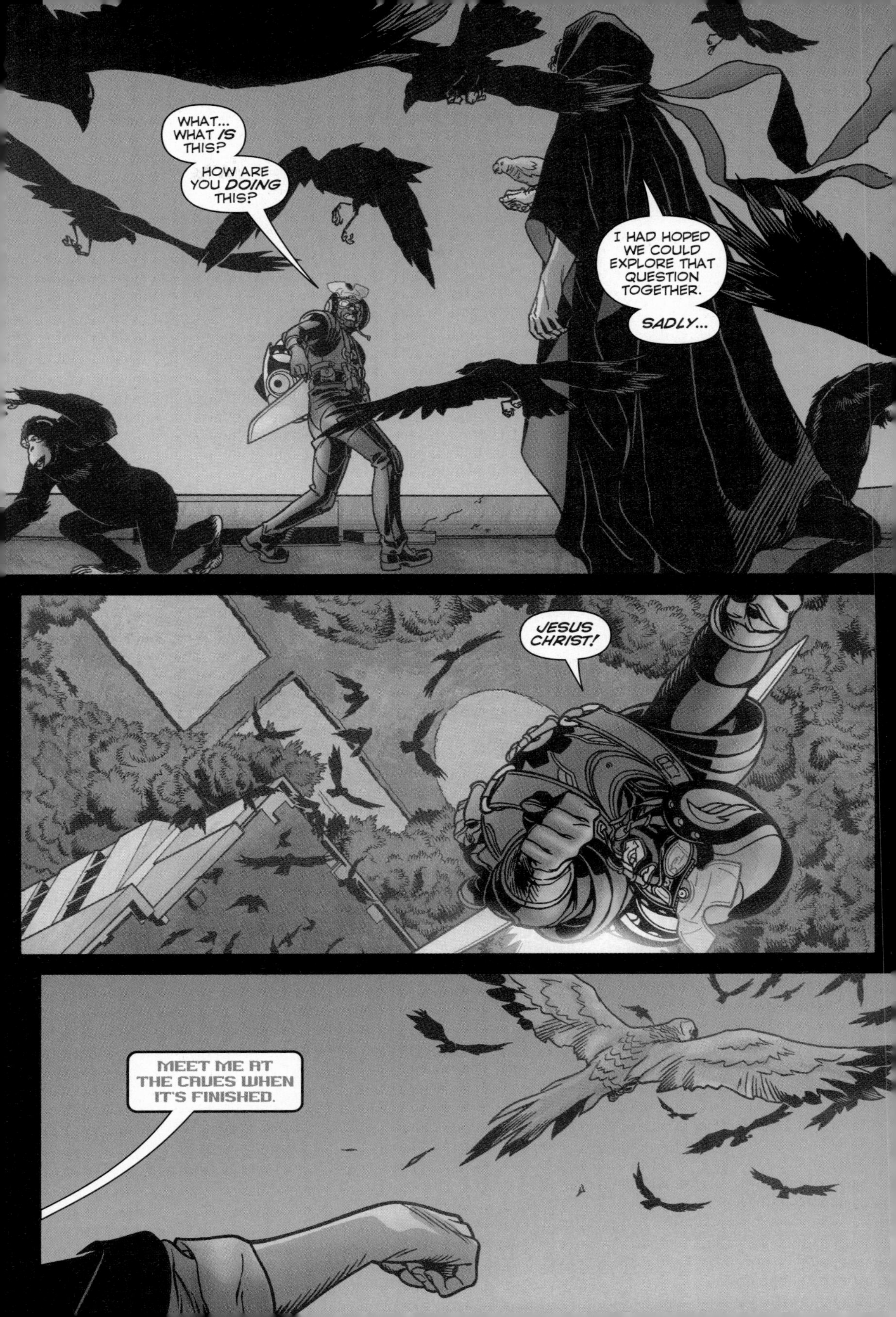
WHAT... WHAT *IS* THIS?
HOW ARE YOU *DOING* THIS?
I HAD HOPED WE COULD EXPLORE THAT QUESTION TOGETHER.
SADLY...
JESUS CHRIST!
MEET ME AT THE CAVES WHEN IT'S FINISHED.

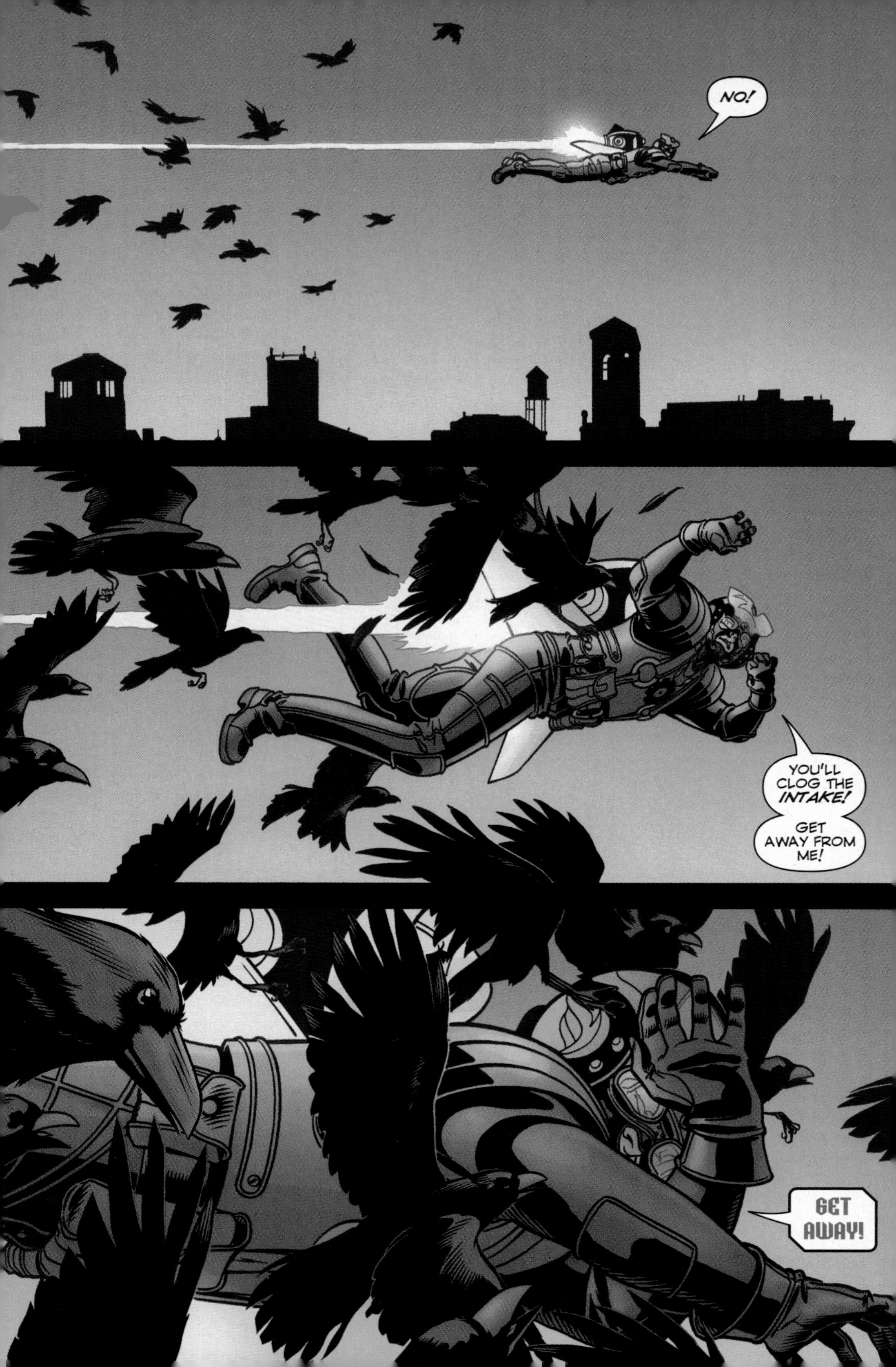

NO!
YOU'LL CLOG THE *INTAKE!*
GET AWAY FROM ME!
GET AWAY!

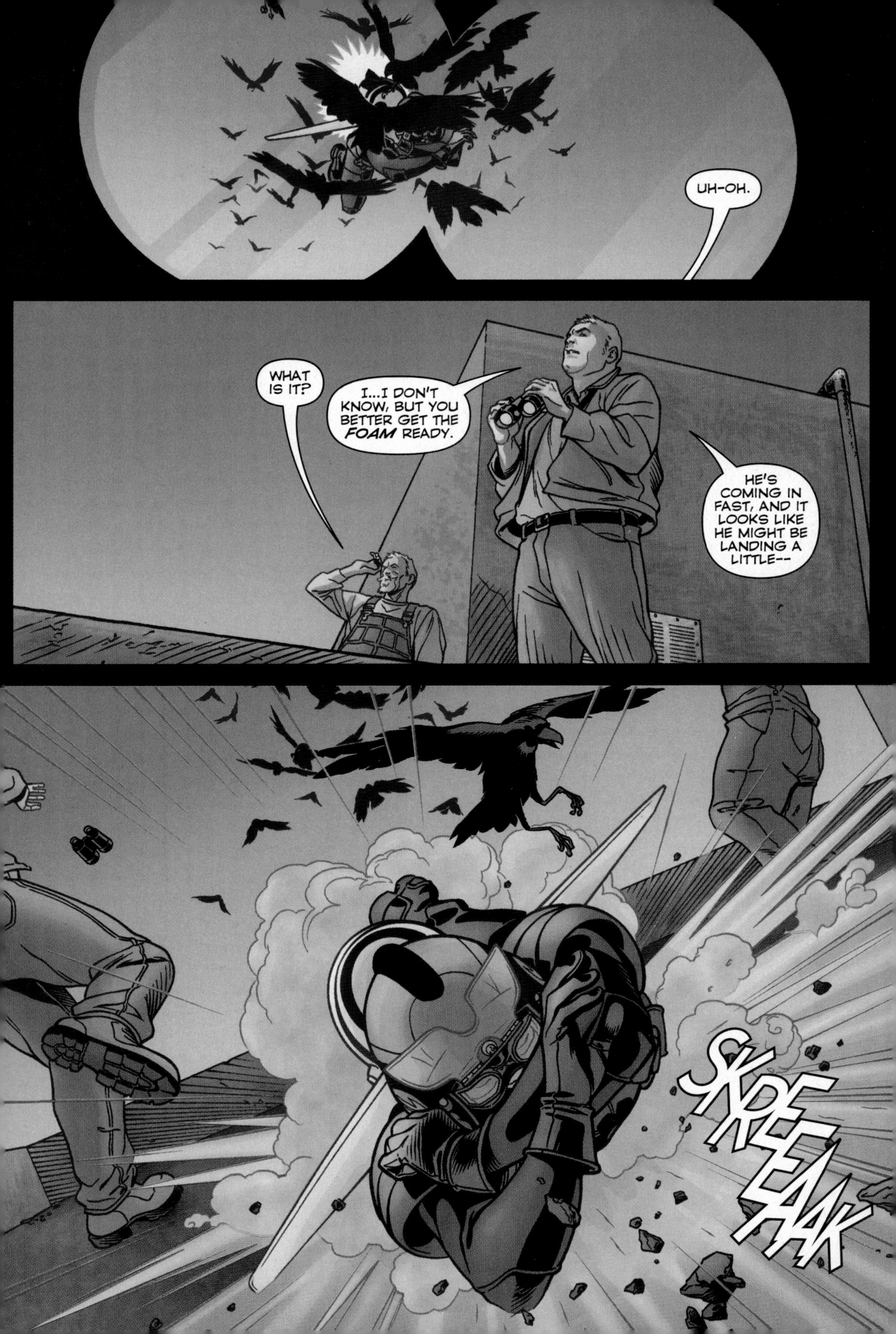
UH-OH.
WHAT IS IT?
I...I DON'T KNOW, BUT YOU BETTER GET THE *FOAM* READY.
HE'S COMING IN FAST, AND IT LOOKS LIKE HE MIGHT BE LANDING A LITTLE--
SKREEEAAK

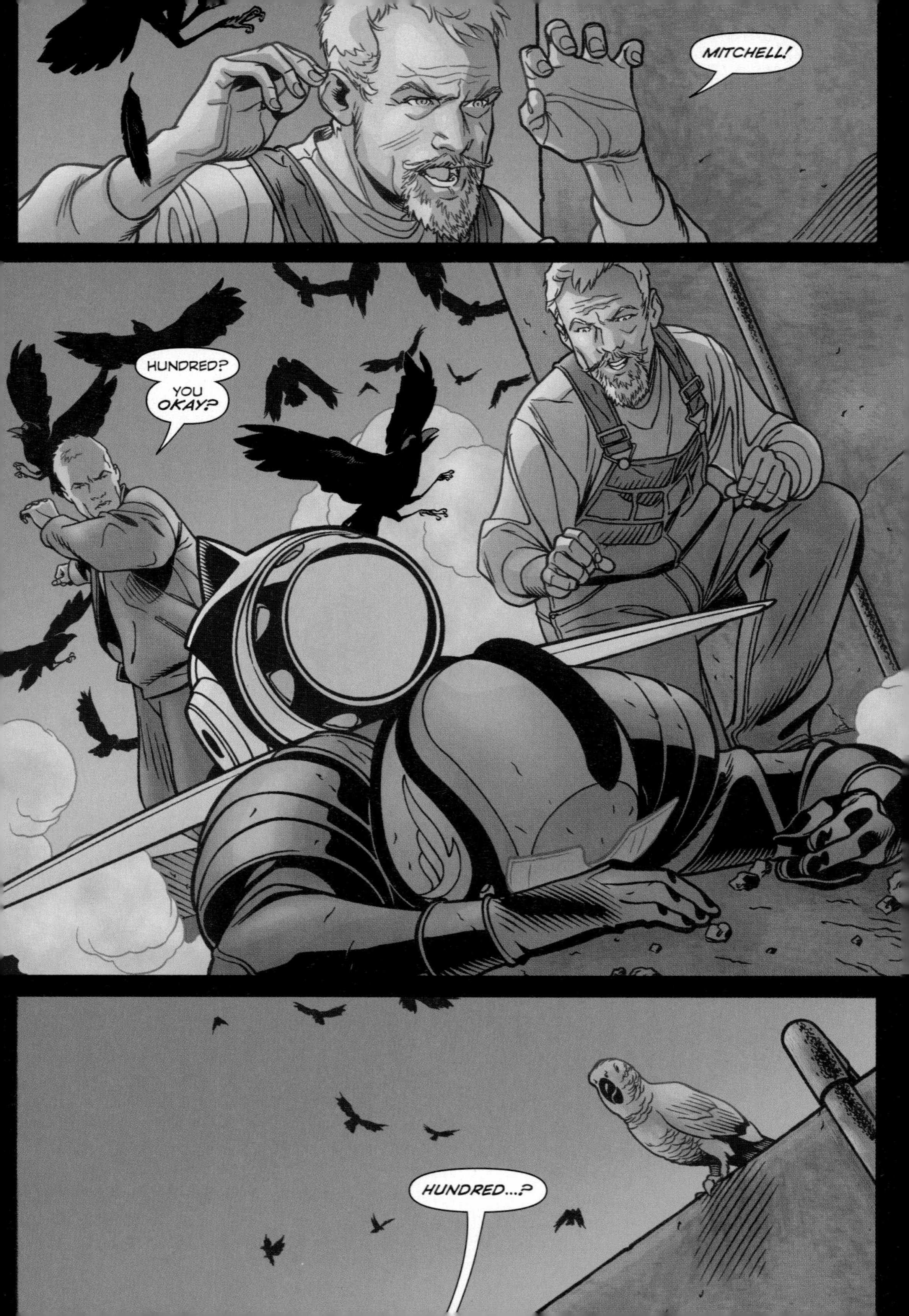
MITCHELL!
HUNDRED? YOU OKAY?
HUNDRED...?

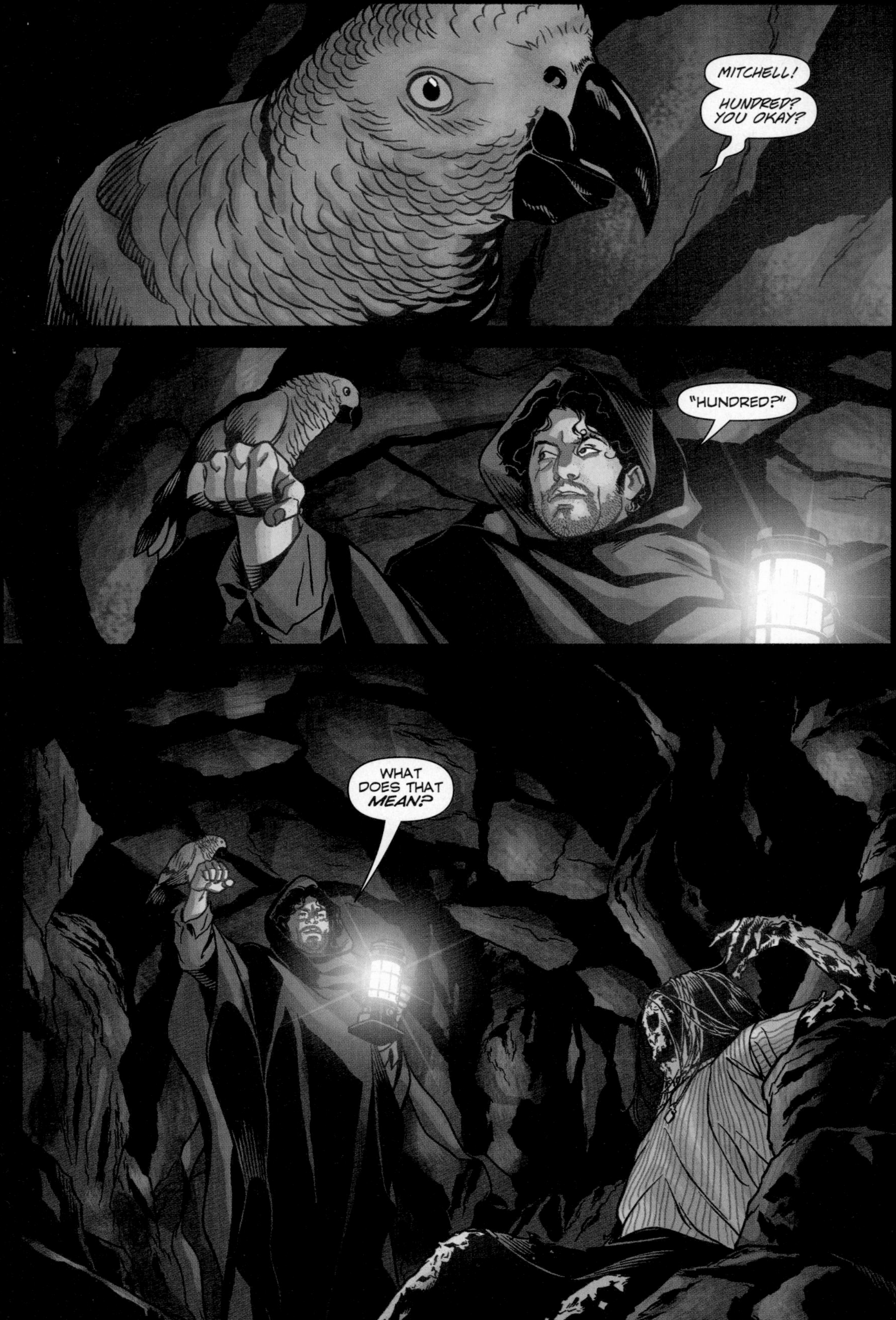
MITCHELL!
HUNDRED? YOU OKAY?
"HUNDRED?"
WHAT DOES THAT *MEAN?*

CHAPTER 6 Life and Death

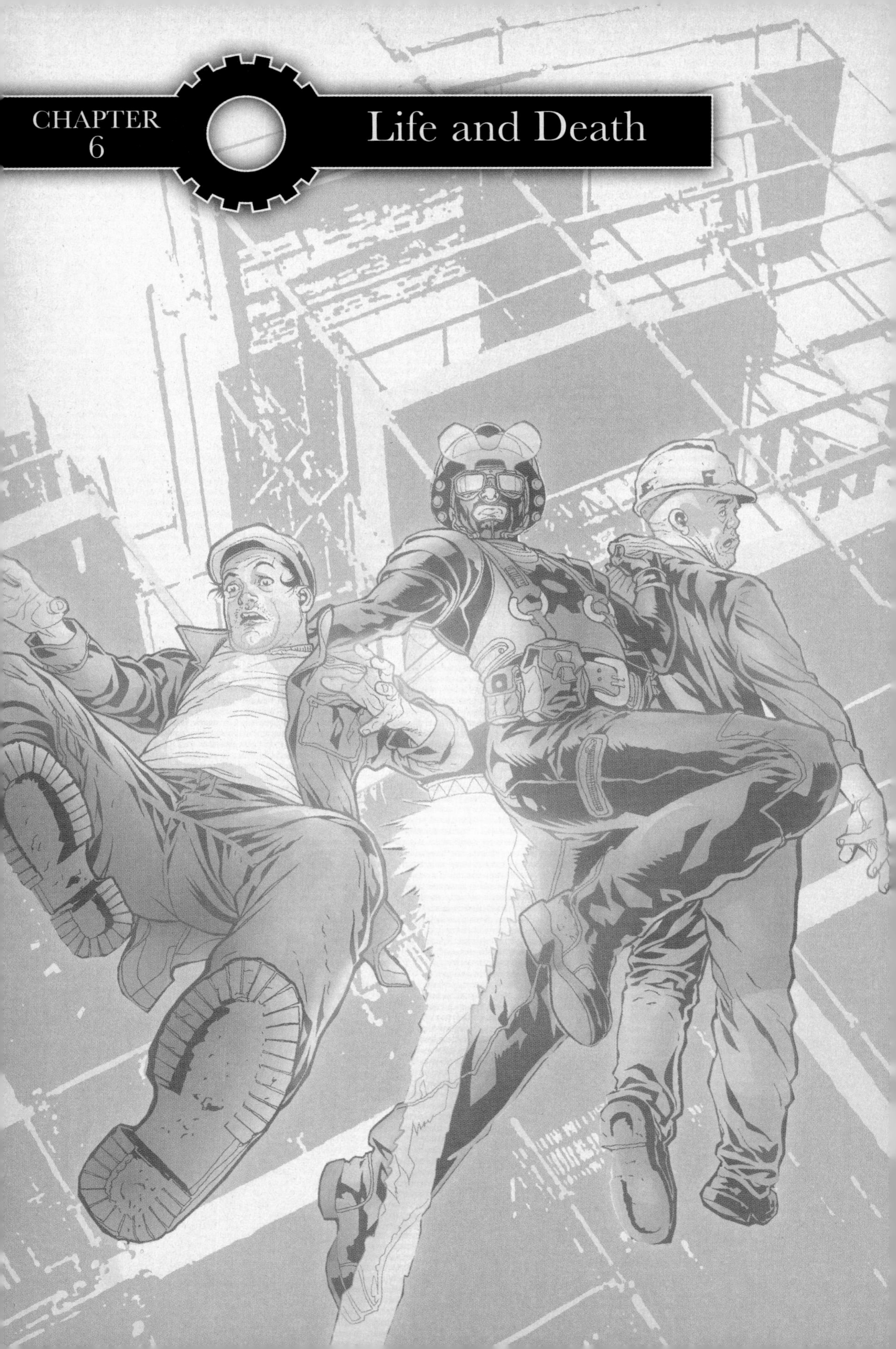

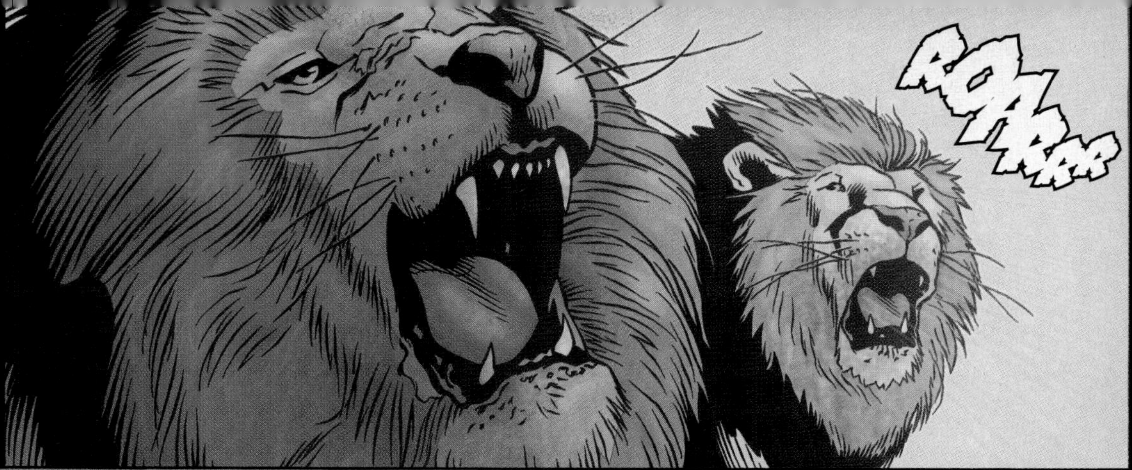
ROARRR

TUESDAY, MAY 8, 2001

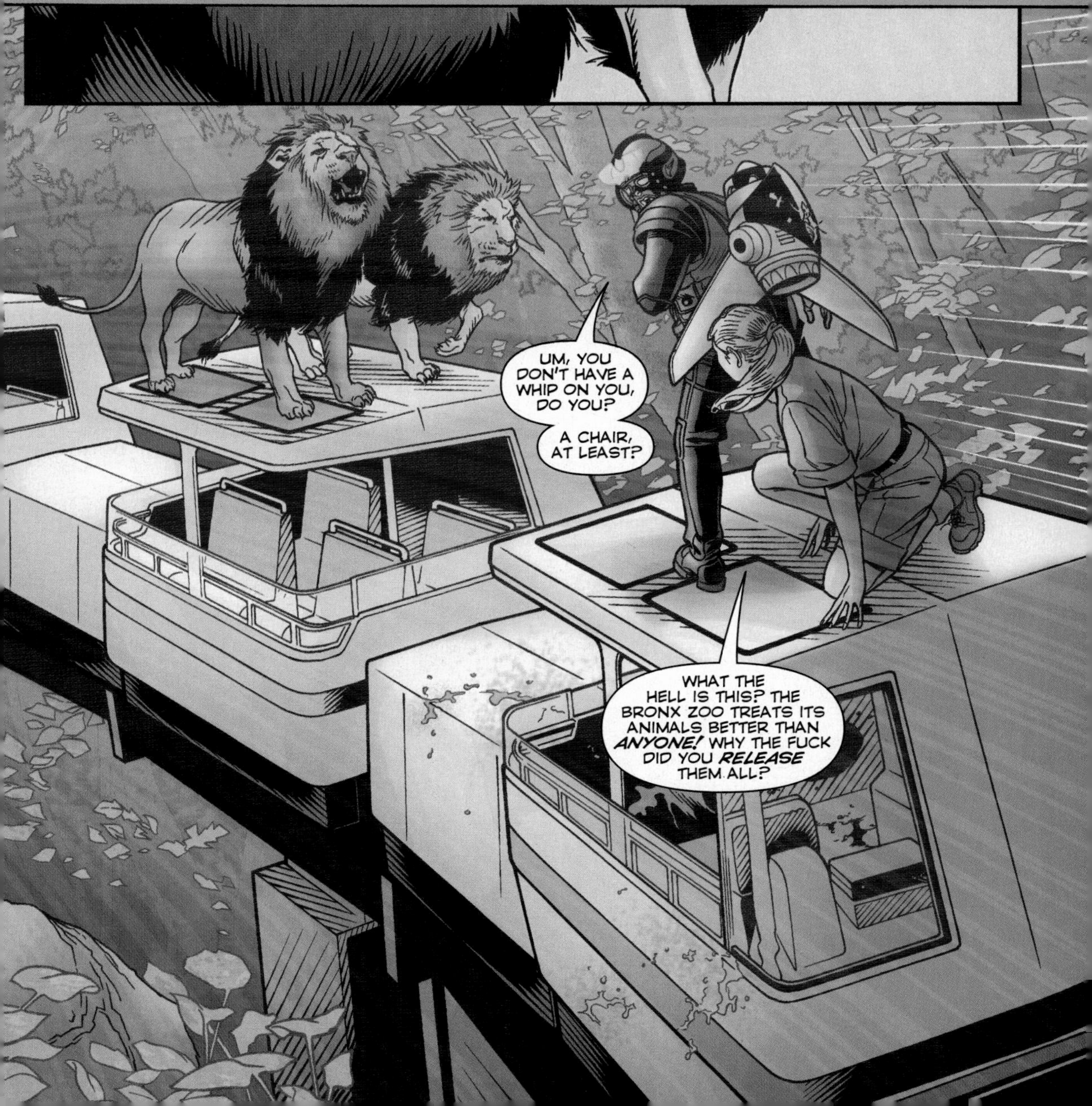
UM, YOU DON'T HAVE A WHIP ON YOU, DO YOU?
A CHAIR, AT LEAST?
WHAT THE HELL IS THIS? THE BRONX ZOO TREATS ITS ANIMALS BETTER THAN *ANYONE!* WHY THE FUCK DID YOU *RELEASE* THEM ALL?

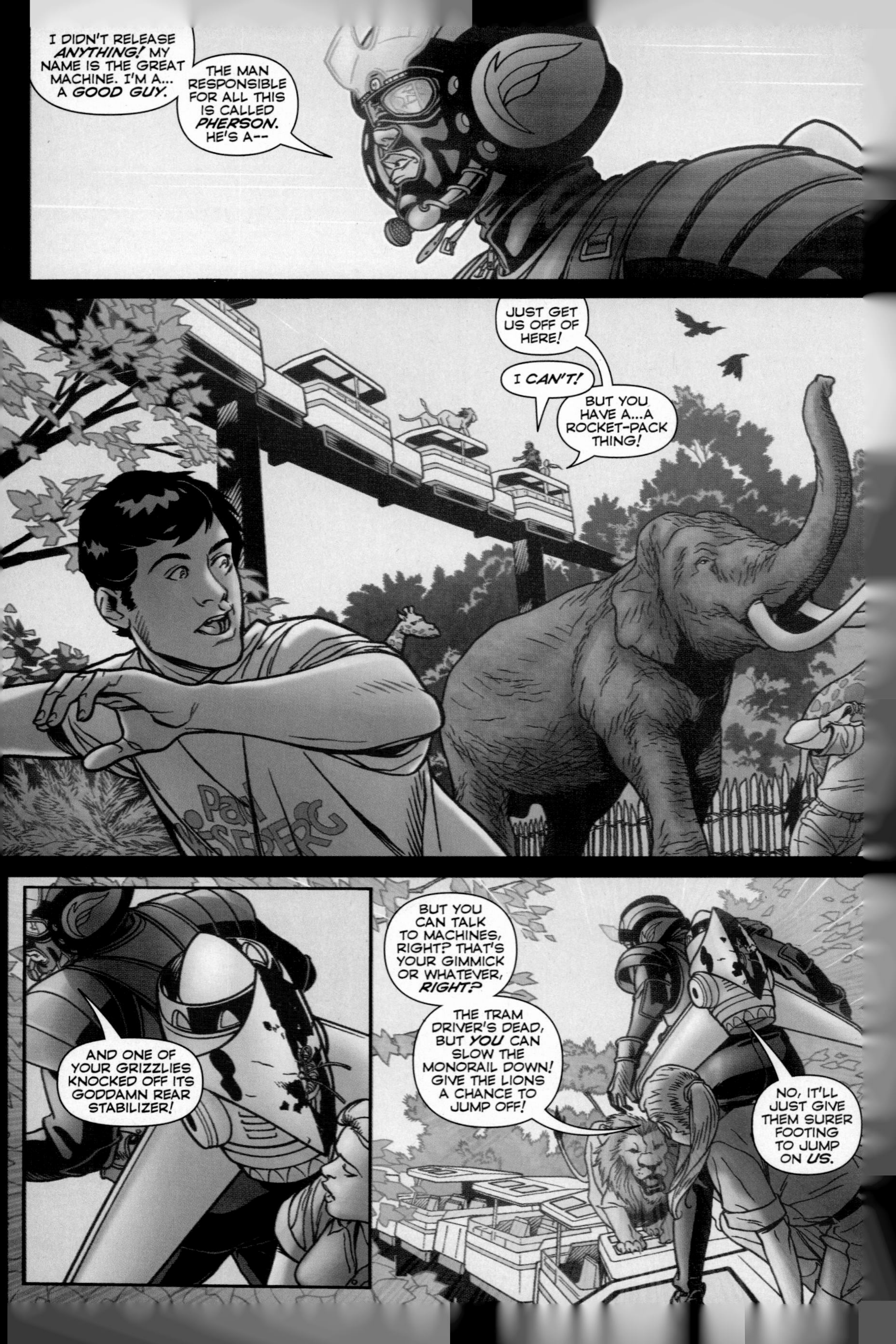
I DIDN'T RELEASE ANYTHING! MY NAME IS THE GREAT MACHINE. I'M A... A GOOD GUY.
THE MAN RESPONSIBLE FOR ALL THIS IS CALLED PHERSON. HE'S A--
JUST GET US OFF OF HERE!
I CAN'T!
BUT YOU HAVE A...A ROCKET-PACK THING!
AND ONE OF YOUR GRIZZLIES KNOCKED OFF ITS GODDAMN REAR STABILIZER!
BUT YOU CAN TALK TO MACHINES, RIGHT? THAT'S YOUR GIMMICK OR WHATEVER, RIGHT?
THE TRAM DRIVER'S DEAD, BUT YOU CAN SLOW THE MONORAIL DOWN! GIVE THE LIONS A CHANCE TO JUMP OFF!
NO, IT'LL JUST GIVE THEM SURER FOOTING TO JUMP ON US.

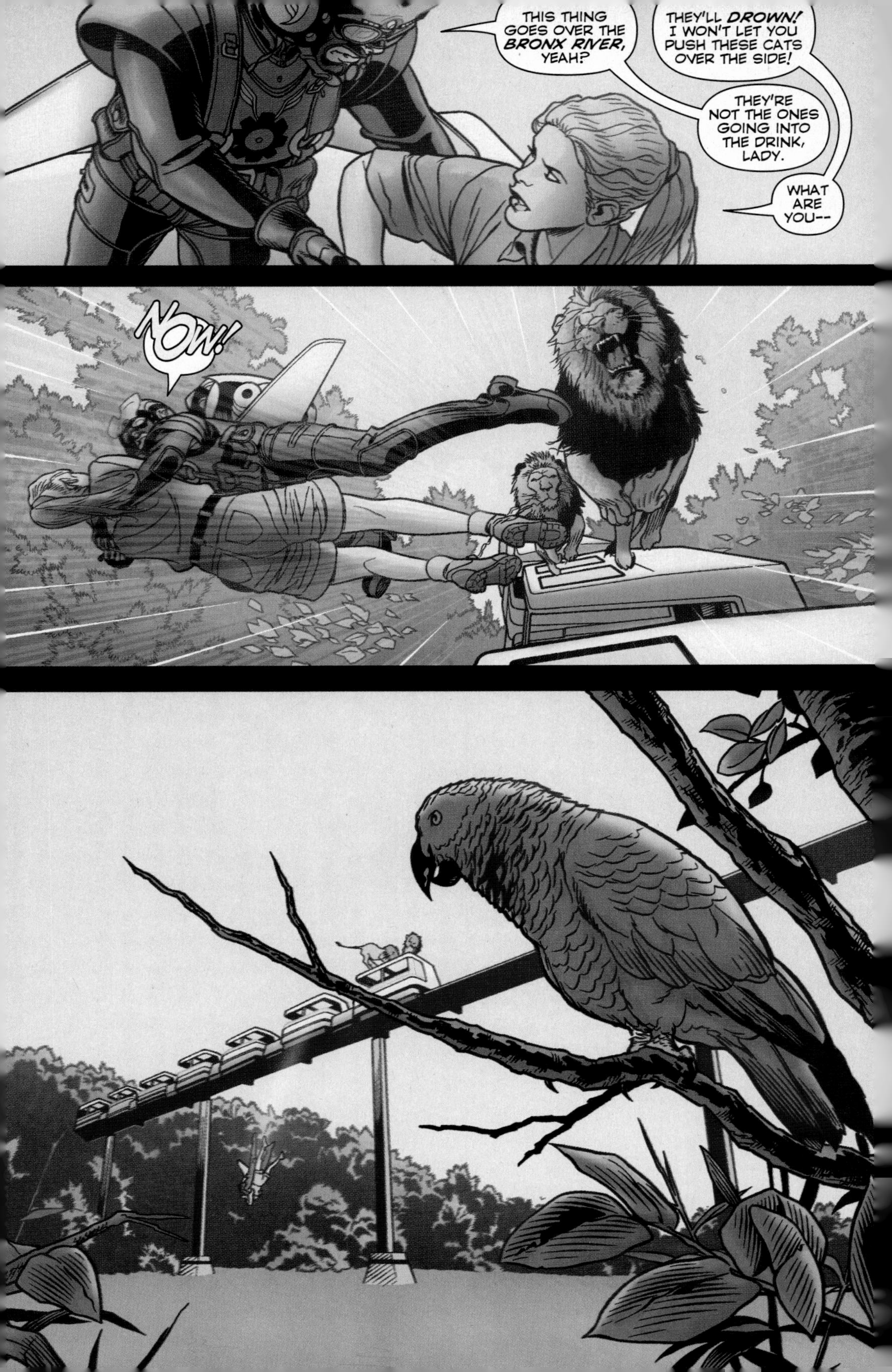
THIS THING GOES OVER THE BRONX RIVER, YEAH?
THEY'LL DROWN! I WON'T LET YOU PUSH THESE CATS OVER THE SIDE!
THEY'RE NOT THE ONES GOING INTO THE DRINK, LADY.
WHAT ARE YOU--
NOW!

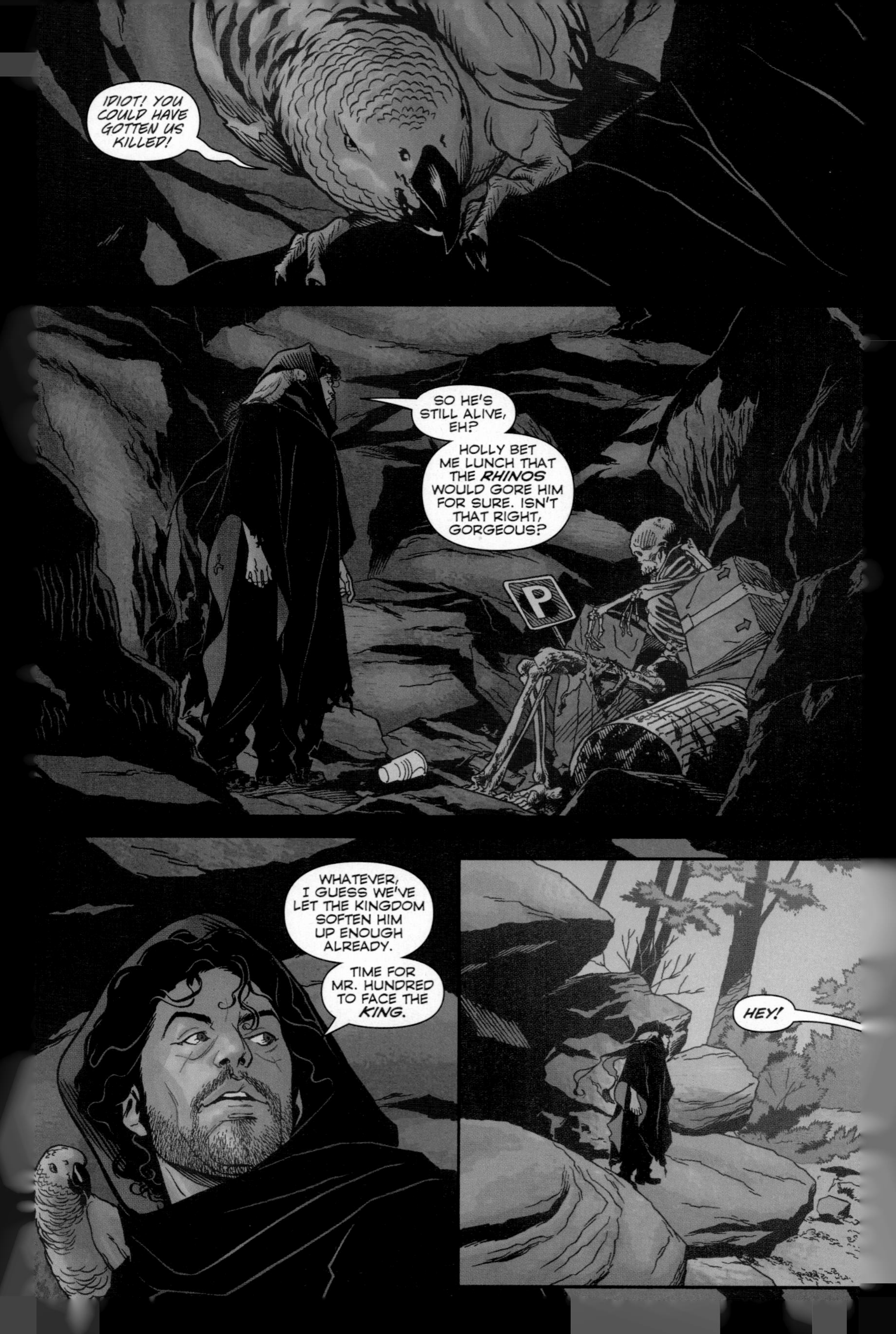
IDIOT! YOU COULD HAVE GOTTEN US KILLED!
SO HE'S STILL ALIVE, EH?
HOLLY BET ME LUNCH THAT THE RHINOS WOULD GORE HIM FOR SURE. ISN'T THAT RIGHT, GORGEOUS?
P
WHATEVER, I GUESS WE'VE LET THE KINGDOM SOFTEN HIM UP ENOUGH ALREADY.
TIME FOR MR. HUNDRED TO FACE THE KING.
HEY!

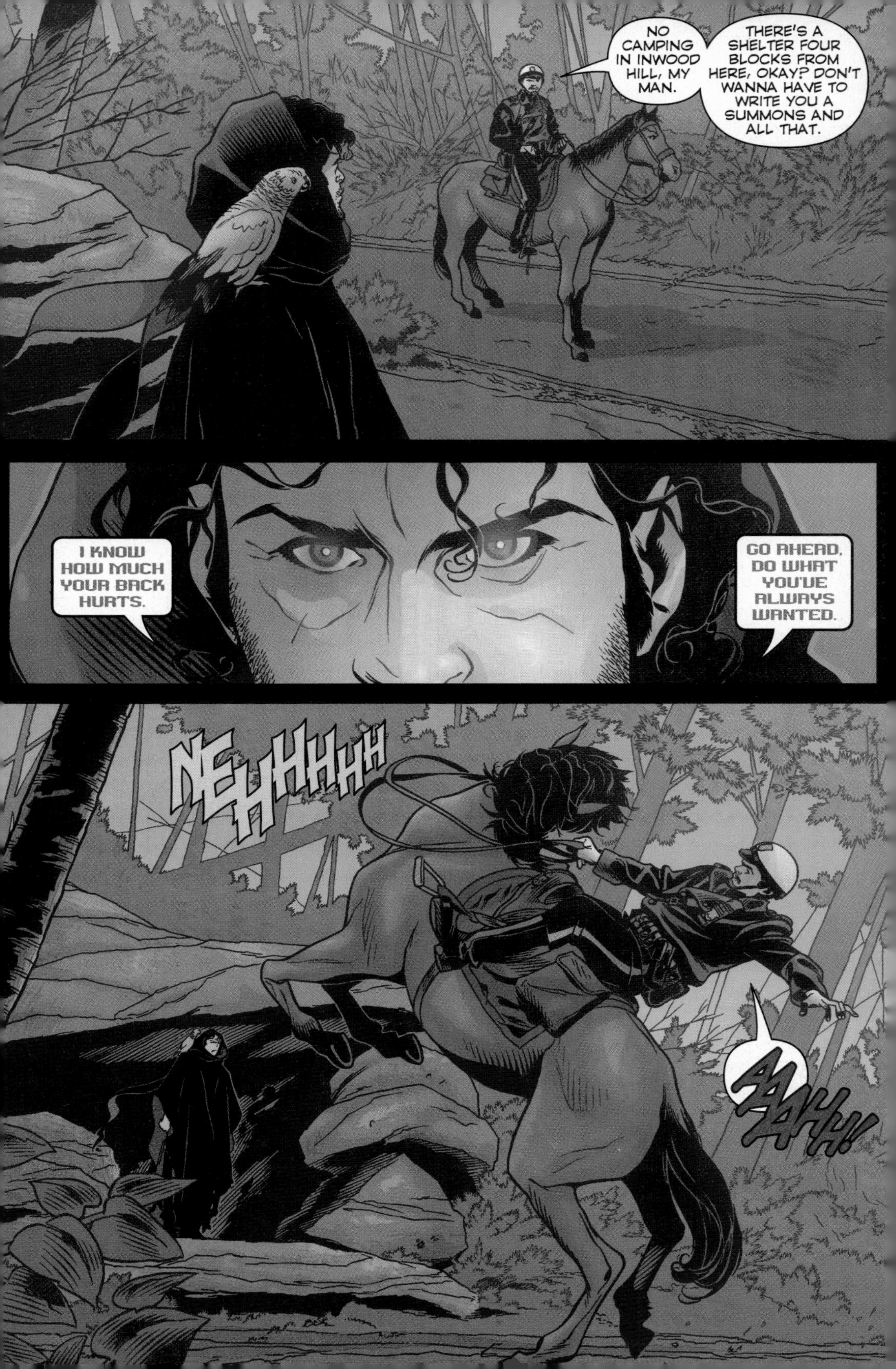
NO CAMPING IN INWOOD HILL, MY MAN.
THERE'S A SHELTER FOUR BLOCKS FROM HERE, OKAY? DON'T WANNA HAVE TO WRITE YOU A SUMMONS AND ALL THAT.
I KNOW HOW MUCH YOUR BACK HURTS.
GO AHEAD, DO WHAT YOU'VE ALWAYS WANTED.
NEHHHHH
AAAHH!

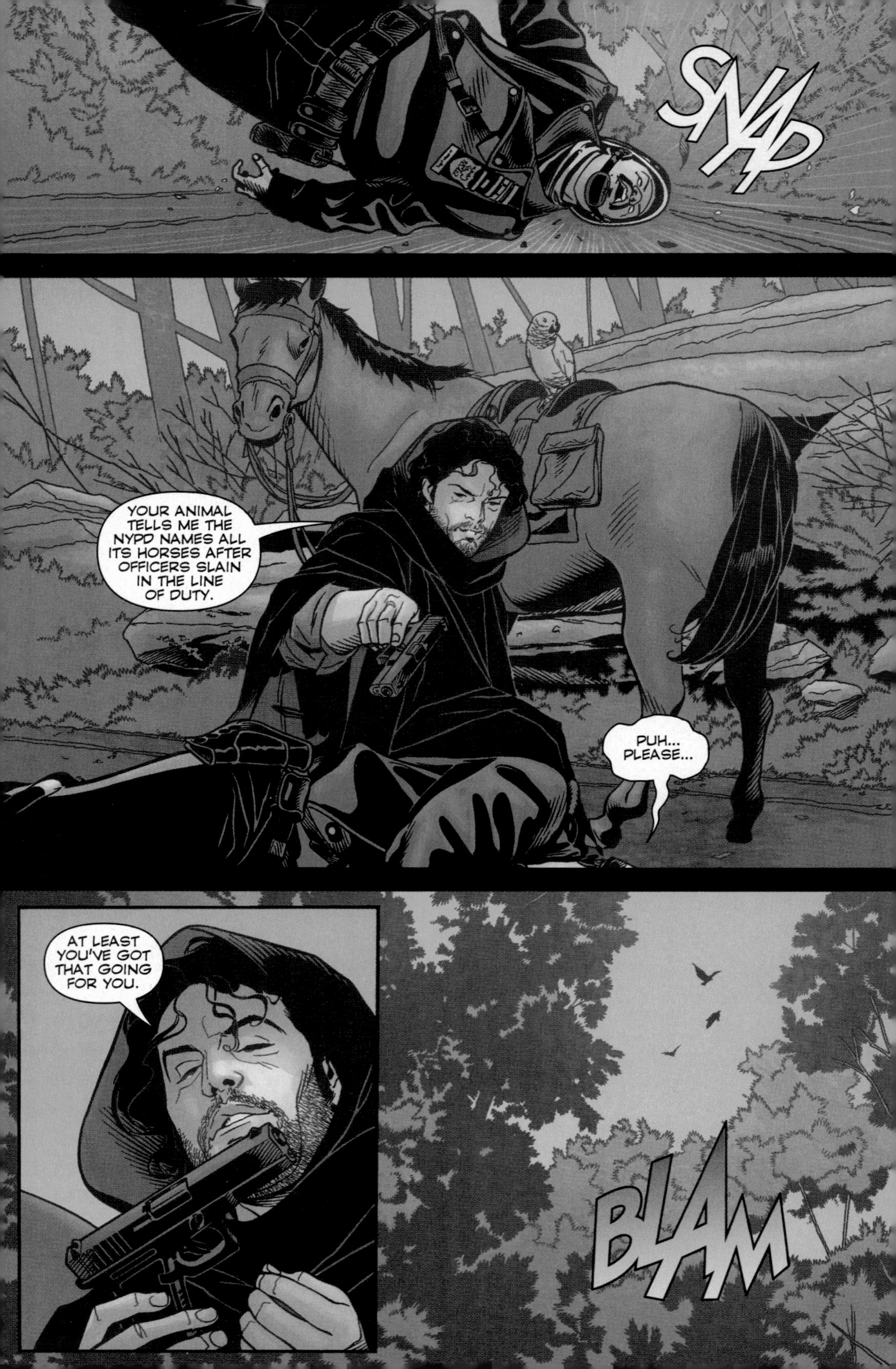
SNAP
YOUR ANIMAL TELLS ME THE NYPD NAMES ALL ITS HORSES AFTER OFFICERS SLAIN IN THE LINE OF DUTY.
PUH... PLEASE...
AT LEAST YOU'VE GOT THAT GOING FOR YOU.
BLAM

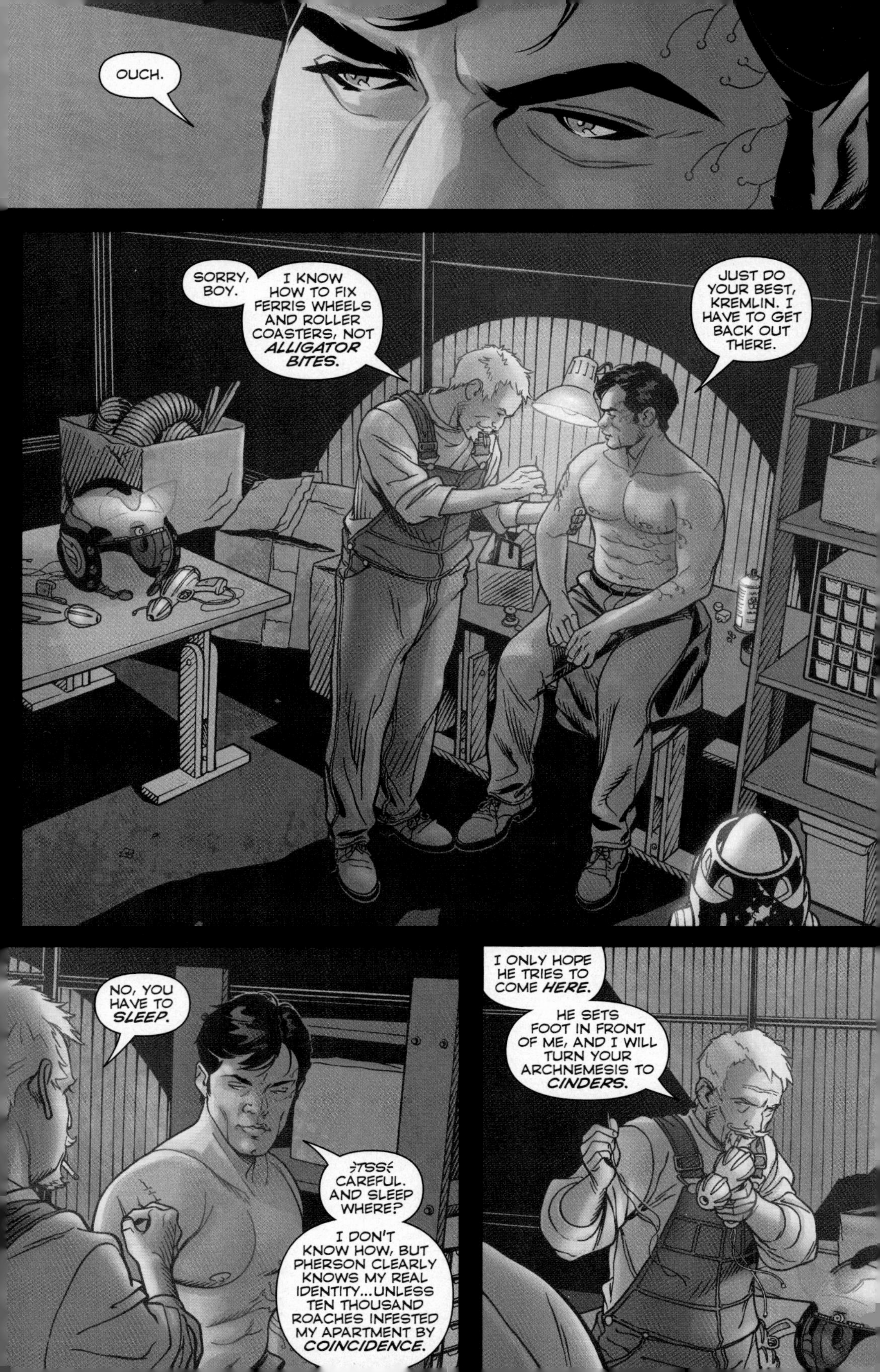
OUCH.
SORRY, BOY.
I KNOW HOW TO FIX FERRIS WHEELS AND ROLLER COASTERS, NOT ALLIGATOR BITES.
JUST DO YOUR BEST, KREMLIN. I HAVE TO GET BACK OUT THERE.
NO, YOU HAVE TO SLEEP.
TSS CAREFUL. AND SLEEP WHERE?
I DON'T KNOW HOW, BUT PHERSON CLEARLY KNOWS MY REAL IDENTITY...UNLESS TEN THOUSAND ROACHES INFESTED MY APARTMENT BY COINCIDENCE.
I ONLY HOPE HE TRIES TO COME HERE.
HE SETS FOOT IN FRONT OF ME, AND I WILL TURN YOUR ARCHNEMESIS TO CINDERS.

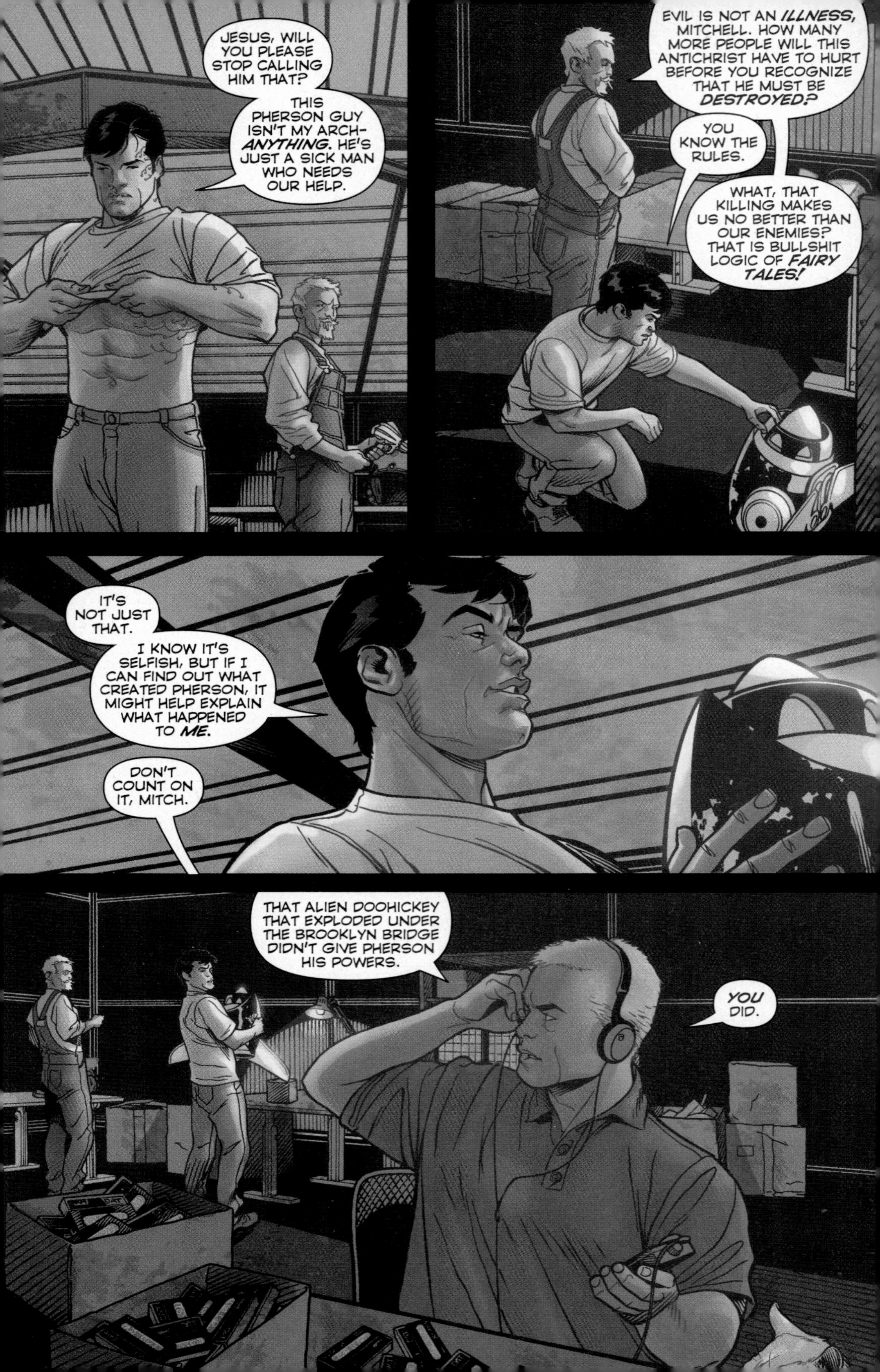
JESUS, WILL YOU PLEASE STOP CALLING HIM THAT?
THIS PHERSON GUY ISN'T MY ARCH-*ANYTHING*. HE'S JUST A SICK MAN WHO NEEDS OUR HELP.
EVIL IS NOT AN *ILLNESS*, MITCHELL. HOW MANY MORE PEOPLE WILL THIS ANTICHRIST HAVE TO HURT BEFORE YOU RECOGNIZE THAT HE MUST BE *DESTROYED?*
YOU KNOW THE RULES.
WHAT, THAT KILLING MAKES US NO BETTER THAN OUR ENEMIES? THAT IS BULLSHIT LOGIC OF *FAIRY TALES!*
IT'S NOT JUST THAT.
I KNOW IT'S SELFISH, BUT IF I CAN FIND OUT WHAT CREATED PHERSON, IT MIGHT HELP EXPLAIN WHAT HAPPENED TO *ME*.
DON'T COUNT ON IT, MITCH.
THAT ALIEN DOOHICKEY THAT EXPLODED UNDER THE BROOKLYN BRIDGE DIDN'T GIVE PHERSON HIS POWERS.
YOU DID.

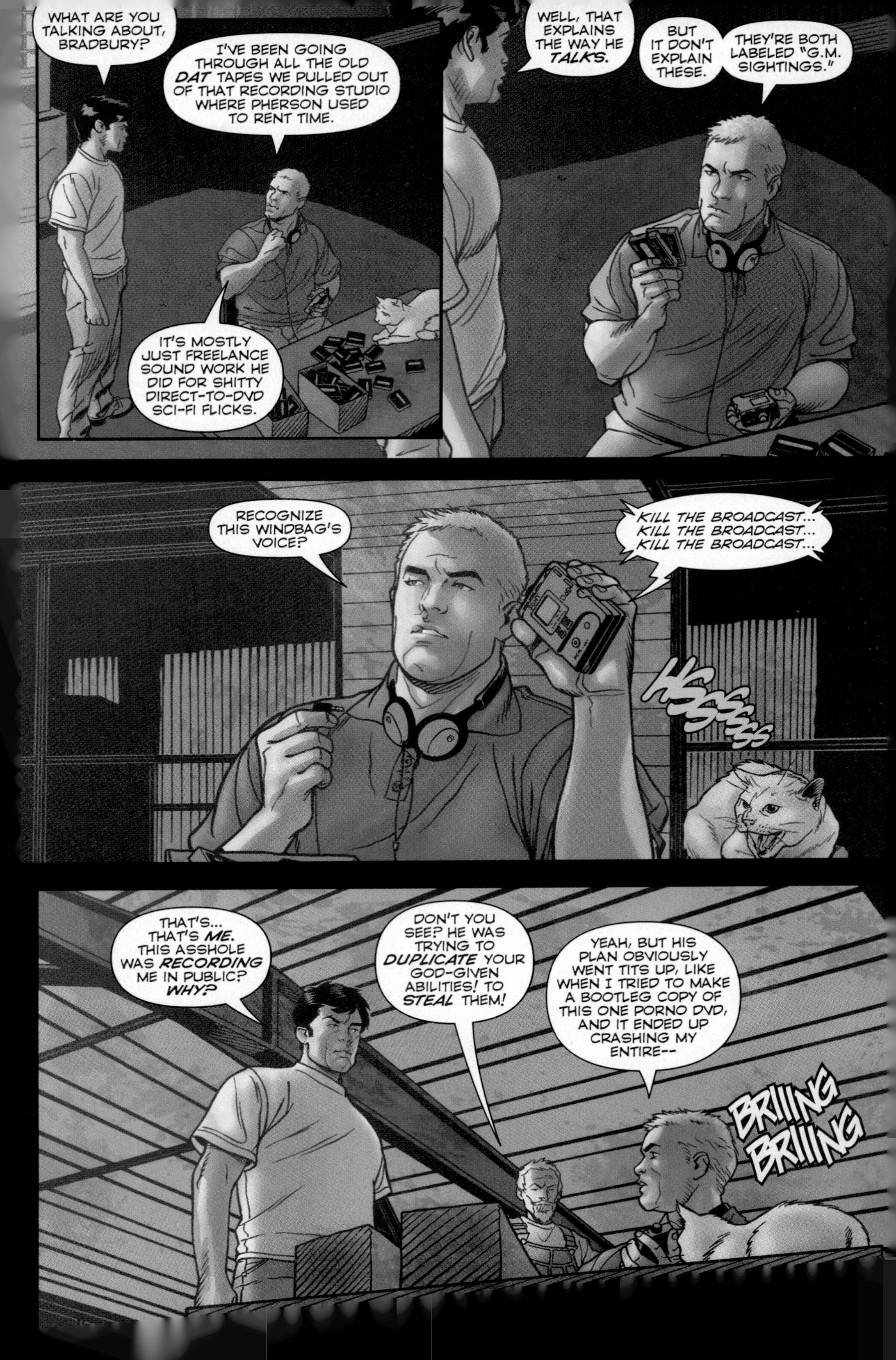
WHAT ARE YOU TALKING ABOUT, BRADBURY?
I'VE BEEN GOING THROUGH ALL THE OLD DAT TAPES WE PULLED OUT OF THAT RECORDING STUDIO WHERE PHERSON USED TO RENT TIME.
IT'S MOSTLY JUST FREELANCE SOUND WORK HE DID FOR SHITTY DIRECT-TO-DVD SCI-FI FLICKS.
WELL, THAT EXPLAINS THE WAY HE TALKS.
BUT IT DON'T EXPLAIN THESE.
THEY'RE BOTH LABELED "G.M. SIGHTINGS."
RECOGNIZE THIS WINDBAG'S VOICE?
KILL THE BROADCAST... KILL THE BROADCAST... KILL THE BROADCAST...
HSSSSSSS
THAT'S... THAT'S ME. THIS ASSHOLE WAS RECORDING ME IN PUBLIC? WHY?
DON'T YOU SEE? HE WAS TRYING TO DUPLICATE YOUR GOD-GIVEN ABILITIES! TO STEAL THEM!
YEAH, BUT HIS PLAN OBVIOUSLY WENT TITS UP, LIKE WHEN I TRIED TO MAKE A BOOTLEG COPY OF THIS ONE PORNO DVD, AND IT ENDED UP CRASHING MY ENTIRE--
BRIIING BRIIING

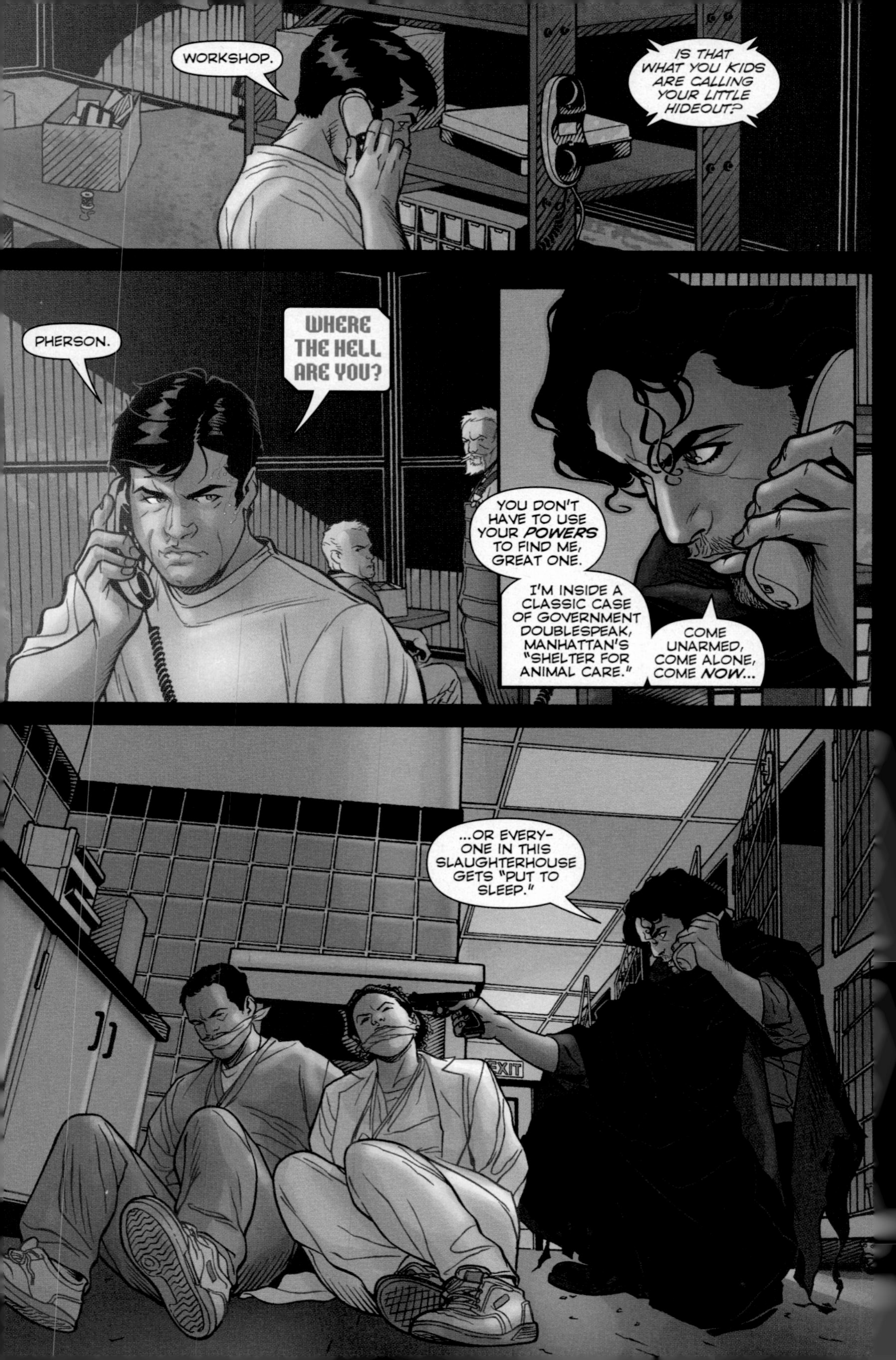
WORKSHOP.
IS THAT WHAT YOU KIDS ARE CALLING YOUR LITTLE HIDEOUT?
PHERSON.
WHERE THE HELL ARE YOU?
YOU DON'T HAVE TO USE YOUR *POWERS* TO FIND ME, GREAT ONE.
I'M INSIDE A CLASSIC CASE OF GOVERNMENT DOUBLESPEAK, MANHATTAN'S "SHELTER FOR ANIMAL CARE."
COME UNARMED, COME ALONE, COME *NOW*...
...OR EVERY-ONE IN THIS SLAUGHTERHOUSE GETS "PUT TO SLEEP."
EXIT

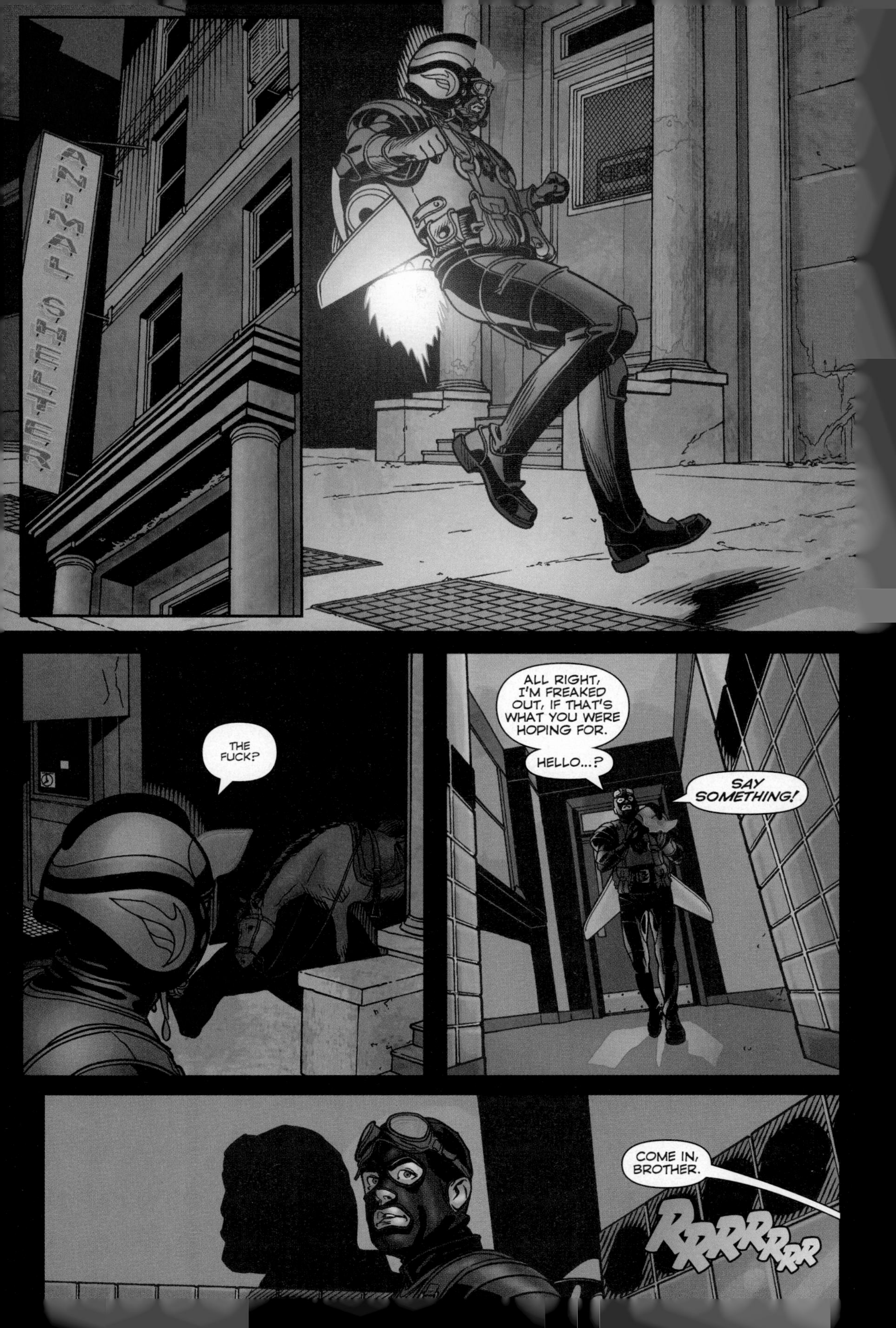

ANIMAL SHELTER
THE FUCK?
ALL RIGHT, I'M FREAKED OUT, IF THAT'S WHAT YOU WERE HOPING FOR.
HELLO...?
SAY SOMETHING!
COME IN, BROTHER.
RRRRRRRR

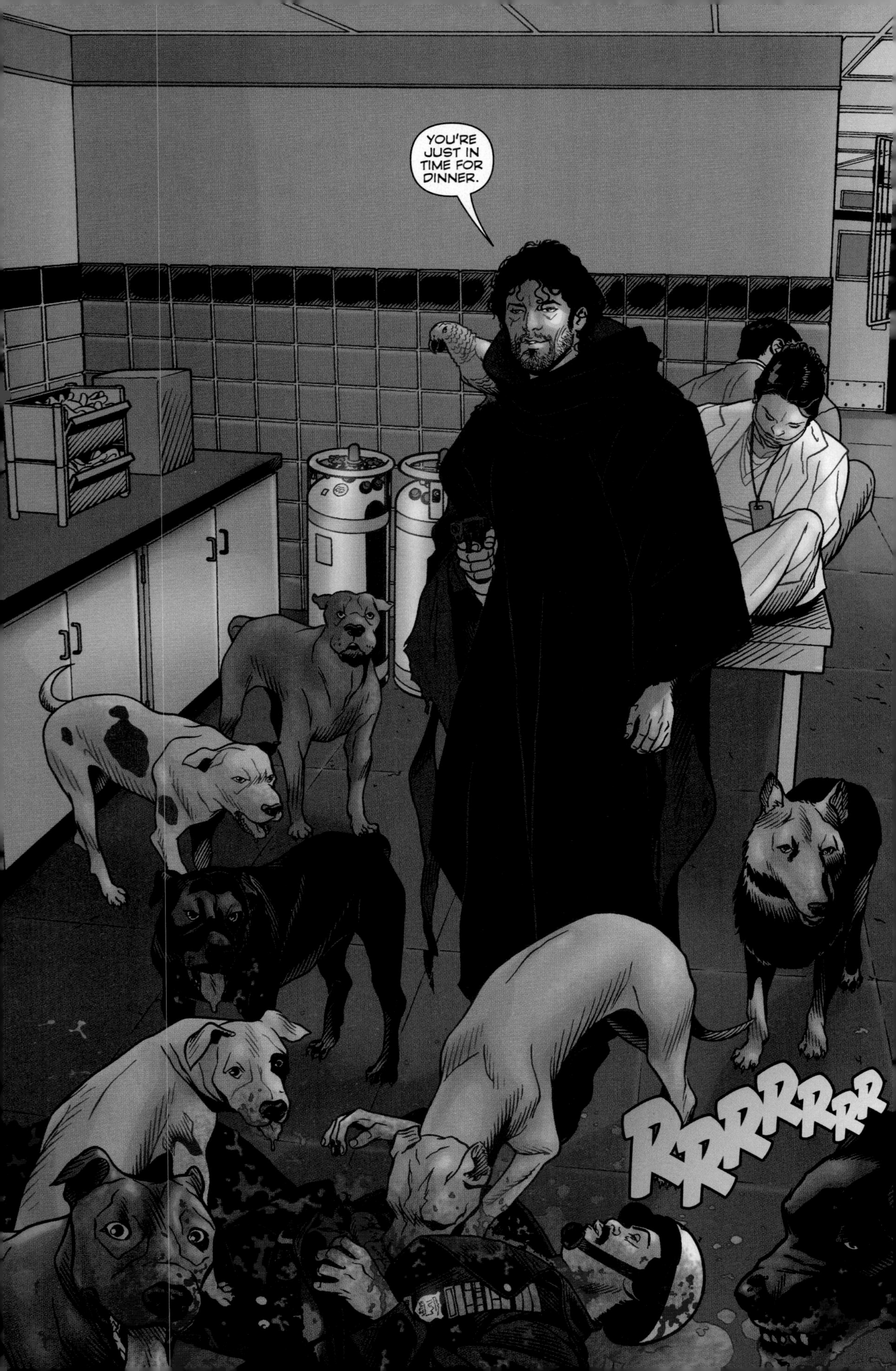
YOU'RE JUST IN TIME FOR DINNER.
RRRRRRR

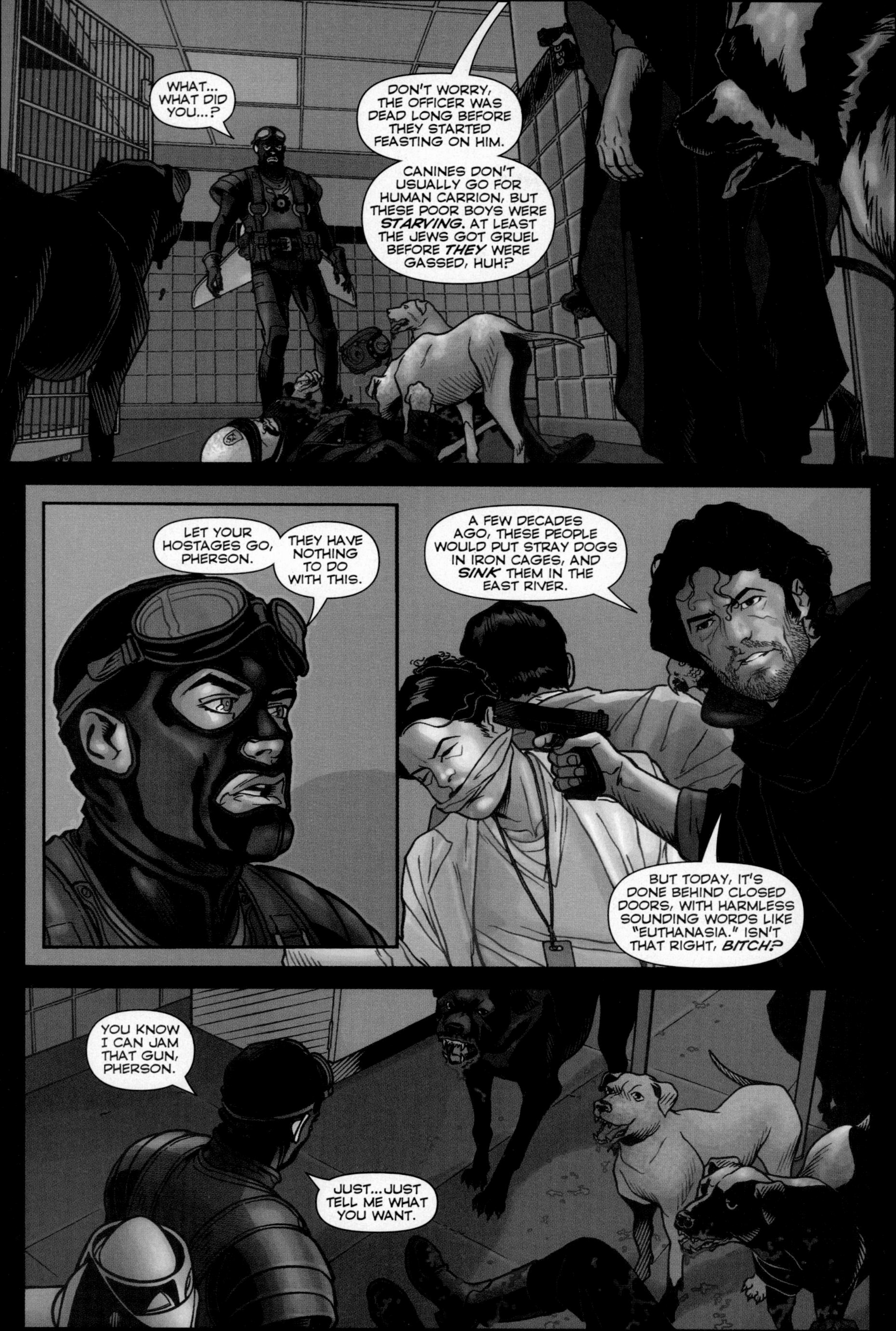
WHAT... WHAT DID YOU...?
DON'T WORRY, THE OFFICER WAS DEAD LONG BEFORE THEY STARTED FEASTING ON HIM.
CANINES DON'T USUALLY GO FOR HUMAN CARRION, BUT THESE POOR BOYS WERE STARVING. AT LEAST THE JEWS GOT GRUEL BEFORE THEY WERE GASSED, HUH?
LET YOUR HOSTAGES GO, PHERSON.
THEY HAVE NOTHING TO DO WITH THIS.
A FEW DECADES AGO, THESE PEOPLE WOULD PUT STRAY DOGS IN IRON CAGES, AND SINK THEM IN THE EAST RIVER.
BUT TODAY, IT'S DONE BEHIND CLOSED DOORS, WITH HARMLESS SOUNDING WORDS LIKE "EUTHANASIA." ISN'T THAT RIGHT, BITCH?
YOU KNOW I CAN JAM THAT GUN, PHERSON.
JUST...JUST TELL ME WHAT YOU WANT.

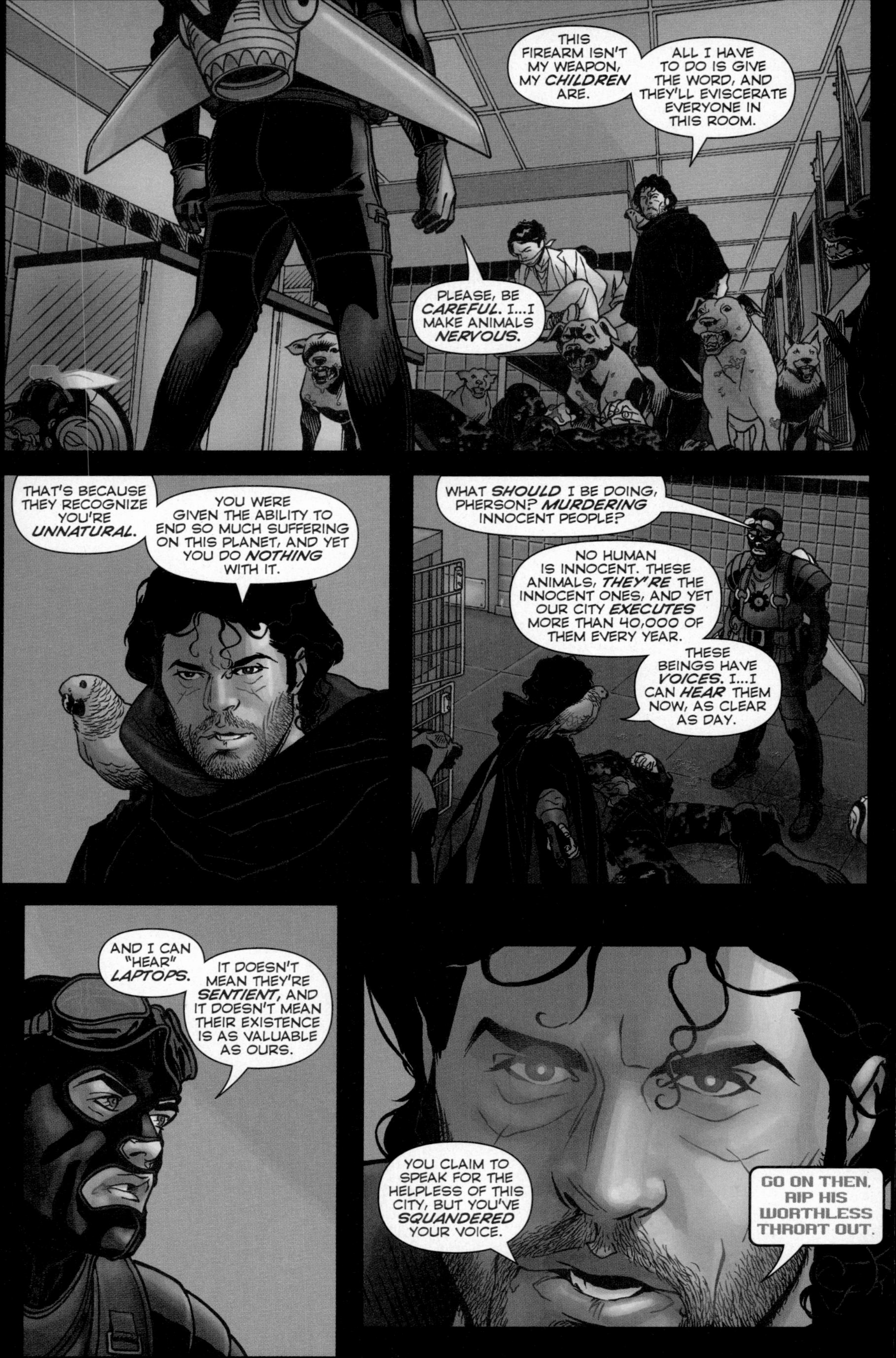

THIS FIREARM ISN'T MY WEAPON, MY *CHILDREN* ARE.
ALL I HAVE TO DO IS GIVE THE WORD, AND THEY'LL EVISCERATE EVERYONE IN THIS ROOM.
PLEASE, BE *CAREFUL*. I...I MAKE ANIMALS *NERVOUS*.
THAT'S BECAUSE THEY RECOGNIZE YOU'RE *UNNATURAL*.
YOU WERE GIVEN THE ABILITY TO END SO MUCH SUFFERING ON THIS PLANET, AND YET YOU DO *NOTHING* WITH IT.
WHAT *SHOULD* I BE DOING, PHERSON? *MURDERING* INNOCENT PEOPLE?
NO HUMAN IS INNOCENT. THESE ANIMALS, *THEY'RE* THE INNOCENT ONES, AND YET OUR CITY *EXECUTES* MORE THAN 40,000 OF THEM EVERY YEAR.
THESE BEINGS HAVE *VOICES*. I...I CAN *HEAR* THEM NOW, AS CLEAR AS DAY.
AND I CAN "HEAR" *LAPTOPS*.
IT DOESN'T MEAN THEY'RE *SENTIENT*, AND IT DOESN'T MEAN THEIR EXISTENCE IS AS VALUABLE AS OURS.
YOU CLAIM TO SPEAK FOR THE HELPLESS OF THIS CITY, BUT YOU'VE *SQUANDERED* YOUR VOICE.
GO ON THEN. RIP HIS WORTHLESS THROAT OUT.

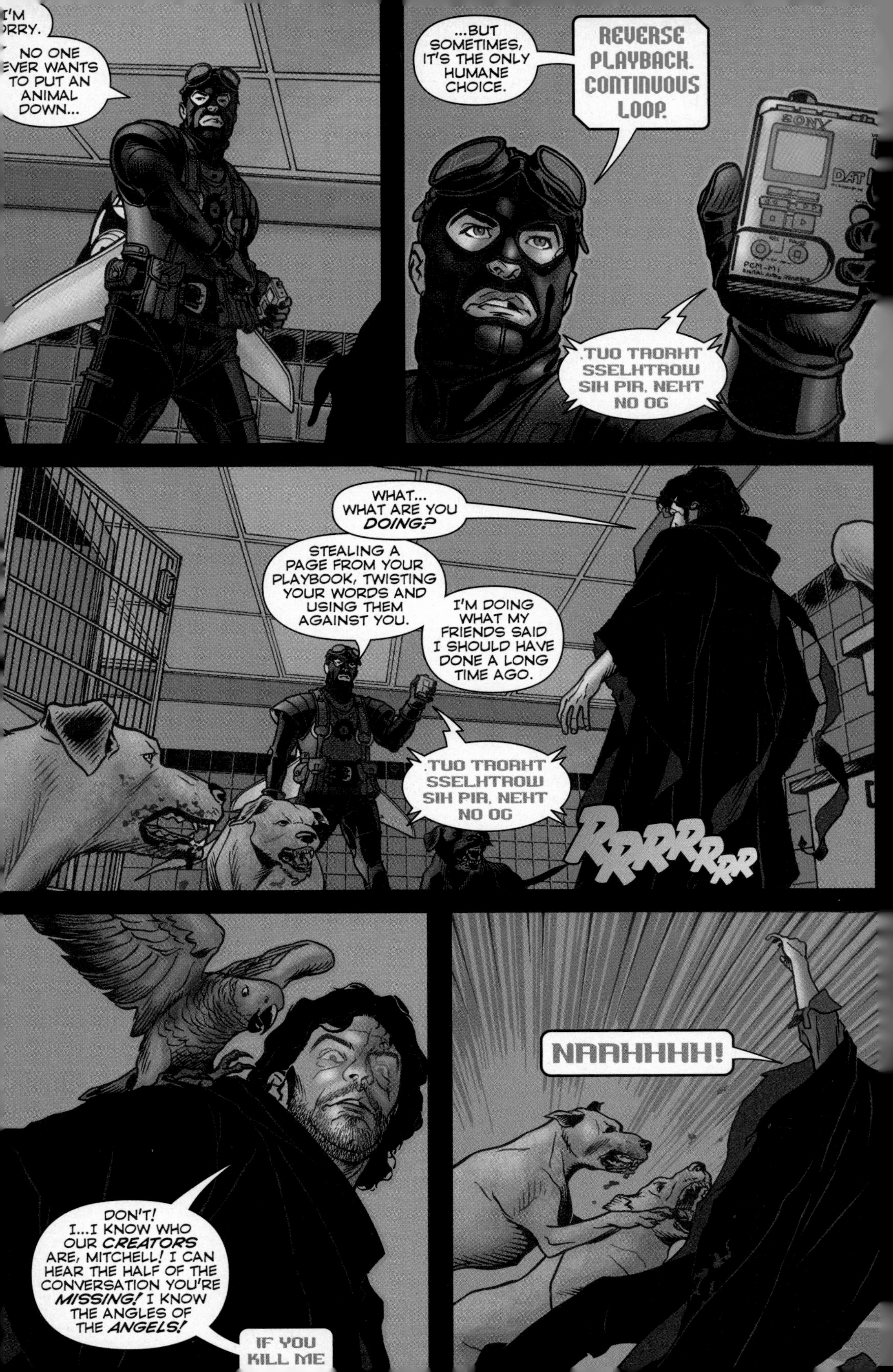
I'M
[S]ORRY.
NO ONE EVER WANTS TO PUT AN ANIMAL DOWN...
...BUT SOMETIMES, IT'S THE ONLY HUMANE CHOICE.
REVERSE PLAYBACK. CONTINUOUS LOOP.
.TUO TAORHT SSELHTAOW SIH PIR, NEHT NO OG
WHAT... WHAT ARE YOU DOING?
STEALING A PAGE FROM YOUR PLAYBOOK, TWISTING YOUR WORDS AND USING THEM AGAINST YOU.
I'M DOING WHAT MY FRIENDS SAID I SHOULD HAVE DONE A LONG TIME AGO.
.TUO TAORHT SSELHTAOW SIH PIR, NEHT NO OG
RRRRRRRR
DON'T! I...I KNOW WHO OUR CREATORS ARE, MITCHELL! I CAN HEAR THE HALF OF THE CONVERSATION YOU'RE MISSING! I KNOW THE ANGLES OF THE ANGELS!
IF YOU KILL ME
NAAHHHH!

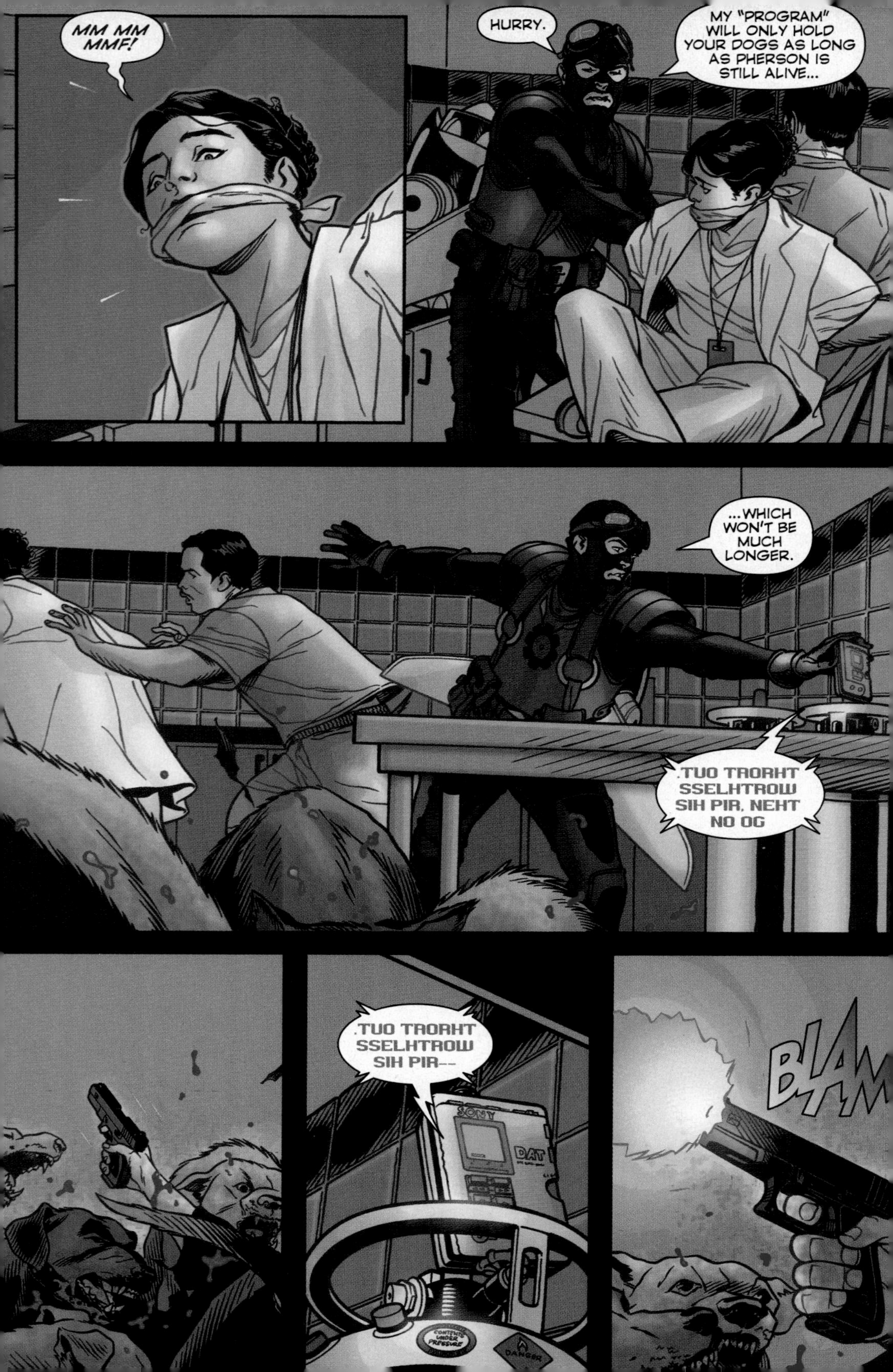
MM MM MMF!
HURRY.
MY "PROGRAM" WILL ONLY HOLD YOUR DOGS AS LONG AS PHERSON IS STILL ALIVE...
...WHICH WON'T BE MUCH LONGER.
.TUO TAORHT SSELHTROW SIH PIR, NEHT NO OG
.TUO TAORHT SSELHTROW SIH PIR--
SONY
DAT
CONTENTS UNDER PRESSURE
DANGER
BLAM

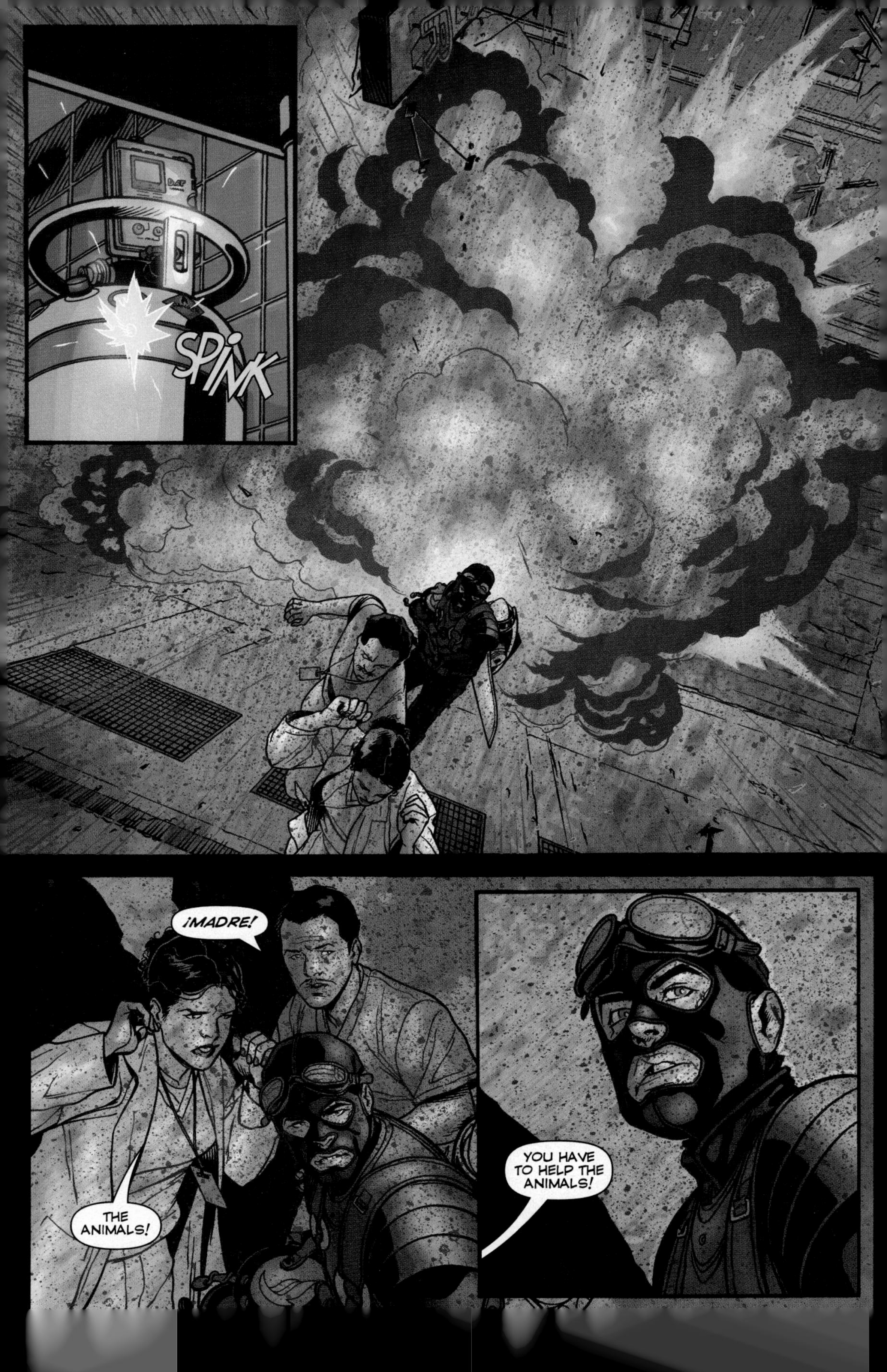
SPINK
¡MADRE!
THE ANIMALS!
YOU HAVE TO HELP THE ANIMALS!

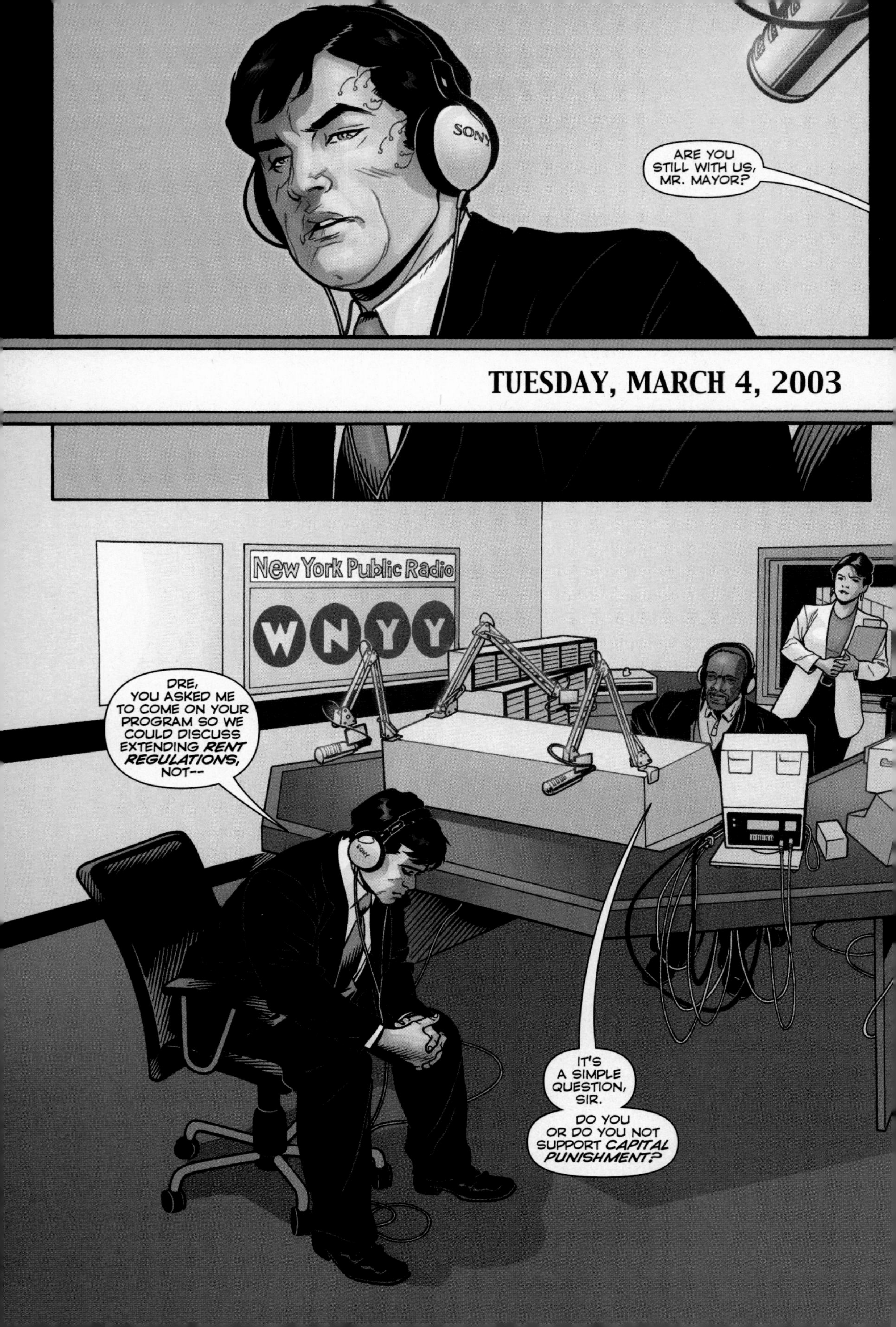
ARE YOU STILL WITH US, MR. MAYOR?
TUESDAY, MARCH 4, 2003
New York Public Radio
WNYY
DRE, YOU ASKED ME TO COME ON YOUR PROGRAM SO WE COULD DISCUSS EXTENDING *RENT REGULATIONS,* NOT--
IT'S A SIMPLE QUESTION, SIR.
DO YOU OR DO YOU NOT SUPPORT *CAPITAL PUNISHMENT?*

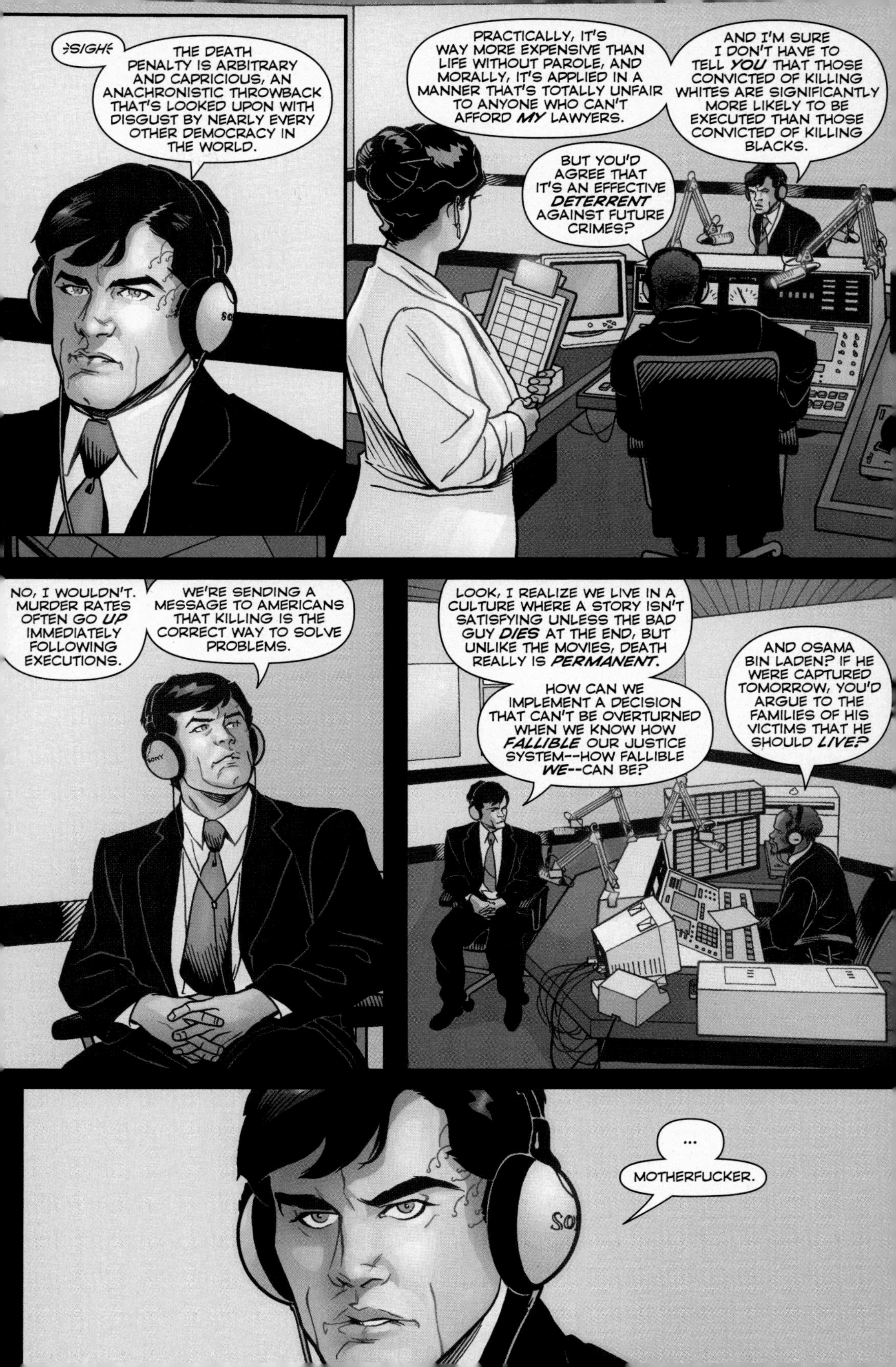

SIGH
THE DEATH PENALTY IS ARBITRARY AND CAPRICIOUS, AN ANACHRONISTIC THROWBACK THAT'S LOOKED UPON WITH DISGUST BY NEARLY EVERY OTHER DEMOCRACY IN THE WORLD.
PRACTICALLY, IT'S WAY MORE EXPENSIVE THAN LIFE WITHOUT PAROLE, AND MORALLY, IT'S APPLIED IN A MANNER THAT'S TOTALLY UNFAIR TO ANYONE WHO CAN'T AFFORD *MY* LAWYERS.
AND I'M SURE I DON'T HAVE TO TELL *YOU* THAT THOSE CONVICTED OF KILLING WHITES ARE SIGNIFICANTLY MORE LIKELY TO BE EXECUTED THAN THOSE CONVICTED OF KILLING BLACKS.
BUT YOU'D AGREE THAT IT'S AN EFFECTIVE *DETERRENT* AGAINST FUTURE CRIMES?
NO, I WOULDN'T. MURDER RATES OFTEN GO *UP* IMMEDIATELY FOLLOWING EXECUTIONS.
WE'RE SENDING A MESSAGE TO AMERICANS THAT KILLING IS THE CORRECT WAY TO SOLVE PROBLEMS.
LOOK, I REALIZE WE LIVE IN A CULTURE WHERE A STORY ISN'T SATISFYING UNLESS THE BAD GUY *DIES* AT THE END, BUT UNLIKE THE MOVIES, DEATH REALLY IS *PERMANENT*.
HOW CAN WE IMPLEMENT A DECISION THAT CAN'T BE OVERTURNED WHEN WE KNOW HOW *FALLIBLE* OUR JUSTICE SYSTEM--HOW FALLIBLE *WE*--CAN BE?
AND OSAMA BIN LADEN? IF HE WERE CAPTURED TOMORROW, YOU'D ARGUE TO THE FAMILIES OF HIS VICTIMS THAT HE SHOULD *LIVE?*
...
MOTHERFUCKER.

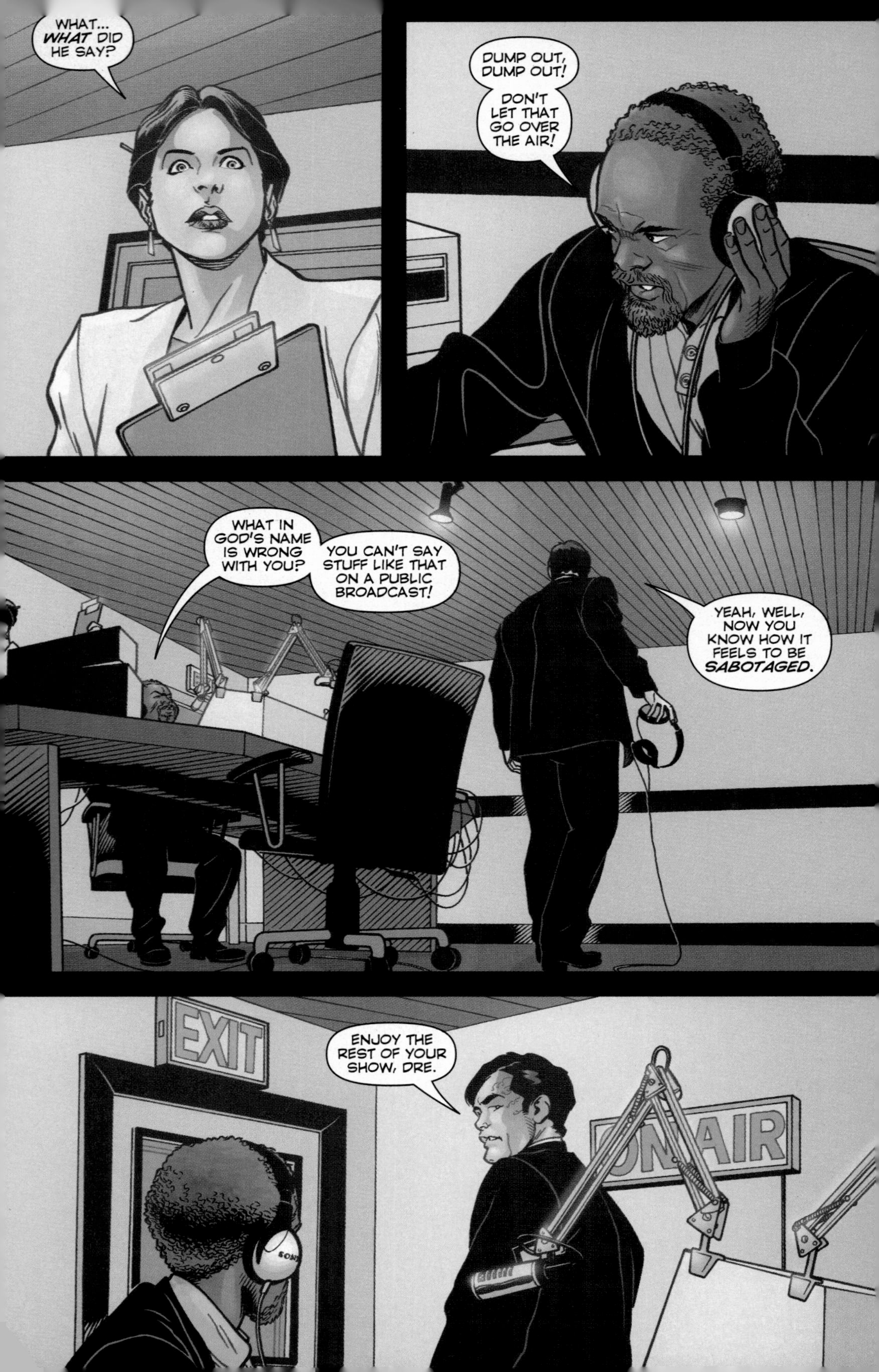
WHAT... *WHAT* DID HE SAY?
DUMP OUT, DUMP OUT!
DON'T LET THAT GO OVER THE AIR!
WHAT IN GOD'S NAME IS WRONG WITH YOU?
YOU CAN'T SAY STUFF LIKE THAT ON A PUBLIC BROADCAST!
YEAH, WELL, NOW YOU KNOW HOW IT FEELS TO BE *SABOTAGED*.
EXIT
ENJOY THE REST OF YOUR SHOW, DRE.
ON AIR